Skills for Social Work Practice

Second Edition

EDITED BY ANDY MANTELL

Series Editors: Jonathan Parker and Greta Bradley

SAGE | LearningMatters

Los Angeles | London | New Delhi
Singapore | Washington DC

Learning Matters
An imprint of SAGE Publications Ltd
1 Oliver's Yard
55 City Road
London EC1Y 1SP

SAGE Publications Inc.
2455 Teller Road
Thousand Oaks, California 91320

SAGE Publications India Pvt Ltd
B 1/I 1 Mohan Cooperative Industrial Area
Mathura Road
New Delhi 110 044

SAGE Publications Asia-Pacific Pte Ltd
3 Church Street
#10–04 Samsung Hub
Singapore 049483

Editor: Luke Block
Production controller: Chris Marke
Project management: Deer Park Productions, Tavistock, Devon
Marketing manager: Tamara Navaratnam
Cover design: Wendy Scott
Typeset by: C&M Digitals (P) Ltd, Chennai, India
Printed and bound by Henry Ling Limited, at the Dorset Press, Dorchester, DT1 1HD

Library of Congress Control Number:
2013940923

British Library Cataloguing in Publication Data

A catalogue record for this book is available from the British Library

ISBN 978-1-44626-733-2 (pbk)
ISBN 978-1-44626-732-5

Contents

Editor and contributors

This book is written by staff of the Childhood, Social Work and Social Care Team, University of Chichester, the University of Winchester, Glasgow Caledonian University and colleagues from the West Sussex Social Services, Hampshire Social Services and Kingston-Upon-Thames.

Sue Bull is a Senior Lecturer in Social Work, University of Chichester.

Gill Constable is a Lecturer in Social Work at Glasgow Caledonian University.

Jane Donson is a Senior Lecturer at the University of Winchester.

David Gaylard is a Senior Lecturer in Social Work at the University of Chichester.

Colin Goble is a Senior Lecturer in Child, Youth and Community Studies at the University of Winchester.

Barbara Hall is an Associate Lecturer at the University of Chichester.

Viv Killner is a Senior Social Worker in West Sussex.

Rebecca Long is a trainer in the voluntary sector.

Andy Mantell is a Senior Lecturer in Social Work at the University of Chichester.

Janet McCray is a Reader in Social Care at the University of Chichester.

Bob Price is an Independent Reviewing Officer for Kingston-upon-Thames.

Marie Price is a Senior Lecturer in Social Work at the University of Chichester.

Jenny Robson is a Senior Social Work Practitioner in West Sussex.

Terry Scragg is a Practice Educator working with the University of Chichester.

Debbie Smallbones is a Senior Social Worker in West Sussex.

Chris Smethurst is Senior Lecturer in Social Work at the University of Chichester.

Paul Tavender is a Senior Practitioner in Hampshire.

Grahame Tooth was a Senior Practitioner and Training and Development Officer for West Sussex County Council and is now a Buddhist monk.

Acknowledgements

I would like to thank the contributors and their families and Jane Cowper. I would particularly like to thank the staff at Learning Matters for their unstinting help, especially Luke Block and Helen Fairlie. Finally, I would like to thank the service users, carers and practitioners who have shown us the way.

This book is dedicated to Rachael – I know you prefer flowers!

Introduction

Social work skills define the distinctive nature and determine the effectiveness of social work practice. Many of these skills are generic and can be transferred to a wide range of social work practice settings. Whether you are working with young people or an older person you are usually working with families and their life cycle. However, each area has its own distinctive challenges that influence the skills that social workers need to develop. Unlike social work with younger people, social work with adults is guided by a complex raft of legislation spanning over half a century. Practice has evolved, and continues to follow and to shape policy, which has shifted from paternalistic protection to promoting rights and choices.

The personalisation agenda offers a significant challenge to social workers' skill sets. It requires a change from directing to empowering. This will necessitate the development of new skills but also provide the opportunity to rediscover aspects of social work neglected within the era of care management.

Public inquiries into the tragic consequences of policies and practices not working effectively can play a reactive role in shaping practice with children and adults. Yet they can also provide pause for thought, to reflect on our expectations of public services and workers. An emphasis on procedures and targets may serve organisational imperatives, producing outputs far removed from the outcomes that service users seek. This book focuses on those skills that are required for working alongside and for empowering children, young people and adults.

Social work skills are required not just within direct work with carers, service users and other professionals but also in constantly managing and updating our own practice. This fully revised second edition is written primarily for the student social worker and explores the range of skills that are essential in social work and that will be useful across the whole of your programme of study. It has been expanded from the first edition to cover work with children, young people and adults. There is a particular emphasis on how to apply these skills, with the aim of enabling you to gain an understanding of ways to meet current challenges in the field that will also be invaluable in subsequent years when you move into practice as a qualified social worker. Likewise experienced social workers will also find the book provides an overview of social work skills and discussion of a range of perspectives that can inform and refresh their practice.

Book structure

This book is written by staff of the Childhood, Social Work and Social Care Team, University of Chichester, the University of Winchester, Glasgow Caledonian University and colleagues from the West Sussex Social Services, Hampshire Social Services and Kingston-upon-Thames. As you will see below, the book is divided into four sections. It starts where any social worker's journey must begin, with themselves. After considering reflective practice we explore how to present yourself in person and in writing and skills for self-management. Having looked at *managing self*, we then move on in Chapters 5, 6 and 7 to *building relationships* with others. Our emphasis is on developing empowering and meaningful relationships through engagement. We then explore the nuts and bolts of communication. In looking to self and how we relate to others, these first six chapters provide essential foundations for empowering social work practice. We then focus on particular aspects of *working with others* in Chapters 8, 9 and 10. The need for better collaboration, multi-disciplinary and multi-agency working is emphasised in most recent public inquiries and legislation relevant to social work. Group work by contrast has become neglected, yet is at the heart of how we manage the dynamics within multi-disciplinary teams and a valuable therapeutic tool for working with children, young people and adults. Negotiation skills are, like collaborative working, viewed as essential, yet are often taken for granted, belying their complexity. In the final four chapters we try to unravel how we *make sense of a complex world*, from using the, at times, byzantine legislation, the thorny issues of assessing needs and risks and our ever evolving decision-making processes.

Part 1 – Managing self

Chapter 1 explores how to develop reflective practice, the essential component of competent and safe practitioners. It provides an overview of its main elements and what it means in social work practice. It considers some of the potential benefits from using this technique and offers you practical ways that you can develop your reflective thinking.

Chapter 2 focuses on how workers present themselves. However, it moves beyond simply considering your physical appearance to explore the impact of your behaviours, thoughts, belief systems and values on your practice. Self-presentation is considered as part of your developmental journey, where your destination is becoming a competent, empathic and reflective practitioner.

Chapter 3 considers written presentations of self, for example through the report writing and recording skills required of all social workers. This neglected area of social work practice has been the subject of numerous reports from public inquiries that have highlighted the need for better case recording. This chapter identifies the attributes necessary for effective case recording, what should be included and what to avoid. This exploration situates written communication in the context of the societal, organisational and professional significance attached to documents and ethical and value considerations such as confidentiality and the power of documents.

Chapter 4 considers the skills required for self-management. The pressures of current social work practice require students/practitioners to be efficient and effective at managing their time, often needing to respond to competing priorities. This chapter considers some of the skills relevant to your 'survival tool kit' in the changing social work environment. At the heart of the chapter is the concept and implications of the 'psychological contract' between the employer and the employee, informed by the Social Work Reform Board 'Standards for Employers of Social Workers in England and Supervision Framework' (2010).

The chapter also looks at practical approaches to reduce stress issues concerning time management, and an exploration of the management of change.

Part 2 – Building relationships

Chapter 5 explores the attitudes, knowledge and skills necessary to promote empowerment and participation. It then considers how social workers can act as advocates, identifying the tensions and practice dilemmas and the need to explicitly recognise the social worker's power. This chapter addresses the difficulties social workers can face in promoting anti-oppressive and anti-discriminatory practice, with particular reference to the social model of disability, the experience of people with learning disabilities and empowering practice with children and young people.

Chapter 6 examines the essential interpersonal skills involved in the process of engaging with others. The chapter particularly focuses upon creating effective one-to-one relationships. It explores establishing rapport, listening, developing trust, being clear about the aims of our interventions, maintaining momentum and managing endings.

Chapter 7 builds from Chapter 6 to explore the communication skills necessary for nurturing effective relationships. It applies the skills that promote open one-to-one communication to challenging areas of practice. Particular attention is paid to situations that may challenge our attitudes, may be distressing or can be threatening. In doing so it illustrates the importance of non-verbal communication, silence and reflective practice.

Part 3 – Working with others

Chapter 8 identifies the components of good collaborative practice, including: valuing roles, knowledge of different contexts, building trust and credibility, managing boundaries, and conflict management.

Collaboration as a practice action is explored while other language and terms often used interchangeably are clarified. Key policy and legislation, general protocols and practice requirements are critically reviewed and barriers to collaboration are considered. During the chapter attention is paid to ethical frameworks to aid anti-oppressive and appropriate social work practice.

Chapter 9, after identifying the range of groups within which social workers find themselves, discusses the nature and roles of group working. It highlights the process involved with groups, their life cycle and dynamics. The significance of each stage, from first beginning to managing ending, is emphasised. Factors that encourage or inhibit group development are discussed, with planning recognised as an essential precursor to successful group work.

Chapter 10 reviews the negotiation skills necessary for effective social work practice. Negotiation is an integral but often overlooked aspect of social work. This chapter will provide an exploration of the skills that can be utilised to facilitate and influence negotiations. In so doing it highlights the risks, conflicts, ambiguity and ethical dilemmas that can accompany negotiations.

Part 4 – Making sense of a complex world

Those new to using legislation often focus on 'the facts' of the law, but neglect the significant skill that is required in applying it. Legislation can offer an illusion of certainty which ignores such subtleties as the difference between the spirit and letter of the law. Chapter 11 explores the interface between your understanding of the principles of the legislative context in which you are working, and applying your knowledge of the law effectively and ethically on behalf of service users. This includes recognising how and when to seek legal advice, being confident in your professional expertise in your field and making decisions, with management support, based on that advice.

Chapter 12 examines the assessment process and how it is linked to the broad repertoire of social work skills. Assessment of need is considered within the complex legislative framework for adults, and for children focuses on section 17 of the Children Act 1989 (section 47 is considered in Chapter 13). The chapter highlights the contentious nature of assessments and how they can be led by procedures, needs, rights and risks. This chapter should be considered in conjunction with Chapter 13 and vice versa.

Chapter 13 looks at risk assessment, which has arguably become the key preoccupation and core activity of social workers in statutory settings. When assessing need (see Chapter 12), it is the degree of risk that is often the deciding factor in resource allocation. This chapter will explore what is meant by risk, its impact on social work practice and the skills social workers require to assess and work with risk. It also includes a more detailed exploration of section 47 of the Children Act 1989, which relates to children at risk of significant harm.

Chapter 14 explores the building blocks for effective decision-making in social work. It considers the impact of competing evidence and opinions and emphasises the importance of values and anti-oppressive practice in shaping effective decisions. It aims to equip you with an understanding of the skills necessary for appraising and applying evidence in complex decision-making situations and provides pointers for how to care for yourself in this often stressful process.

Learning features

This book is interactive, drawing on practice-based examples and research to aid your learning. You are encouraged to work through the book as an active participant, taking responsibility for your learning, in order to increase your knowledge, understanding and ability to apply this learning to your practice. You will be expected to reflect creatively on how your immediate learning needs can be met in working with children, young people, adult service users and carers. It is also essential to look beyond your immediate needs to how your longer-term professional learning can be developed in your future career.

We have devised activities that require you to reflect on experiences, situations and events and help you to review and summarise learning undertaken. In this way your knowledge will become deeply embedded as part of your development. When you come to practise learning in an agency the work and reflection undertaken here will help you to improve and hone your skills and knowledge.

This book intends to develop your skills in social work, but we realise that there are many other sources of information that you may wish to access that provide more detailed information on specific aspects of your work and we have suggested further reading at the end of each chapter for you to follow up.

This book has been carefully mapped to the new Professional Capabilities Framework for Social Workers in England and will help you to develop the appropriate standards at the right level. These standards are:

- **Professionalism**

  Identify and behave as a professional social worker committed to professional development.

- **Values and ethics**

  Apply social work ethical principles and values to guide professional practice.

- **Diversity**

  Recognise diversity and apply anti-discriminatory and anti-oppressive principles in practice.

- **Rights, justice and economic well-being**

  Advance human rights and promote social justice and economic well-being.

- **Knowledge**

  Apply knowledge of social sciences, law and social work practice theory.

- **Critical reflection and analysis**

  Apply critical reflection and analysis to inform and provide a rationale for professional decision-making.

- **Intervention and skills**

  Use judgment and authority to intervene with individuals, families and communities to promote independence, provide support and prevent harm, neglect and abuse.

- **Contexts and organisations**

  Engage with, inform, and adapt to changing contexts that shape practice. Operate effectively within your own organisational frameworks and contribute to the development of services and organisations. Operate effectively within multi-agency and inter-professional settings.

- **Professional leadership**

  Take responsibility for the professional learning and development of others through supervision, mentoring, assessing, research, teaching, leadership and management.

  References to these standards will be made throughout the text and you will find a diagram of the Professional Capabilities Framework in an Appendix on page 251.

Part 1
Managing self

Chapter 1
Reflective practice

Terry Scragg

A C H I E V I N G   A   S O C I A L   W O R K   D E G R E E

This chapter will help you to develop the following capabilities from the **Professional Capabilities Framework**.

- **Professionalism**. Identify and behave as a professional social worker, committed to professional development.
- **Knowledge**. Apply knowledge of social science, law and social work practice theory.
- **Critical reflection and analysis**. Apply critical reflection and analysis to inform and provide a rationale for professional decision-making.

It will also introduce you to the following standards as set out in the 2008 social work subject benchmark statement.

5.5.2   Gathering information
5.5.3   Analysis and synthesis
5.8   Skills in personal and professional development
6.2   Reflection on performance

Introduction

This chapter will introduce you to the concept of reflective practice, which is an essential skill you will need to develop during your social work course. It will also provide definitions of reflective practice and describe its roots and the different techniques that can be adopted to enhance reflection. Examples of how reflective practice can be used are illustrated through activities and case studies, with recent research findings. Particular emphasis is placed on the supervisory relationship, whether with a practice educator or practice supervisor.

What is reflective practice?

Reflective practice has long been seen as an essential part of social work education at qualifying and post-qualifying levels, as it is in other professions such as nursing and teaching. Reflection is formalised in academic assignments and in activities undertaken while on placements, with the intention of enabling you to critically examine your practice. At its most straightforward, reflection plays an important part in helping you learn from the experiences of different interventions and other significant events. This is particularly important in enabling you to make links between what you actually *do* when you are working with a client and what you hope to achieve by a particular intervention and, importantly, your feelings about yourself in the practitioner role. In making the connection between these aspects and analysing your thoughts, actions and intentions you can, particularly with support from your tutor or supervisor, gain greater understanding of your own performance and refine your future practice. With these foundations reflection can become an integral part of your everyday practice and part of your lifelong learning as a professional social worker.

Definitions of reflective practice

We have seen that reflective practice is an essential part of your development as a student social worker and, to help you understand more fully what this involves, the following two definitions capture the essence of reflective practice:

A general definition by Boud *et al.* (1985, p43) states that:

> *Reflection is an important human activity in which people recapture their experience, think about it, mull over and evaluate it. It is this working with experience that is important in learning.*

A more recent definition from the Social Work Benchmark Statements, which focus on the activities of the social work student, states that:

> *Reflection is a process in which a student reflects critically and evaluatively on past experiences, recent performances, and feedback, and applies this information to the process of integrating awareness (including awareness of the impact of self on others) and new understanding, leading to improved performance.*

> (QAA, 2008)

These definitions help to focus on what are seen as the essential elements of reflective practice: returning to a past experience, thinking about what took place in a particular intervention and reflecting on your thoughts and actions, and identifying what you might do differently in the future. The definitions suggest that reflection is also a process that leads to learning and improved practice.

ACTIVITY **1.1**

Think back to an event while you were on placement where you were asked to undertake a particular task for the first time and where you felt uncertain about your ability to complete the task effectively.

Comment

You will probably find yourself thinking about recent experiences, particularly if they were new or novel, or where you were concerned about your ability. These could be described as common-sense reflections and do not necessarily promote learning. On the other hand, if your reflection is structured, through the use of a reflective diary where you record your thoughts and feelings, or through dialogue with your supervisor, then it can be an active and critical process with the potential to improve your performance in the future.

Roots of reflective practice

An early exponent of reflective practice was John Dewey, an educational philosopher. Writing in the twentieth century, he identified in reflective thinking many of the key elements that we still use today in the reflective process. For Dewey, reflection is particularly important when we are confronted by a problem that perplexes us or about which we feel uncomfortable. We then reflect on the problem to develop a fuller understanding of it and its possible solutions. We do this through critical reasoning and testing our understanding in practice (Dewey, 1938). In using this approach Dewey argued that it enabled people to avoid becoming trapped by routine thinking and actions driven by external forces or authorities. We can relate this latter view of Dewey's to those social work organisations where emphasis is placed on following standardised procedures, which practitioners find stifles creative work with clients.

Dewey's work laid the foundations for the later seminal work of Donald Schön (1983), who sought to understand how practitioners developed their knowledge bases and then applied this knowledge to their practice. He described the person who consciously thinks about his or her practice as the 'reflective practitioner'. In exploring the work of different professions he described two types of reflection. The first, *reflection in action*, is where you think on your feet while you are engaged in an intervention, drawing on experience and theories, and improvise and modify your practice to achieve a better outcome. The second type is *reflection on action*, where the process is undertaken retrospectively, away from the event, starting with recall, a description of what happened, and leading to the integration of theory and practice to better inform future practice through critical analysis of the event.

Schön's work demonstrated that practitioners often encountered situations that were complex, messy and challenging – the 'swampy lowlands of practice', as he described it – where theory or standard procedures were of little help in making sense of a situation. He recognised that reflecting on their practical experience and applying this learning allowed practitioners to 'revise, modify and refine their expertise' (Finlay, 2008, p4). Through this process practitioners developed 'professional artistry', with an ability to integrate the knowledge gained through reflection with formal scientific theories.

A missing element in Schön's work, according to Greenwood (1993), is the important preparatory element of reflective practice where the practitioner pauses to think before acting in order to avoid errors. *Reflection for action* takes place prior to an intervention, with the practitioner planning what they intend to do and how they will do it. Thompson and Thompson (2008) see value in the practitioner thinking ahead to what they might encounter, and what precautions they need to take (for example, in meeting a client who has a history of unpredictable behaviour), so that they are much better prepared when they meet the client. This stage of reflection is helpful in that the practitioner anticipates potential difficulties, leading to a greater sense of control and confidence, with the consequent positive effect on morale and motivation.

Of course, *reflection for action* can be helpful at any stage in your development as a student, but it will become more useful as you gain experience of different interventions. You will then be able to look back to previous experiences as your knowledge and understanding grow and you become more confident about what you might anticipate in a particular situation and the steps to consider before you act.

Before we leave the roots of reflective practice it is important to briefly consider the term *reflexivity*. You may see this term used sometimes interchangeably with reflection, but although they are related terms there are important differences between them. Fook (2002) sees reflexivity as taking into account as many different perspectives in a situation as possible, whereas Jude and Regan (2010) see reflexive thinking as the basis for developing multiple hypotheses, as opposed to a fixed, unchanging view of a situation. According to Finlay (2008), reflexive practitioners engage in critical self-reflection: critically reflecting on the impact of their own background, their assumptions and feelings, as well as wider organisational, ideological and political dimensions. Finlay suggests there are contentious issues about how much practitioners should use reflection to focus on themselves as individuals rather than on the larger social context. Considering the fact that the majority of people who use social work services are in receipt of state benefits it is essential that the wider social and economic context is fully explored when reflecting on work with clients (Walker and Walker, 2009).

Creating conditions for reflection on your practice

In order to develop your skills as a reflective practitioner it is important to have a 'personal reflective space' where you can engage with the process of reflection without distractions, focusing on your own thoughts and feelings that you experience during practice interventions and other significant practice events. This means both the physical space and sufficient time to spend on reflective activity. This is where the support of your practice supervisor can be helpful in ensuring you have the facilities and time to use for reflection. You may also need to negotiate for personal reflective space in your personal life, particularly if you are sharing accommodation with others. Sometimes this space will mean time when you are travelling or doing domestic tasks. This form of reflection is described by

Finlay (2008) as *introspection* and is seen as the dominant model of reflection. It means you are taking personal responsibility for making time to reflect on your practice and becoming more confident as a reflective practitioner.

Because you are using an introspective approach when you are reflecting in your personal space, it is important to ensure that you adopt a critical stance. This means recognising the importance of self-awareness (Thompson and Thompson, 2008). It includes identifying what impact you have on a situation, for example, when working with a client where you have been dissatisfied with your performance, or where the situation has left you with uncomfortable feelings. By using these questions as a starting point when you are in your personal space, you can begin to explore what they mean for you in terms of more effectively developing yourself and your practice. The more honestly you can explore these questions, and it may mean some discomfort (Taylor, 2006), the more the reflective process will challenge your thinking about your practice.

Reflection in a supervisory relationship

Although reflection in your personal space will be the main approach to thinking about your practice, your development will be enhanced by working with a skilled and experienced supervisor. This will normally be your practice educator and/or practice supervisor, who is able to facilitate your learning through reviewing your work with clients, challenging you as you describe your practice, giving you feedback on your practice, and identifying future learning needs. For supervision to be effective it relies on the quality of the relationship and open communication between supervisor and student, undertaken on a regular basis, where there is sufficient time, in an appropriate setting, with conditions of privacy and without interruptions.

To create the right conditions for reflection your supervisor needs to be familiar with your practice, understand the main social work theories and the processes involved in reflective practice. They also need to be able to ask the right questions – the *who, what, where* and *when* of practice – that will help you analyse your practice in a way that leads to greater insight into and understanding of your actions and those of others. You should not expect them to have all the answers to practice issues, but rather to be able to facilitate an increased awareness of the range of possible approaches that you can test out in the future.

Your supervisors should also ensure that there is clarity about the purpose of reflection, that it is an activity concerned with professional learning and development, that personal issues are only addressed in so far as they affect your professional practice, and that you are comfortable discussing your performance (Fook and Askeland, 2007) within carefully established boundaries (Hunt, 2001). In a supportive and trusting learning environment, disclosure about aspects of your performance where there is personal discomfort, if managed sensitively by your supervisor, can offer the potential for enhancing learning in a non-judgmental environment.

To ensure that you are able to use the opportunity to reflect with your supervisor it is helpful to do some preparatory work before you meet. Think about the experiences you have had, review them in your mind so that you are prepared for the session, and offer suggestions for experiences you would like to use for reflection. Here it is helpful to keep a reflective diary, as you are unlikely to be able to rely on your memory for the details of the event, particularly if you have undertaken subsequent work with other clients. If you record in your diary what took place, as soon after the event as possible, you are more likely to capture the issues that are important to take into the supervision session.

Working with your supervisor needs to take place in an atmosphere where you feel safe to express your feelings about your practice. You should be able to acknowledge what you feel are weaknesses in your practice, and where you feel you have made mistakes, so that these can be discussed without any feeling of recrimination. In these conditions you can begin to develop confidence that the feedback you are given, although challenging, is essentially supportive and enables you to develop your practice skills and help you become more self-aware. With the right conditions reflection can be a constructive process and help enhance your confidence and skills, but where conditions are inappropriate then these can inhibit self-development (Yip, 2006).

Creating a suitable environment for learning

It is understandable that you will feel anxious at times during your placement, and while this can be a positive factor in enhancing performance, too much anxiety can inhibit your learning. Anxieties can arise from a number of sources, including adapting to an unfamiliar environment, taking on a new role, establishing a relationship with your supervisor and being responsible for working with clients. You also have to cope with the feeling of being observed and assessed by your supervisor. To help you deal with this anxiety the following conditions should be present in your placement:

- Your supervisor creates a supportive learning environment.

- Your supervisor models appropriate professional behaviour.

- Your supervisor communicates any problems about your performance as soon as they are identified.

- You receive honest feedback that is supportive and provides clear guidelines for improving your performance.

- You are given clear and realistic targets.

- Your supervisor achieves a balance between support and appropriate challenge.

(adapted from McClure, 2002)

These conditions are more likely to be met where the student–supervisor relationship is based on openness, caring, mutually meeting each other's needs, honesty, tolerance and respect for each other.

You are more likely to experience these conditions where the organisational culture values learning and development and encourages its staff to engage in reflection about their own practice (Gould and Baldwin, 2004). An organisation that values feedback on its performance, particularly from those who use the service, and is non-defensive in its evaluation of practice is likely to provide greater opportunities for reflection by its staff.

Reflective techniques

There are a range of different techniques that you can adopt when developing your skills as a reflective practitioner. These will provide you with different opportunities to use different reflective processes and each has its own strengths and limitations.

Reflection for action

Our starting point is *reflection for action*: this is where you gather information through discussion with your supervisor, read case records to try to anticipate the issues you may face, and become aware of the skills and knowledge you will need to feel confident in meeting a client for the first time. This is essentially about thinking ahead and anticipating the important things that you need to be aware of when you meet the client.

Reflection in action

The next stage is *reflection in action*, which involves reflecting on a situation as it occurs, for example, when meeting a client for the first time. In this situation you make connections between your feelings and what social work theories inform you about the situation. When you are engaging with a client and building rapport it is particularly important to be aware of your feelings as this will enable you to be more in touch with the power of the client's emotions (Shulman, 1999). The more you can recognise clients' emotions, particularly around power, status and anxiety, the more successful you are likely to be in your practice (Morrison, 2006).

CASE STUDY

John is visiting Bernard, who has a severe physical disability. As Bernard describes how he manages many aspects of his life, with limited support from a personal carer, John is made aware that severe disability does not mean the person is necessarily restricted in living their life as normally as possible. John also recognises that he has tended to place too much focus on Bernard's physical impairment and how this impinges on his life, and has failed to see him more holistically. John also begins to realise that the seminar he attended on the social model of disability now makes sense as Bernard describes his life experience and how he manages his disability.

Comment

When you are faced with a new situation you are observing and listening to what the client is saying and this begins to influence how you view the person and their needs. It can also trigger thoughts about theories that you have read that begin to make sense when you reflect on the experience, and influence how you view similar situations in the future.

Maclean and Harrison (2009, p121) suggest that reflection in action involves:

- thinking ahead ('Right, if that happens, I need to . . .');
- being critical ('That didn't seem to work very well . . . ');
- storing up experiences ('I could have dealt with that better; next time I'll try . . .');
- analysing what happened ('She is saying that to test me – I think I should . . .').

Of course, reflection in action is taking place continually if you are focusing on being as effective as possible in an intervention and this helps you develop an awareness of the needs of clients and your practice. As Maclean and Harrison (2009) point out, there are limitations. You are only seeing things from your own perspective and the timescale can be extremely short, with decisions having to be made quickly. The scope for reflection may be limited and you may have to exercise judgment in a fast-changing situation and often under extreme conditions (Ixer, 1999).

CASE STUDY

Ben is a student on placement in a learning disability service and has been asked by his supervisor to visit Graham, a client who has recently moved into his own flat and is being supported to live independently for the first time. When Ben meets Graham he feels unsure about how he should respond as Graham speaks very slowly and is difficult to understand. Ben remembers what he has read about communicating with a person with a learning disability and, 'thinking on his feet', he slows down, using short, simple sentences and giving Graham time to respond. He also focuses on what Graham is saying and what he is trying to express through his non-verbal gestures. Ben becomes more relaxed, waiting for Graham to answer and is slowly able to understand what Graham is saying and begins to form a picture of how he is coping in his new flat.

Comment

This situation demonstrates the value of reflection in action, where you can pause and rethink your approach, drawing on previous experience (in this example, discussion with your supervisor and reading about the needs of people with learning disabilities). It is all too easy to be overwhelmed by the situation and forget what you have been told or read when you are sitting in front of the client thinking, 'What do I say next?' Pausing to rethink your approach helps you begin to refine your practice and, most importantly, improves your response to the needs of the client.

Reflection on action

In contrast, *reflection on action* is undertaken subsequent to the intervention. The main difference is that you are no longer under pressure to respond in a particular way and have more time to reflect on the intervention. Here you are able to explore why you acted in the way you did and what was happening during an intervention. When you are reflecting on the action with your supervisor you overcome the limitation of only seeing your practice from your own perspective. Working with another person who can clarify and challenge your assumptions about your practice adds a further critical dimension to the process of reflection.

CASE STUDY

Sarah is completing her placement in a local authority children and families service and she has been asked to work with Lindsay, a single parent, whose daughter Leah is the subject of a Child Protection Plan. Lindsay has a history of substance misuse, but has been abstinent for some time following a Drug Rehabilitation Requirement imposed by the court. Sarah is visiting her to ensure that Leah is not at risk of neglect due to her mother's history of substance misuse. Lindsay is very guarded in her responses to Sarah, who is trying to build her relationship with Lindsay in order to work more effectively with her and support her, so that she doesn't slip back into using illegal substances. During the interview Sarah feels inhibited in asking specific questions about Leah and is frustrated at not being able to make a more effective judgment about Lindsay's care for her daughter. When Sarah subsequently meets her supervisor she reflects on the intervention and voices her concern that she has not achieved the correct balance between engaging effectively with Lindsay and recognising how much Lindsay is working to manage her addiction, and at the same time asking more questions and probing more deeply into the care of Leah. Sarah is concerned that she is not able to ask more challenging questions that would enable her to understand whether Lindsay is being evasive about her lifestyle and her daughter's care. Sarah acknowledges that she has strong feelings about women who use illegal substances and who have childcare responsibilities.

Comment

Through the process of reflection Sarah is able to explore her feelings about substance misuse and her ambivalent feelings about Lindsay and her care for her daughter. Through a series of questions from her supervisor she is able to understand how her feelings might be inhibiting her in adopting a more positive relationship with Lindsay and consequently a more effective way of working with her that recognises the progress that Lindsay has made to manage her addiction. Challenging her to explore her personal beliefs, assumptions and biases about people who use substances can help Sarah to be a more effective social worker. Her supervisor also suggests that she rehearse some of the challenging questions (reflection for action) she would like to use when she next visits Lindsay so that she can develop a more informed understanding of the quality of care that Leah receives.

Using a framework to aid reflection

When you are reflecting on action you are thinking back to an experience, to what happened and how you felt. This means going beyond simply recalling and describing the event to thinking critically about the different aspects of the experience. Using a framework to guide your reflection can be important as it provides a structure which, with time, can become an established part of the reflective process. There are many similar frameworks in the literature on reflective practice that are intended to help you order your thoughts when thinking about an experience you want to use for reflection. A model of structured reflection based on Johns (2006) should help you to focus on the essential elements that you need to consider when reflecting on a particular experience.

Description of the experience

Stage 1: Reflection

- What was I trying to achieve?
- What were the consequences of my actions?
- How did I feel about the experience as it was happening?
- How do I think the service user felt about it?
- What worked well and what could have been improved?

Stage 2: What factors influenced the way I acted in the situation?

- My thoughts and feelings?
- Knowledge and information I considered?
- The reaction of the service user?
- Other external factors?

Stage 3: Future action

- How might I act differently next time?
- What might be the consequences of a different approach for myself and for the service user?
- What factors might inhibit my acting in a new way?

Stage 4: Learning

- How do I feel now about the experience?

- What have I learned from reflecting on this experience?

This series of questions offers the opportunity to thoroughly consider a range of thoughts, feelings and assumptions about your practice that together with questions from your supervisor will enable you to develop your reflective capabilities. A framework can be helpful when first learning how to reflect, and as you gain experience you should not feel restricted to using a particular model but develop your own particular approach that sits more easily with your own needs and priorities.

RESEARCH SUMMARY

Research by Ruch (2005) has demonstrated the value of reflective practice in work with children and families. She argues that 'holistic reflective practice', where social workers adopt a relationship-based approach to their practice, challenges bureaucratic responses to the complexity, risk and uncertainty inherent in such work, and encourages more creative and thoughtful practice. Reflection enables practitioners to recognise the diverse sources of knowledge embedded in their practice as well as theoretical perspectives. Similarly team discussions were used to consider different theoretical perspectives and evidence alongside responses grounded in practice wisdom and intuition. Ruch sees reflective practice as the key determinant in the successful application of relationship-based practice, but for this to be successful practitioners need to work in a supportive organisational context, with clear professional boundaries, collaborative and communicative working relationships, and multi-faceted reflective forums.

Keeping a reflective diary

Keeping a reflective diary is a valuable process that can help you develop your practice, particularly if you are able to maintain it over the duration of your placement, and if you use it to describe accounts of particular experiences that are significant to you. It is a particularly useful vehicle for increasing your self-awareness as you acknowledge the limits to your understanding of practice situations. Writing things down is particularly helpful in enabling you to clarify your thoughts and emotions and to work out future strategies. It can also help you to measure your progress over the duration of a placement (Cottrell, 2003).

Some students keep diaries on an ongoing basis while others write up specific experiences that are significant to them, or when requested by their tutor or supervisor. As diaries are a personal account and a private record you can use them to report your thoughts, feelings and views about your experiences, not just the factual details. It is particularly important that you also consider issues of confidentiality and that diary entries are not written in a way that enables individual clients to be identified.

There is no right or wrong way to write a reflective diary. Your approach will be one that is right for you, but it is helpful to go beyond pure description and incorporate your reactions, thoughts, theories, learning and hoped for outcomes (Parker, 2004). How you write your diary entries is your personal choice but it can nevertheless be helpful to consider some general guidelines that enable you to capture the essential elements of a particular experience and event. The following suggestions are helpful.

- Set some time aside each week for writing up your diary, but remember that it is advisable to write down your experiences while they are still fresh in your memory. The longer you leave it after an experience the harder it is to recall exactly what happened and how you felt about it.

- Give yourself sufficient time to mull over your thoughts and ideas.

- Don't worry about style or presentation as this is your personal diary.

- Describe what happened, but also ask yourself critical questions about the 'how', 'why' and 'what' of a situation.

Reflective questions

You could use the following set of questions to assist your thinking when writing up your diary or when you are thinking back over an experience and discussing your practice with your supervisor.

- What was I aiming to do when (for example) I met the person?

- What exactly did I do (describe it precisely)?

- Why did I choose that particular action?

- What theories or models informed my action?

- How successful was I?

- Could I have dealt with the situation better?

- How could I do things differently next time?

- Has the review of my practice changed the way I intend to do things in the future?

(adapted from Allin and Turnock, 2007)

---

*ACTIVITY **1.2***

In order to develop your skill in writing reflectively, think back to a situation that challenged you in some way and feel free to write whatever thoughts and feelings come into your head. By doing this you are giving yourself permission to engage with your emotions and not censor your thoughts and feelings as you become aware of them when you recall the experience.

Comment

Freeing up your writing can enable you to be honest about your practice; something that you might not want to do when you discuss a situation with your supervisor, for fear of being judged not to be sufficiently 'professional'. For a discussion on the value of writing reflectively see Archambeault (2009).

Reflection in groups

An additional opportunity to reflect on practice can take place in group settings, where you are able to learn alongside other students. Reflection in these settings is particularly useful as you are able to see how others deal with issues in their interventions. Thompson and Thompson (2008) suggest that group learning experiences offer some particular benefits, including learning about how others use their skills. Realising that they too may have anxieties about their practice can help you feel better about your own limitations and concerns, and can help you put things into perspective. They also recommend that during group discussions you use the opportunity to undertake some *reflection in action*, by focusing on other presentations and being proactive in seeking out the learning that can be gained from trying to identify explicit learning points from the discussions. Here you are using your analytic skills to make sense of the experience and relate discussion points to your own practice. One caution when using groups for reflection is to ensure that confidentiality is acknowledged as it can be more of a problem than in one-to-one situations. Jude and Regan's (2010) research offers some useful ground rules when working in a reflective group, including the following points.

- Connect your comments to the material being presented.

- Be mindful of negative feedback.

- Present your ideas tentatively.

- Don't mirror the presenter's points but offer alternatives to enable differences to emerge from the process. Too many similar ideas are not helpful.

- Offer as many explanations for a situation as possible.

RESEARCH SUMMARY

A recent research project by Jude and Regan (2010) explored reflective practice in a multi-disciplinary 5–19 years prevention team. Members of the team participated in a 'fortnightly reflective space' where cases they were working on were presented to the group with an opportunity to explore a variety of options, to facilitate learning and help transform practice. A range of methods were used to reflect on practice, including imagery, toys and role play. From this work key themes emerged, including the value

(Continued)

(Continued)

*of multiple perspectives, the benefits of using a systematic reflective space where prac-
titioners use a collective approach to reflect on their practice, the adoption of different
techniques, and approaching work with families with more curiosity. Jude and Regan's
findings suggest that the reflective space created opportunities for new ways of thinking
and enabled team members to transform their practice.*

Developing both analytic and intuitive skills

As a student your practice will be informed by a range of theories, mainly from
your academic studies, while other learning will arise from the experience of different interventions during placements. At first this can be difficult as you will
not have had sufficient direct practice to appreciate how theoretical perspectives
can be synthesised with practice experience. As you gain more experience, and
particularly where you use your reflection to explore critical incidents, you will
develop a more sophisticated understanding of how you can integrate practice
knowledge with social work theories. This will enable you to gradually construct
a body of informal knowledge, or experiential wisdom, from your practice (Parker
and Bradley, 2007), adding another layer of knowledge and skills, along with the
social work theories and intervention methods you have learned during your academic work and while in placements.

In her review of child protection Professor Eileen Munro (2011) describes how
social workers use both analytic and intuitive reasoning in their work and
together these enable the practitioner to make assumptions that result in decisions based on sound judgments. Analytic skills are those that are developed
through academic studies and guided reading, particularly interpreting findings
from research and practice that enable the worker to make sense of situations.
Intuitive reasoning on the other hand is primarily derived from experience and is
generally considered to be an unconscious process that occurs when the worker
experiences situations. These lead to beliefs or 'gut feelings' about situations that
provide some security when operating in a world of uncertainty. Munro (2011,
p90) gives an example of how the experienced social worker visiting a family
quickly has *an intuitive awareness of the state of the dynamics in the family – the
warmth of the relationship between family members, or level of fear felt by a
child*. This intuitive reasoning blends with conscious awareness and enables the
worker to shape the way they progress an interview with the family.

Reflecting on intuitive reasoning

Although Munro sees intuitive reasoning as important, she argues that experience on its own is insufficient, and that using reflection, where the practitioner
can make time to mull over the experience and learn from it, is also important,

particularly when undertaken in supervision and in discussion with colleagues. This is where reflection can help practitioners draw out their intuitive reasoning so that it can be reviewed and challenged, rather than remaining unspoken, with the danger that biases and errors are not replaced by more considered approaches. Munro suggests that we may cling to our beliefs despite observing evidence to the contrary, and act without evaluating whether the most effective course has been followed. Because social workers often find themselves having to make rapid decisions and act under pressure from a range of sources, there is the tendency to revert to intuitive reasoning when overloaded or exhausted. This is where reflection is important in helping the practitioner articulate their feelings about their practice and indentify the bases for particular beliefs which may not previously have been consciously verbalised.

The importance of recognising emotions

In her report Munro (2011) also recognises that there is an important emotional dimension to how social workers reason and act. We have also seen, when reflecting both 'in' and 'on' practice, how work with service users can lead to strong emotional feelings and that it is important to recognise that these play a crucial role in social work, in terms of the awareness of both service users' feelings and your own as a practitioner. Where a practitioner lacks self-awareness and suppresses their emotions it may result in less effective engagement and relationship building with service users (Morrison, 2006). Morrison also suggests that service users, many of whom may have experienced multiple problems, can detect the practitioner's emotional state faster than the practitioner can elicit the emotions of the service user. The ability to empathise and communicate skilfully is therefore seen as an important attribute in helping service users feel positive about their relationship with the practitioner. Here there is value in understanding the concept of 'emotional intelligence' (Goleman, 1996) with its potential to offer insights into the ability to monitor one's own and others' feelings and emotions that are an important guide to thinking and action. Being able to reflect on your emotions in a supervisory relationship is important for the insights it can provide into not only how you develop self-awareness, but also how you can build more successful relationships when you are in touch with service users emotional states. In their discussion of the value of emotional intelligence Thompson and Thompson (2008) argue that if we are not attuned to the emotional aspects of our work then there is the risk that we can be insensitive to the needs of people we are trying to help and may also put ourselves at risk by not recognising emotionally harmful situations.

ACTIVITY **1.3**

Can you think of an example of practice where you experienced strong emotional feelings when working with a service user and where the quality of the relationship was an important factor in helping the person change?

Comment

This activity suggests that successful practice can be strongly influenced by recognising the power of emotions (your own and the service user's) and how this can be an important factor in helping to engage with a service user and develop a relationship that results in a more positive intervention.

CHAPTER SUMMARY

This chapter has introduced you to the concept of reflective practice, drawing on the work of the early proponents and more recent writers on the subject. It has also provided you with a range of practical approaches that you can use, both in a personal capacity and in supervisory relationships when on placement. The research examples have highlighted the importance of reflection in enabling social workers to find more creative ways of working with clients, drawing particular attention to the importance of intuitive feelings and emotional awareness. Developing an understanding of reflective practice and the confidence to use a range of techniques during your programme of study can lay the foundation for lifelong learning and development as a social worker.

FURTHER READING

Knott, C and Scragg, T (eds) (2013) *Reflective practice in social work.* 3rd edition. Exeter: Learning Matters.

This is an introductory text on reflective practice, with clear explanations of different approaches, widely illustrated with activities, case studies and research summaries, and provides you with a thorough understanding of the value of using reflection to develop your practice.

REFERENCES

Allin, L and Turnock, C (2007) *Assessing student performance in work-based learning: Making practice-based assessment work.* www.practicebasedlearning.org, accessed 12 November 2012.

Archambeault, J (2009) *Reflective reader: Social work and mental health.* Exeter: Learning Matters.

Boud, D, Keogh, R and Walker, D (1985) *Reflection: Turning experience into learning.* London: Kogan Page.

Cottrell, S (2003) *Skills for success.* Basingstoke: Palgrave Macmillan.

Dewey, J (1938*) Logic: The theory of inquiry.* Troy, MN: Rinehart and Winston.

Finlay, L (2008) Reflecting on 'Reflective Practice', BPPL Paper 52. www.open.ac.uk/cetl-workspace/ceticontent (accessed 14 November 2012).

Fook, J (2002) *Social work: Critical theory and practice.* London: Sage.

Fook, J and Askeland, GA (2007) Challenges of critical reflection: Nothing ventured, nothing gained. *Social Work Education,* 26 (5), 520–33.

Goleman, D (1996) *Emotional intelligence: Why it can matter more than IQ.* London: Bloomsbury.

Gould, N and Baldwin, M (2004) *Social work, critical reflection and the learning organisation.* Aldershot: Ashgate.

Greenwood, J (1993) Some considerations concerning practice and feedback in nursing education. *Journal of Advanced Nursing*, 18, 1992–2002.

Hunt, C (2001) Shifting shadows: Metaphors and maps for facilitating reflective practice. *Reflective Practice*, 2 (3), 275–87.

Ixer, G (1999) There's no such thing as reflection. *British Journal of Social Work*, 29 (4), 513–27.

Johns, C (2006) *Engaging reflection in practice: A narrative approach.* Oxford: Blackwell Publishing.

Jude, J and Regan, S (2010) *An exploration of reflective practice in a social care team.* Leeds: Children's Workforce Development Council.

Knott, C and Scragg, T (eds) (2013) *Reflective practice in social work.* 3rd edition. Exeter: Learning Matters.

Maclean, S and Harrison, R (2009) *Theory and practice, a straightforward guide for social work students.* Rugeley: Kirwin Maclean Associates.

McClure, P (2002) Reflection on practice. www.practicebasedlearning.org (accessed 19 December 2012).

Morrison, T (2006) Emotional intelligence, emotion and social work: Context, characteristics, complications and contribution. *British Journal of Social Work*, 37 (2), 245–63.

Munro, E (2011) *The Munro report: Final report – a child centred system.* London: Department of Education. www.education.gov.uk/publications/Munro-Review.pdf (accessed 2 December 2012).

Parker, J (2004) *Effective practice learning in social work.* Exeter: Learning Matters.

Parker, J and Bradley, G (2007) *Social work practice: Assessment, planning, intervention and review.* 2nd edition. Exeter: Learning Matters.

Ruch, G (2005) Relationship-based practice and reflective practice: Holistic approaches to contemporary child care social work. *Child and Family Social Work*, 10 (2) May, 111–23.

Schön, D (1983) *The reflective practitioner: How professionals think in action.* New York: Basic Books.

Shulman, L (1999) *The skills of helping: Individuals and groups.* Illinois: Peacock.

Taylor, C (2006) Narrating significant experience: Reflective accounts and the production of (self) knowledge. *British Journal of Social Work*, 36 (2), 189–206.

Thompson, S and Thompson, N (2008) *The critically reflective practitioner.* Basingstoke: Palgrave Macmillan.

Quality Assurance Agency for Higher Education (2008) *Subject benchmark statement: Social work.* Gloucester: QAA.

Walker, A and Walker, C (2009) Social policy and social work. In Adams, R, Dominelli, L and Payne, M (eds) *Social work themes: Issues and critical debates.* 3rd edition. Basingstoke: Palgrave Macmillan.

Yip, K (2006) Self-reflection in reflective practice, a note of caution. *British Journal of Social Work*, 35 (5), 777–88.

Chapter 2
Self-presentation

Gill Constable

A C H I E V I N G   A   S O C I A L   W O R K   D E G R E E

This chapter will help you to develop the following capabilities from the **Professional Capabilities Framework.**

- **Professionalism.** Identify and behave as a professional social worker, committed to professional development.
- **Values and ethics.** Apply social work ethical principles and values to guide professional practice.

It will also introduce you to the following standards as set out in the 2008 social work subject benchmark statement.

5.8   Skills in personal and professional development

Introduction

In this chapter we will be looking at self-presentation. This is not simply about our appearance, but our behaviours, thoughts, belief systems and values that impact on how we present to ourselves and others, and what this means as a social worker. The approach that will be adopted is thinking about our development as part of a journey where our destination is to become a competent, empathic and reflective practitioner. But in some senses of course the journey never ends and the gaining of *practice wisdom* (Hardiker and Barker, 1981, p2) incrementally increases with experience. So, while reading this chapter you will need to be focused on enhancing your own self-awareness, and the impact that you have on others. We will start by looking at self-identity and the concept of professionalism through exploring belief systems, and how these impact on our *metaphor of life* (Cottrell, 2003, p39). We will move on to the development of critical and analytical skills and assertive behaviour as this is empowering to us and others.

The importance of self-awareness in social work

Thompson (2005) seeks to define social work, and summarises it as the performance of statutory duties, the management of both caring for and controlling people. Social work resides between people's personal difficulties and issues that cause public concern. He states that social work can be seen as doing *society's dirty work* (p6), so it is paramount that social work is committed to social justice. The Professional Capabilities Framework for Social Workers in England (2012) states that by the end of their first placement student social workers should be able to apply ethical principles and values to guide their professional practice. The following capabilities are listed:

- Understand and, with support, apply the profession's ethical principles;

- Recognise and, with support, manage the impact of own values on professional practice;

- Identify and, with guidance, manage potentially conflicting values and ethical dilemmas;

- Elicit and respect the needs and views of service users and carers and, with support, promote their participation in decision-making wherever possible;

- Recognise and, with support, promote individuals' rights to autonomy and self-determination;

- Promote and protect the privacy of individuals within and outside their families and networks, recognising the requirements of professional accountability and information sharing.

Thompson (2005) confirms the importance of an ethical value base for practitioners as it provides: a guide to action; framework to understand practice; process to determine decisions; motivation and commitment to practice. Gilbert (2005, p33), when writing about the leadership of self, states:

> *Crucial to this is whether the leader has positive values, is aware of them, can nurture them and turn them into positive behaviours.*

The link between values and behaviour is clearly stated here. Social work offers numerous challenges. There is a fine balance between care and control within people's lives, as can be seen for example in child protection assessments. How important is self-awareness in social work? Can you be a social worker during your working hours and at other times engage in activities or hold beliefs that are in contradiction to social work values?

CASE STUDY

Steve was a mature student in his first semester at university. He was generally regarded in his circle of friends as the 'funny man'. He recognised that sometimes his humour was 'a bit near the mark', but he always rationalised this to himself by thinking that people should 'lighten up'. Steve was genuinely surprised to be challenged about his sexism by his friend Iain, after he called a female student 'Nice Legs' in the student bar.

ACTIVITY **2.1**

1. Do you think that when this type of behaviour occurs socially it is less of an issue than if it takes place during teaching time, or on a social work placement?
2. Why do you think that Steve was surprised at being challenged by Iain?

Comment

One way to respond to this case study is to assess Steve's comment against the social work values as set down in the Professional Capabilities Framework, and determine how it measures up against them. Steve's surprise indicates that he assumed that Iain would think there was nothing amiss about this behaviour, and anyway this was not Iain's issue. In fact the challenge made by Iain had a profound impact on Steve and gave him the opportunity to have an *auto-biographically critical moment* (Mason, 2002, p20) to reflect on the incident, his assumptions, and how another man, whom he liked, viewed his behaviour.

If a sexist, racist or homophobic comment or joke is made should it be up to those groups to challenge it, as it is at their expense, or do we not all have a duty to challenge discrimination, and form an alliance with groups of people who on a routine basis are discriminated against? Part of Iain's subsequent discussion with Steve revolved around the lack of congruence between Steve's values and those of their social work course. In that moment Parsloe and Wray's (2001, p173) view rang true for Steve, that:

> People only take self-development seriously when they recognize either an immediate tangible benefit or a credible negative consequence of not doing so.

He did not want to lose Iain's friendship, and he started to reflect on his relationships with some of his peers, and whether he accorded people the respect that they deserved. Steve apologised to the student for his comment.

Belief systems

A component of developing self-awareness is to identify what are our belief systems. Cottrell (2003, p38) identifies the use of metaphors to illustrate how we view life. This reveals what our current belief systems are, and whether we generally have an optimistic and hopeful outlook, or whether we have a tendency towards pessimism.

Our belief systems are developed throughout our childhood and adolescence. If you grew up in an environment where there was tension and anxiety this might have affected your overall view of life, and for you the metaphor of life as a trial or burden may resonate, whereas if you remember your childhood as mainly happy, your metaphors may be about life as fun and a gift. Our philosophy of

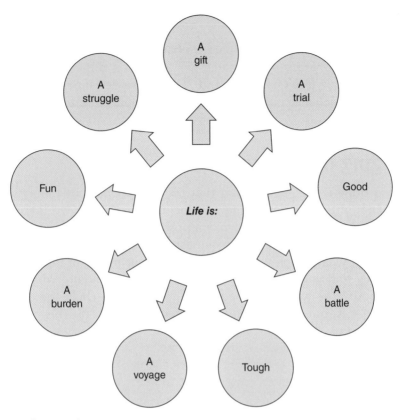

Figure 2.1 Life metaphors

life is often revealed in how we present ourselves to other people. Koprowska (2005, p41) suggests an activity that enables us to reflect on the messages that we give to others.

ACTIVITY 2.2

Think about yourself for a moment. What is your usual posture? What is your speed or pace when you are walking? Here are some possibilities (picture the posture and facial expression that goes with each as you read them).

- *Always in a hurry.*
- *Easygoing, relaxed.*
- *Tense, worried.*
- *Cheerful, friendly.*
- *High energy, enthusiastic and excited.*

If you were to ask a friend, family member or colleague, how would they describe your usual posture and facial expression? What do they think is your life metaphor? Do you agree?

Comment

We all need to think about the impact we have on others. A social worker who looks permanently harassed or irritated will experience difficulty in establishing rapport with people (see Chapters 6 and 7). Once we develop self-awareness we can change, and enhance our strengths, and one approach is to develop positive thinking habits.

Managing our thoughts

Butler and Hope (2007, p9) explain that cognitive behaviour theory suggests it is our thoughts that determine our feelings, and once we learn how to manage our thoughts we can provoke a positive emotional change. For example, if you have a sudden feeling of sadness you need to ask yourself what you were thinking; what image was going through your mind? In the same way, if you suddenly find yourself feeling elated, ask yourself again, what were you thinking about? The way we manage our thoughts is to challenge our internal dialogue, that is, our self-talk (Back and Back, 1999, p12). This can be illustrated as follows:

Noticing our thoughts

Situation	Feelings	**What went through my mind at the time:** *what was I telling myself, what images was I seeing?*
Cindy and Don Peters contacted the Team Manager in my placement and said that they were not prepared to see me as I was too young and inexperienced.	Surprised, upset, confused	• I must have appeared incompetent when I first met them. • I may fail my placement.
Joy phoned me and said that I had really helped her to get some things straight in her own mind by listening, and talking through with her what she can do to manage her two-year-old daughter's temper tantrums.	Happy	• I am able to help people. • I am able to get alongside young parents.

You can become aware of your thoughts by noticing what you say to yourself, especially in moments when you experience intense emotions. A feeling is always preceded by a thought. Catch the thought and you will understand where the feeling came from. To develop self-esteem and emotional resilience you need to adopt self-talk that is balanced, proportionate to the situation and supportive, in contrast to self-talk that is critical and judgmental.

Butler and Hope (pp72 and 74) have identified *thirteen kinds of crooked thinking*. They are very common and most of us at some time have had these thoughts, so you may recognise some of them either in yourself or in other people:

• Catastrophising – automatically thinking that a disaster will happen, for example: *My partner is late home, maybe there has been a multi-vehicle accident on the motorway.*

- Overgeneralising – if something happens once, thinking it will happen again: *She is always unreliable.*

- Exaggeration – making difficulties worse than they really are: *I am devastated my team lost.*

- Dismissing positive statements and events: *It was really just a bit of luck that my dissertation achieved the highest mark in the year group.*

- Mind reading – thinking that you know what other people are thinking: *I know what he was thinking, that I am incompetent.*

- Making predictions about the future: *I can see exactly what will happen; it will be a disaster, mark my words.*

- Using extreme language without any balance: *If she doesn't stay with him, he will die of a broken heart.*

- Taking things personally: *I know why I was allocated this case, I'm hated by management.*

- Taking the blame when it is not your fault: *It's down to me that Phillip got hit by Tina. I spoke to her two weeks ago about her aggression.*

- Mistaking feelings for facts: *Lauren dislikes me intensely; she ignored me on the stairs today.*

- Name calling: *What a fool I am. There is no fool like an old fool.*

- Making a situation into a crisis: *What if the plane is hijacked?*

- Thinking things would be better if they were different: *If only I was wealthy I would be happy.*

Are some of these thoughts familiar to you? Have you heard other people express them?

If we keep repeating negative and often fearful ideas to ourselves, they reinforce a gloomy perspective. The good news is that we can change our thinking patterns and beliefs into positive, life-affirming approaches (Seligman, 2003).

Self-talk can be changed by challenging negative thoughts with questions such as the following.

- What other ways of looking at this are there?

- Am I being too hard on myself?

- What would a friend say to me at a time like this?

- Is there any evidence for my negative thoughts?

- What are the facts?

- What is the worst that could happen, even if things do not go the way I want them to?

- I have coped with difficulties before and I will cope again.

- In six months' time will this matter to me?

CASE STUDY

Gerry started working in a community project for people with mental health needs. Her role was to develop a number of support groups. A priority area that had been identified was for people with depression. Gerry decided to utilise cognitive behaviour therapy as the theory to underpin the work of the group. She delivered some workshops that explained the theory to the service users and asked them to keep thought records to become familiar with their self-talk, and to track when they had sudden mood changes. Over time the group became familiar with their self-talk, and developed the habit of turning negative statements into positive ones. They could also identify and feed back to each other examples of 'crooked thinking'. Set out below is one of the tasks that Gerry set the group.

Ways of seeing

	Pessimistic statement	Optimistic statement
1	It never rains but it pours	The sun is always behind the clouds
2	I'm a worrier, always will be	
3	There is too much change going on	With change come new opportunities
4	Things are bleak	
5	Don't bother trying to improve things	
6	We've tried that, it didn't work	
7	Luck never comes our way	

ACTIVITY 2.3

Take the negative statements that have not been reworded and think how you could make them positive.

How easy or difficult did you find this?

Comment

Seligman (2003) characterises pessimism as a belief that sees misfortunes as pervasive and permanent. Another concept developed by Peterson *et al.* (1993) is learned helplessness, where the person believes that whatever they do will have no impact. Seligman maintains that optimism and hope can be learned through challenging our thoughts. So, returning to the statements above, these can be challenged in the following way.

Ways of seeing

Pessimistic statement	Comment about the pessimistic statement	Change to an optimistic statement
It never rains but it pours	Pervasive statement	*The sun is always behind the clouds*
I'm a worrier, always will be	Learned helplessness Permanent statement	*On occasions I worry, but most of the time I tend to get on with things*
There is too much change going on	Pervasive statement	*With change come new opportunities*
Things are bleak	Pervasive and permanent statement	*Things are difficult at the moment but nothing goes on for ever*
Don't bother trying to improve things	Learned helplessness	*Where there is a problem there is a solution*
We've tried that, it didn't work	Learned helplessness	*Now it's time to resolve this using our previous experience*
Luck never comes our way	Permanent statement	*Most of the time we are very lucky*

Butler and Hope (2007, pp73 and 74) identify *extremist words* that, said to ourselves or other people, sound blaming, create guilt and increase intra-personal and interpersonal stress. These words highlight Seligman's identification of pessimistic thoughts as seeing difficulties as all-pervasive and permanent.

- I *always* get asked to do the boring, routine things in the team.

- I will *never* be able to change.

- *Nobody* takes any interest in my achievements.

Particular words add stress and pressure, as in the following examples.

- Should: I *should* offer to help more. We often say this when we feel some guilt.

- Must: I *must* do this right now.

- Have to: I *have to* stay here otherwise my manager says the whole service will fall apart.

- Ought: I *ought to* go round and see him.

If these words are changed as suggested by Dibley (1986) we can see how they empower us, as we are in control and making choices.

- *I can choose* to offer to help more.

- *I might* do this.

- *I could* stay here, but the decision *will* be mine.

- *I may* go round and see him.

Managing stress through our behaviour

We have considered the importance of developing self-awareness and being clear about our values, and how our thoughts impact on feelings. We now need to make the link with behaviour. A significant issue that social workers need to be mindful of is the stressful nature of their occupation, and their responsibility to take care of their health.

RESEARCH SUMMARY

In the course of the last decade self-reported injuries in the health and social care sector have declined, but employer-reported injuries have increased.

In 2010/11 there were about 4.7 million lost working days (1.6 days per worker) due to self-reported work-related illness or workplace injury. Almost 90 per cent of these were illness related. This is the highest number of days lost per worker in any sector and significantly higher than the average of 0.98 days per worker for all industries. There were an estimated 104,000 new cases of work-related ill health, with rates for stress in particular significantly above the average for all industries. There were 11,390 reported injuries to employees in the health sector and 6,453 in social care. The majority of the reported injuries were handling injuries (39 per cent for health and 29 per cent for social care) and a quarter were slips and trips (RIDDOR). Furthermore, over half of all the reported injuries involving assault arose in the health and social care sector (RIDDOR).

(Health and Safety Executive website, 2012)

Social workers often deal with uncertainties and complexities. Self-awareness enables us to develop coping strategies to deal with pressures to ensure that our behaviour is appropriate and positive. One coping strategy for stress is the development of assertiveness behaviour (Thompson *et al.*, 1994). There can be confusion, particularly about what is assertive behaviour as opposed to aggression.

Back and Back (1999, p1) give the following definitions.

Assertive behaviour

- Standing up for your own rights in such a way that you do not violate another person's rights.

- Expressing your needs, wants, opinions, feelings and beliefs in a direct, honest and appropriate way.

Non-assertive behaviour

- Not standing up for your rights, or doing so in such a way that others can easily disregard them.

- Expressing your needs, wants, opinions, feelings and beliefs in apologetic, diffident or self-effacing ways.

- Not expressing honestly your needs, wants, opinions, feelings and beliefs.

Aggressive behaviour

- Standing up for your own rights, but doing so in such a way that you violate the rights of other people.

- Ignoring or dismissing the needs, wants, opinions, feelings or beliefs of others.

- Expressing your needs, wants and opinions (which may be honest or dishonest) in inappropriate ways.

People do not fit into these categories neatly, and we can all move between them depending on the situation and who we are with. For example, Sonia was seen at work as being 'strong-minded' and assertive in her approach, and the staff team and tenants of the bail hostel where she was the manager thought her approach was fair and appropriate. Her deputy manager Angus was surprised at how different Sonia was towards her adolescent son, who appeared to 'run rings' around his mother. She tolerated his casual discourtesy to her without dissent. This can be explained by returning to people's belief systems. In Sonia's case she has an understanding of what is required in her professional role to support and prepare the tenants to move on from the hostel, but her beliefs about herself as a mother, and what she must tolerate, impact on her behaviour towards her son, which Angus perceives as passive.

People who exhibit aggressive behaviour believe that their own needs and rights are more important than those of others. Non-assertive people believe that other people's needs and rights matter more than their own. In contrast, assertive people believe that their own and other people's rights and needs should be recognised, and that we are all entitled to contribute and participate.

The consequences of non-assertive behaviour

People who behave in a passive manner may be motivated by a wish to reduce conflict and feelings of guilt. Sometimes there is also some pride in putting other people's needs before their own, which can be experienced as being like a 'martyr'. Back and Back (1999) identify the consequences that this behaviour has on the person, other people and practice. Non-assertive behaviour may lead to a lowering of self-esteem and feelings of powerlessness. Anger, resentment, self-pity and hurt feelings can become internalised. This may lead to feelings of stress which are manifested in physical health problems such as headaches and muscular cramps. Ironically, non-assertive people often want to be liked, but their behaviour creates the reverse.

People who are non-assertive show this through their verbal and non-verbal communication. For example, instead of directly asking for something they may elaborate at great length, apologise for the request and their sentences may tail off at the end. Other examples include putting their hand over their mouth, crossing their arms for protection and adopting a slouched posture. The metaphor to fit this behaviour could be 'life is a struggle'.

Initially other people may feel sorry for the non-assertive person due to their lack of agency and see them as a doormat, but this leads to feelings of irritation as the person does not articulate their views or what they want. Non-assertive people may be ignored and avoided by others. The effect on their practice is that conflicts are not dealt with and decisions may not be made.

The consequences of aggressive behaviour

The hallmark of aggressive behaviour is a rigid approach to what the person will or will not do. At times other people will admire this approach as it can appear that the person is standing up for themselves. There is a sense of power and control and the release of repressed emotions. In the longer term this behaviour may produce feelings of guilt, or the person might start to become cynical and negative in outlook. Other people may dislike the person, avoid them and undermine them obliquely. The life metaphor that would fit this behaviour is 'life is a battle'. Long-term health consequences can occur, such as high blood pressure.

Aggressive behaviour in extreme moments can show itself in fast, fluent speech that may be abrupt. Bodily movements are fast, table-thumping may occur, fingers are pointed at other people, eyes stare and arms are crossed. The person is not always approachable, or easy to be with. This can have negative and dangerous effects on practice, as people may not be prepared to report significant information to the person due to concerns about how it might be received.

The consequences of assertive behaviour

People who are assertive use concise statements, clearly stating what it is that they want. They 'own' their views and start statements with 'I' or 'My' and clearly state their preferences. For example:

- *It is my view . . . but what do you think?*
- *I think we should . . .*
- *I prefer . . .*

Statements are to the point and not hedged as they are with someone who is non-assertive. Other people's views are sought; rational and constructive approaches are used to problem-solve, underpinned by a respectful and inclusive attitude. People who are assertive adopt open, relaxed body language; they smile appropriately and are characterised by their affability, respectful approach to others and consistency in manner. They are able to articulate their views but in such a way that they do not diminish other people.

Assertiveness in practice has positive benefits for service users and carers, as advocacy is more likely to be successful. Partnership and inter-disciplinary working is based on co-operation, trust, honesty and openness, where good working relationships can be developed and sustained. Assertive people are more confident and able to take the initiative. Their energy is effectively utilised as they deal with difficulties in a straightforward and immediate way.

In *The development of assertiveness*, Townend (1991, pp7 and 8) includes a list of rights. Our own and other people's behaviour can be assessed against them.

My rights

1. I have the right to express my thoughts and opinions, even though they may be different from those of others.
2. I have the right to express my feelings and take responsibility for them.
3. I have the right to say 'Yes' to people.
4. I have the right to change my mind without making excuses.
5. I have the right to make mistakes and to be responsible for them.
6. I have the right to say 'I don't know'.
7. I have the right to say 'I don't understand'.
8. I have the right to ask for what I want.
9. I have the right to say 'No' without feeling guilty.
10. I have the right to be respected by others, and to respect them.
11. I have the right to be listened to and taken seriously.
12. I have the right to be independent.
13. I have the right to be successful.
14. I have the right to choose not to assert myself.

ACTIVITY **2.4**

How would you assess your behaviour against this list of rights?

Does your behaviour change depending on the people you are with and the situation that you are in?

If there are occasions when your behaviour is either non-assertive or aggressive, think of three things that you could do to make it assertive.

How to manage situations that create negative feelings

We will now use a case study to illustrate how Saura, a student social worker, managed difficulties in her placement.

> **CASE STUDY**
>
> *Saura was a first-year social work student placed in a small residential home for young asylum seekers. The home sought to support the young people to develop social and practical skills, as well as enabling them to access education either through school or college. Saura was nineteen years old, small in stature and very slight. She realised that she had to assert herself to be taken seriously by the staff.*
>
> *Most of the young people and staff were male. There was one female young person, Fen, who told Saura that she wished there were other girls for her to make friends with, as she felt isolated. Furthermore, another male resident, Armend, kept asking Fen to be his girlfriend, and she did not like the attention that he was giving her.*
>
> *Saura noticed that she and Fen often found themselves doing the cooking and tidying in the home, although this should have been shared by the young people and staff working together. Everyone at the home had been very welcoming towards Saura, and she had received positive feedback about her contribution from Charles, the manager, but she felt that his attitude was rather patronising as he emphasised how much he enjoyed the Indian meals she prepared. He did not take seriously Fen's concerns about Armend, describing it as a 'boy–girl thing'.*

Comment

Saura had recently been looking at transactional analysis (TA). Payne (2005) states that people communicate in terms of their parent–adult–child ego states. The ego is our sense of our self and it *manages relationships with people and things, outside ourselves* (Payne, 2005, p76). Saura drew a diagram (see Figure 2.2) to describe the way she saw her relationship with Charles. She was the child and Charles the parent, as he tended to tell her what to do rather than ask her. She felt disempowered by his approach; although he was consistently friendly and approachable, he was overprotective, which prevented her developing her practice.

Having established where she saw herself in relation to Charles, Saura explored this further using Harris (1973) and Townend (1991, p7) to set down her underlying beliefs about the situation. Charles was confident, but did not relate to Saura on the basis of equality. She felt there were underlying issues of gender and age difference, cultural assumptions and stereotypes that Charles was making about her as an Asian woman. She did not feel OK in this relationship and, thinking about the 'list of rights', she was able to realise that her rights were not being recognised. Saura wanted to move her relationship with Charles so that it was adult to adult. This would enable her to be more influential in her support of Fen, who felt sexually harassed by Armend.

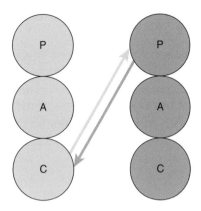

Figure 2.2 Saura's relationship to Charles using transactional analysis

Linking beliefs to behaviour

Life position	Meaning	Type of behaviour
Adult to adult	I'm OK – you're OK	Assertive
Parent to child	I'm OK – you're not OK	Aggressive
Child to parent	I'm not OK – you're OK	Non-assertive
Child to child	I'm not OK – you're not OK	Non-assertive

Saura decided to take the following action.

- Discuss the situation with her practice educator, and request a three-way meeting to include Charles to discuss her role and responsibilities in the placement.

- Place in writing to Charles her concerns that Fen was being sexually harassed, and that this was in opposition to the home's equalities policy, and this behaviour was adversely affecting Fen's health and well-being (see Chapter 3).

- Feed back constructively to Charles about the changes that would need to occur between them, so that they could start to relate to each other on the basis of equality and respect.

- Agree a plan of work at the three-way meeting so that she could meet the Professional Capabilities Framework.

Saura was highly motivated to achieve these changes. Her expectations were that these issues could be resolved, as her approach was focused, positive and optimistic because she was able to provide the evidence for her concerns and offer suggestions for a way forward.

CHAPTER SUMMARY

In this chapter there has been an emphasis on the development of self-awareness, and an examination of our beliefs. Links have been made in terms of thoughts, feelings and behaviour, and we have examined the development of assertiveness. Transactional analysis has been considered as one method to assess how we interface with other people. For social workers to be effective they need to be optimistic, creative and energetic. Seligman's (2003) ideas of developing hopefulness for ourselves, and in our work with service users and carers, has been given particular prominence. Making a commitment to our personal and professional development will enhance our self-awareness and our presentation as social workers. Our development is part of our life's journey, and of course the journey never ends as we develop as people. What is crucial about any journey is that we enjoy travelling and remember what we have learned, so that our practice is positive, creative and always developing.

FURTHER READING

Back, K and Back, K (1999) *Assertiveness at work.* 3rd edition. Maidenhead, Berkshire: McGraw-Hill.

This is a highly informative and practical book, which sets out clear approaches to develop assertiveness.

Seligman, MEP (2003) *Authentic happiness.* London: Nicholas Brealey.

This is a very accessible book written by one of the leading proponents of positive psychology. It is essential reading for any social worker.

REFERENCES

Back, K and Back, K (1999) *Assertiveness at work.* 3rd edn. Maidenhead, Berkshire: McGraw-Hill.

Butler, G and Hope, T (2007) *Manage your mind.* 2nd edition. Oxford: Oxford University Press.

Cottrell, S (2003) *Skills for success.* Basingstoke: Palgrave Macmillan.

Dibley, J (1986) *Let's get motivated.* Australia: Learning Performance (Aust) Pty Ltd.

Fook, J (2002) *Social work critical theory in practice.* London: Sage.

Gilbert, P (2005) *Leadership: Being effective and remaining human.* Dorset: Russell House.

Hardiker, P and Barker, M (eds) (1981) *Theories of practice in social work.* London: Academic Press.

Harris, TA (1973) *I'm OK, you're OK (The book of choice).* London: Cape.

Health and Safety Executive (2012) *Work related research and statistics* (online). Available from www.hse.gov.uk/stress/research/htm (accessed 10 July 2012).

Koprowska, J (2005) *Communication and interpersonal skills in social work.* 1st edition. Exeter: Learning Matters.

Koprowska, J (2008) *Communication and interpersonal skills in social work.* 2nd edition. Exeter: Learning Matters.

Mason, J (2002) *Researching your own practice: The discipline of noticing.* London: Routledge.

Parsloe, E and Wray, M (2001) *Coaching and mentoring: Practical ways to improve learning.* London: Kogan Page.

Payne, M (2005) *Modern social work theory.* 3rd edition. Basingstoke: Palgrave Macmillan.

Peterson, C, Maier, S and Seligman, MEP (1993) *Learned helplessness.* New York: Oxford University Press.

Seligman, MEP (2003) *Authentic happiness.* London: Nicholas Brealey.

Thompson, N, Murphy, M and Stradling, S (1994) *Dealing with stress.* Basingstoke: Macmillan.

Thompson, N (2005) *Understanding social work.* Basingstoke: Palgrave Macmillan.

Thompson, N (2006) *Promoting workplace learning.* Bristol: The Policy Press.

Townend, A (1991) *Developing assertiveness.* London: Routledge.

Chapter 3
Written presentation of self

Gill Constable

A C H I E V I N G   A   S O C I A L   W O R K   D E G R E E

This chapter will help you to develop the following capabilities from the **Professional Capabilities Framework.**

- **Professionalism.** Identify and behave as a professional social worker, committed to professional development.
- **Values and ethics.** Apply social work ethical principles and values to guide professional practice.
- **Diversity.** Recognise diversity and apply anti-discriminatory and anti-oppressive principles in practice.
- **Intervention and skills.** Use judgment and authority to intervene with individuals, families and communities to promote independence, provide support and prevent harm, neglect and abuse.

It will also introduce you to the following standards as set out in the 2008 social work subject benchmark statement.

3.2.3 Communication skills

- **Write accurately and clearly in styles adapted to the audience, purpose and context of the communication.**
- **Present conclusions verbally and on paper, in a structured form, appropriate to the audience for which these have been prepared.**

Introduction

In this chapter we are going to focus on writing and its importance for social work as a profession, as well as for people who use services and carers. First though we will reflect on two quotes that you may well hear repeated while you are on placement:

> *I didn't become a social worker because I wanted to be a typist or a computer programmer. I want to work with people, not waste my time in front of a machine.*

(Comment from a social care assessor)

My staff are good at what they do, not what they write down.

(A Director of Social Services)

(Department of Health, 1999, pp 2 and 29)

These comments were made to inspectors during a review of social work case recording procedures and practice in seven local authorities several years ago, but the debate about how much time should be spent recording social work interventions continues (Munro, 2011). Our emphasis in this chapter will be on developing writing skills that are proportionate to the task and support best social work practice. We will begin by thinking about writing as an aspect of communication (see Chapter 7) and the value that society places on it, and the different types of writing that social workers do. This chapter is positioned within the ethical and value base of social work. Confidentiality, sharing and access to records will be discussed. Linkages will be made with the academic work you are required to do at university, and how those skills can be transferred to your practice in placement. Some advice will be given to assist you in the development of effective writing skills, so you can view writing as an ally in your personal and professional development.

What is the purpose of writing?

Thompson (2003) states that writing is a powerful activity, which is demonstrated by the law, policy, guidance, legal documents such as birth certificates and wills being written down. It is the method in modern societies by which events are recorded. Writing is a form of communication and it endures, unlike the spoken word. The skills of listening, speaking and observing non-verbal communication such as body language are core to social work, but so are well-developed writing skills. Healy and Mulholland (2007, p11) identify the differences between speech and writing as follows.

- Writing stands alone and cannot be enhanced by non-verbal communication, unlike speech.

- Speaking involves other people, unlike reading, which is usually a solitary activity. It is important that writing is clear, carefully structured and the reader is guided through the process.

- The writer does not know who might read the document, and therefore areas that need clarification should be anticipated, as people cannot ask questions.

- Written documents allow the reader to reflect on their contents and read them again. This is not the case with the spoken word.

- Writing is permanent and may be referred to in the future.

CASE STUDY

Lilly was 15 years old and living with foster parents. She had spent significant periods of time in care throughout her childhood due to her mother's misuse of substances. Maggie had recently become her allocated social worker and started to talk to Lilly about planning for the future in terms of going on to college or work, with an eventual move into her own accommodation. Lilly found these meetings with Maggie upsetting, especially as her mother, who was living in Birmingham, had lost contact with her over the past 18 months. This had occurred before and it was generally assumed that her mother had started to use substances again.

Maggie realised very quickly that Lilly was struggling to plan for the future as she had such a fragmented sense of her own past. They agreed that they would work on developing a life story book that would give a timeline to Lilly's life. As part of this process, Lilly asked Maggie to find out about her paternal grandmother, whom Lilly remembered with affection. When Maggie sought this information from Lilly's case files she was shocked to find that there was no information that related to either Lilly's father or her paternal grandparents. The case recording focused almost exclusively on her mother's substance misuse and the practical details surrounding Lilly's frequent admissions to care. There was no evidence of any attempts to find out and engage with Lilly's extended family, or detailed assessment and planning for Lilly over the longer term. Lilly and her mother had had a number of social workers over the years and there was a lack of continuity and consistency in the case recording, which at times was minimal, or highly descriptive but with limited analysis.

Comment

Imagine how you might feel if you were Lilly and there was no one who could reliably remember and share your personal history with you, including crucial details about your family. You may well think that no one could be bothered to find out and record this information. This could make you feel that your life and circumstances were unimportant and engender a sense of worthlessness. For some children and adults who use services, written records that are compiled by social workers may be the main or only source of information about significant events in their life. This highlights how important it is to maintain quality records. Poor records can also lead to:

- inappropriate action being taken or no action, such as in Lilly's situation, where access to her paternal extended family would have been supportive to Lilly and may have been an alternative option to foster care;

- complaints being made that might result in litigation (Thompson, 2003).

RESEARCH SUMMARY

What can we learn from child protection case records?

The quality of written records between 1973 and 1994 has been criticised in the report findings of 45 public inquiries into the death of a child where social workers were involved. Key findings were:

- *scarcity of information;*
- *inaccurate information;*
- *no statement about who was seen on the visit;*
- *information not collated or linked together.*

Munro (1998, p94)

Between April and the end of September 2010 the Office for Standards in Education, Children's Services and Skills (Ofsted) reviewed 67 serious case reviews where a child had been seriously harmed or had died. One aspect of the review was an audit of case recordings, which found that the voice of the child was often missing. The findings were as follows.

- *The child was not seen often enough by the professionals, or asked about their views and feelings.*
- *Agencies did not listen to adults who tried to advocate for the child or who had significant information to share.*
- *Parents and carers created barriers to prevent professionals from seeing or hearing the child.*
- *The practitioners' focus was often on the needs of parents, especially if they were seen as vulnerable, without considering the needs of the child.*
- *Agencies did not analyse or interpret their findings well enough to protect the child.*

Comment

In the first research summary the findings suggest that social workers had not developed a systematic process for recording information. Since Munro completed this research both Children and Adults' Services in the statutory sector have sought to improve the design of case files, so that information is easier to access. Moving on to the second piece of research, we see that this demonstrates that practice has not concentrated on the most vulnerable person in the family, the child; rather, their needs have been marginalised. Effective recording is important in tracking and making sense of the experience of children. When records are read back over a period of time this enables patterns and themes to emerge so that through careful analysis the child's experience can be reviewed. It also highlights, as pointed out in Ofsted's review, when the voice of the child is absent. When you are on placement, have a look at some case files and assess the quality of the recording against the findings of Munro's and Ofsted's research. Are there differences between social workers, and if you were allocated the case would you feel confident that you have all the information that you need? Does the voice of the child emerge clearly throughout the case recording? Do you have a sense of the child's needs, and how these can best be met? Later in the chapter we will look in detail at the skills required to produce high-quality and professional case recording.

Defining the types of written communication that social workers do

We will now go on and consider the type of writing that social workers do.

Comment

This is dependent on the organisation for whom they work and the purpose of the writing, which will also impact on the detail and length of the writing. Thompson (2002, pp109, 112) identifies the following types of communication used by social workers.

- Telephone messages. It is important that these are written down and dated, stating the full name of the person calling, concise details of the message, telephone number to ring back and the name of the person who took the message.

- Text messages. This may not be a preferred method of communication but can be very useful in an emergency when the mobile signal is poor. A disadvantage is that text language can obscure rather than clarify meaning.

- Letters to service users, carers, other professionals and external organisations. They should follow a structure, be clear and concise.

- Memos are used when communicating in a formal manner with a manager or another team or department within the same organisation.

- Email is used within an organisation and with other agencies. Email is not appropriate for complex and detailed information. Some disadvantages are that it can be sent or read quickly, which may lead to misunderstandings, and can be sent off sometimes without being checked. Additionally they are often overused, which does cause stress if people have lots of emails to read. They can be used to 'cover your back' by supplying information about a case to another worker or manager. This is not appropriate or safe social work practice. The positives of emails are that they are quick and easy to use, and can assist in the setting up of appointments and meetings, as a group of people can be sent the same email.

- Reports may be required internally, for example in the implementation of the Safeguarding Children Procedures, or formally requested by an external agency such as a mental health tribunal.

- Referral is a request for an assessment or service; for example, a general practitioner requesting assistance to be provided to one of their patients.

- Assessments. Many agencies have standard assessment templates for social workers and other professionals to complete. The development of self-directed or personalised care for service users means that increasingly social workers will be supporting service users and carers to develop the skills to assess their own needs (see Chapter 12).

- Care plans set out how the person's needs are to be met, that is their health, emotional, spiritual, cultural, educational, leisure and employment needs (see Chapter 12).

- Case recording sheets. These are used to record times, dates, people seen and the work that has been achieved with the person who uses services.

- Process recording is detailed writing about the process of the interview. It includes verbal and non-verbal communication and the social worker's reflections and observations on self and others.

- Review documents are used when the person's care plan is reassessed to see if it still meets their needs (see Chapter 12).

- Summaries are completed if a specific piece of work has been achieved, when a case is transferred to another worker or the case is closed. The summary sets out the objectives of the involvement, the current situation, what has been achieved and if further work is required or anticipated.

- Information may be provided about services to prospective recipients or carers.

- Service specifications, contracts or service-level agreements are developed when a service has been purchased; they detail the cost, type and quality of the provision.

Moon (1999) describes the importance of writing to develop critical thinking and reflective skills.

- Writing slows us down and requires us to concentrate.

- It enables us to organise our thinking and feelings.

- It gives us structure and control so we can set about identifying and prioritising issues.

- It can enable our understanding to be enhanced.

- It enables us to problem-solve.

- It supports us to link our thoughts with previous and present experience and knowledge, which we can use in the future.

Social workers need to develop case recording skills to ensure that they can write effectively in a manner that is proportionate to the needs of the case. So we will now consider case recording in some detail.

Case recording

As identified earlier, case recording is a core activity for social workers. We have considered the importance of accurate and concise writing as a component of social work. If we specifically consider case recording its purpose is to:

- provide information about and for children and adults who need and use services;
- provide clarity about their background and current situation;
- provide information for other professionals including inspectors;
- provide evidence that the policies and procedures of the agency have been followed;
- demonstrate that legal requirements are met, and good-quality information is given to the courts when required;
- provide evidence as to how decisions were made;
- show evidence of good practice and that the agency is consistent in its response and methods used to assist children and adults, which will be required if a complaint is made or an insurance claim submitted to the agency;
- provide information that supports the planning, development and commissioning of services, as well as statistical information that is useful to the agency that supports policy development and the allocation of funds: for example, the ethnic origin, age and needs of people accessing services;
- enable managers to audit the quality of work, and identify training and development requirements.

Below is an example of case recording which is concise and has summarised events.

CASE STUDY

Current situation

1 May 2012. Mr Doyle was visited by Melanie Thomas (Community Nurse Dementia Care Team) at 3.30 p.m. at his home. Mr Doyle was undressed, confused and wandering in his garden. Mr Doyle's daughter-in-law Jenny Doyle was contacted. Dr Botang (GP) made an emergency visit and made arrangements for immediate admission to Queen Elizabeth Hospital (QEH) for assessment. Mr Doyle was accompanied by his son Christopher Doyle at 6 p.m. and admitted to Abbey Ward, QEH this evening.

Action required

1. Adam Davis (Student Social Worker) to liaise with the hospital Social Work Team on 2 May 2012 regarding the assessment of Mr Doyle's medical needs and discharge planning.

Recorded by: Norma Rice, Duty Social Worker, 1 May 2012, 6.30 p.m.

Comment

This is a very brief summation of the events leading to Mr Doyle's admission to hospital. In particular note that Norma Rice has identified the names and roles of the people involved, so that anyone could read this recording and be clear who was involved, and the whereabouts of Mr Doyle. You may have spotted that telephone numbers have not been included, which is an omission, but this information may have been included in a contact page with basic details. Social work records are computerised and it is extremely important that basic details are included, names and addresses correctly spelt and information is accurate. If you are unsure about how to spell a person's name or address do ask the service user or carer. Accurate and well-presented records are evidence of professional practice. Norma Rice has indicated what action Adam Davis, the Student Social Worker, needs to take and when this should occur.

The ethical value base of writing as a social worker

Healy and Muholland (2007, p14) state:

> You should always try to represent yourself in your writing as thoughtful, objective, experienced, and careful about what you communicate.

This is a useful maxim to follow. Writing should be underpinned by the professional role and responsibilities, processes and value base of the profession. Included within this is confidentiality. Carers and service users need to be advised that information that may indicate that they are at risk of harm, or that other people are at risk, will be passed on by the social worker. Assurance should be given that information is kept confidential, and will not be exchanged casually with other people. It should be explained that information is gathered on behalf of the agency that employs the social worker, and records are kept. Consent must be sought to pass non-high-risk information to other professionals where appropriate: for example, to request that an occupational therapist assess a child with physical disabilities to enhance their mobility within their home.

Service users are entitled to access their records under the Data Protection Act 1998 and agencies have policies and procedures in place to enable this to happen.

The Data Protection Act 1998

There are eight principles that underpin the Act and social workers should be mindful of these as they record information. Information from a third party that is recorded on case files requires that person's consent to access it. Below are the eight principles.

1. Personal data shall be processed fairly and lawfully.

2. Personal data shall be obtained only for one or more specified and lawful purposes, and shall not be further processed in any manner incompatible with that purpose or those purposes.

3. Personal data shall be adequate, relevant and not excessive in relation to the purpose or purposes for which they are processed.

4. Personal data shall be accurate and, where necessary, kept up to date.

5. Personal data processed for any purpose or purposes shall not be kept for longer than is necessary for that purpose or those purposes.

6. Personal data shall be processed in accordance with the rights of data subjects under this Act.

7. Appropriate technical and organisational measures shall be taken against unauthorised or unlawful processing of personal data and against accidental loss or destruction of, or damage to, personal data.

8. Personal data shall not be transferred to a country or territory outside the European Economic Area unless that country or territory ensures an adequate level of protection for the rights and freedoms of data subjects in relation to the processing of personal data.

When social workers are recording information they need to be aware that a number of people might read it, and should learn to *communicate sensitively* (Thompson, 2003, p33). The tone of the writing and the language should be respectful and formal, as language can reinforce oppressive racist, sexist and homophobic attitudes and negative stereotypes of people. It is important to reflect on the choice of words; for example, can you detect any difficulties with these statements?

> *The gentleman who was accused of sexually abusing the young man at the employment project denied it.*

> *The lady doctor was popular with the social workers in the local team, as she was supportive towards the carers of her older patients.*

The terms 'gentleman' and 'lady' are not neutral: they connote certain attributes and suggest evaluative attitudes on the part of the writer. It is preferable to use descriptive and precise language; in these examples this would be 'man' and 'female'. Of course, 'man' and 'female' or 'male' and 'woman' are also indicators of social constructions and stereotypes, so all language needs to be handled sensitively.

Forms of discourse

There are four forms of discourse that people use in speech (Healy and Mulholland, 2007, p80) although sometimes these are combined.

- Narrative form – speaking as if telling a story.
- Descriptive form – describing the people and actions in terms of how they impacted on the speaker rather than what actually happened.
- Argument form – the person presents what they want and why.
- Statement form – this is a clear description of the situation and the difficulties. The person is able to identify the outcome they want.

CASE STUDY

Joyce is a social worker in the Family Services Team. On Friday morning Tom Piper arrives at the office with his 14-year-old daughter Amy. He tells Joyce:

> *'Amy is out of control – she's wild and very bad, stays out all night and won't go to school. I can't cope – my girlfriend is threatening to leave me, and Amy's mum has had enough too. She has the other kids to look after, and Amy's a bad influence. You must do something – it's not working, all this talking to Amy, which is all you lot seem to do. She's stayed with me one week and that is enough; she needs to be in care.'*

Mr Piper stands up and walks out.

ACTIVITY 3.2

What do you think was Mr Piper's preferred form of discourse?

Comment

Mr Piper's preferred form of discourse is argument. He has come to the office to see Joyce with a clear outcome in mind and reasons to support this. Nevertheless, case recording has to be written in the statement form of discourse, irrespective of the person's preferred form of discourse. It must identify the issues clearly.

Facts, opinions, hearsay, access and confidentiality

Pritchard (2007, pp284, 285), in her writing about adult abuse (although this is relevant for child protection too), states that recording should give the nature and source of the information. Facts should be separated from opinions and hearsay. Social workers must understand and implement the concept of confidentiality and recognise people's entitlement to access records kept about them. Figure 3.1 shows five key concepts that you should be able to identify when you are reviewing your writing. Read the following case study and then answer the questions with reference to the diagram.

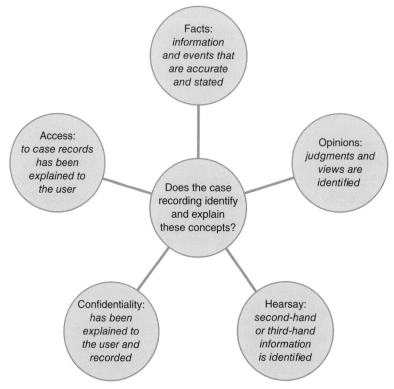

Figure 3.1 Five concepts in social work writing

CASE STUDY

Sylvia was working in a rehabilitation team in the voluntary sector for people who misuse substances. She was allocated a case of a young man, Kevin, who had a long history of both alcohol and drug misuse. The previous worker had left the following transfer summary:

'I have worked with Kevin over the last 18 months; he no longer appears to use drugs, just alcohol. He started misusing substances when he was 14 years old. He has spent most of his life in care and has had a number of prison sentences, mainly relating to theft and possession of Class A drugs. Kevin has three children by two different girlfriends. His relationships are short term, and his interest in his children non-existent. Kevin is seen locally as unpredictable and frightening, especially when he has been drinking. The boyfriend of an ex-girlfriend of Kevin's told me that most of the pubs in the town have banned him. Kevin has taken recently to being tattooed, probably to offset his rather feminine appearance. This makes him appear more alarming. Overall the medical team at the unit think the prognosis for Kevin is very poor and give his life expectancy as about five years. At the present time Kevin is living with a girlfriend, Deb, who has one child under five years old. Children's Services are involved, primarily as Deb has a history of cocaine misuse. Kevin is cooperating with his community order.'

Can you identify what are the facts in this case recording?

What is opinion?

Are there examples of hearsay information?

Have issues of confidentiality and access to records been addressed?

Comment

You are provided with information but the facts are not identified. Facts are based on events that definitely happened and information that you know to be true. The information that is given lacks depth and specificity; for example, we are not told Kevin's age or ethnic origin. There is no information about his children or previous partners. There is no sense of Kevin's family or social networks or employment history. We are not provided with the name of the Children's Services contact or the nature of the work that is taking place and so on.

If an opinion is given in case recording it needs to be identified as such and the following two questions asked: *Whose opinion is this? Is the person qualified to assess/give an opinion?* (Pritchard, 2007, p284). We are told Kevin's life expectancy is five years, but no medical practitioner is named. It is stated that Kevin's *relationships are short term, and his interest in his children non-existent.* Who has made this assessment, and are they qualified to do so?

Hearsay is information that cannot be confirmed. It is said by another person, and passed on to someone else. It is *second- or third-hand information* (p285). An example in this case recording is: *The boyfriend of an ex-girlfriend of Kevin's told me that most of the pubs in the town have banned him.* This information is imprecise and it would be inadmissible in a court of law, but it is powerful as it implies that Kevin's behaviour can be volatile.

The issue of confidentiality and Kevin's entitlement to access his records has not been recorded. Pritchard (2007) reminds us to ask the following questions: *Who might read this record? Will they understand what I am saying?* (p285). The statements *Kevin has taken recently to being tattooed, probably to offset his rather feminine appearance. This makes him appear more alarming* are highly judgmental and opinionated. The concepts of femininity and masculinity are socially constructed, which means they mean different things to different people and cultures over time. They can be oppressive as they implicitly conjure up images in our mind. At this point what is your mental image of Kevin? What impact does the use of terms like *boyfriends and girlfriends* have? It is understandable if you imagine Kevin to be an adolescent, but as a young adult his relationships have not been given due respect. It would be more appropriate to use the term *partner*. Thompson's (2003, p33) *communication sensitivity* stresses the need to integrate anti-oppressive practice in writing. How do you think Kevin might feel if he were to read this case summary about himself and his life? We are told one positive fact about Kevin, that he is co-operating with his community order, and yet this is not expanded upon.

Focusing on strengths in recording

Social work seeks to enable and support people to achieve change in their lives, so attention should focus on what is positive with a balanced view of challenges and negatives. We have to address this within ourselves: do you identify the strengths within people and situations, or does your focus rest on the difficulties?

Tanner and Harris (2008, p146) have developed a template that can be used to assess our writing practice in terms of whether we are using a perspective that identifies the strengths. We will use this approach in revising a small proportion of the case recording about Kevin as an example (see Table 3.1).

Table 3.1 Revising Kevin's transfer summary

Principles

Write so that:

- the behaviour is described rather than using judgmental statements;
- strengths rather than difficulties are emphasised;
- language is clear, concise and easy to understand without jargon.

Negative statements	More positive statements
He no longer appears to use drugs, just alcohol.	Kevin is tested regularly as part of his community order, and there is no evidence that he is using drugs. Work is focused on helping Kevin to reduce his consumption of alcohol. Kevin estimates that he has reduced his consumption from 55 units to 30 units per week. He states that he no longer drinks spirits, but consumes longer drinks such as lager. He is aware that the continuation of this level of consumption will cause ill health.
He has had a number of prison sentences.	Kevin has had three prison sentences in the last seven years, the longest being six months. He has not had a custodial sentence in the last two years.
Kevin is co-operating with the community order.	Kevin is fully engaged in working with the project. This involves attending two groups a week, and meeting his key worker on a fortnightly basis. To date he has not missed any appointments, and the project is now supporting Kevin to find work.

Has the mental image you have of Kevin changed? If it has, this is likely to be due to the additional information that you have been given, and how it has been presented. This gives a more rounded picture of Kevin. It is important to stress that focusing on strengths does not mean that risks are ignored. These should be recorded and assessed. We will now look at how these skills can be used to write reports.

Report writing

It was earlier stated by Thompson (2003) that the capacity to write gives authority and is potentially powerful. It is disempowering not to be able to read or write. Social workers hold this power as they are required to write reports for a wide number of uses such as: to access resources; for child protection conferences; to provide information for courts in childcare proceedings; for mental health review tribunals; to obtain funding from charitable bodies; to respond to complaints, and so on. Many of the skills that you have acquired at university when writing assignments are transferable to report writing, such as the presentation of evidence to support an argument and summarising complex ideas. The same concepts are used in report writing as in case recording.

Healy and Mulholland (2007, p90) identify the importance of the following qualities.

- Reports should be objective and factual. You need to be clear about the information that you can verify. If it is second-hand information you need to state this, for example:

Sylvia Smith, head teacher of Upton Junior School, describes Stacey Middleton's behaviour towards her seven-year-old son Ashley as either 'off-hand or impatient'. Sylvia Smith says that Stacey Middleton is often late dropping him off at school, and expects him to walk the two miles home at the end of the school day. The school are concerned as Ashley has to walk down narrow country lanes where there is a lot of traffic.

- Reports should be coherent and systematic in their order and structure. There are a number of ways that you can structure your report: by chronology, by significant events, and by its usefulness to the reader. The language used should be accessible and understandable to the subject of the report and other professionals, so avoid jargon, and explain any services or concepts that the reader/s may not understand.

- Reports should comprise essential information. Make a list of the information that is required and prioritise what the reader needs to know. Core information will include the name, gender, ethnic origin, age of the person, the range of agencies involved, family and social networks, employment details, housing and so on.

- Reports should be concise. The report will be more influential if it is to the point, contains a clear, evidence-based summary and makes recommendations with action attached.

CASE STUDY

Victor had recently been appointed as a newly qualified social worker in a community mental health team. He was asked by the manager to help a colleague complete a report for the Mental Health Tribunal on an 18-year-old Japanese student, Kazumi, who had been compulsorily admitted to hospital and was seeking to be discharged. The allocated social worker was on compassionate leave due to a family bereavement.

How should Victor set about this task?

How can Victor empower Kazumi?

Comment

Victor decided to undertake some research. He accessed the Mental Health Tribunal website (2012), and downloaded general information about the role and responsibilities of the Mental Health Tribunal, and the standard template for social inquiry reports. He then asked the manager if he could see good examples of other reports that social workers in the team had completed.

Victor then planned the process that he would use to gather the information. This included visits to Kazumi, reading the nursing and medical notes and case file. He also accessed information from the BBC website to find out about Japan, so that he would have some understanding of Kazumi's culture and country of origin (BBC website, 2012). He checked with Kazumi to see if he wanted an interpreter, and that he had an appropriate advocate and legal advice.

Victor undertook further research into the support services within the college where Kazumi was studying, as well as community provision, to determine if there were options for discharge. He ensured that he shared this with the psychiatric team in the hospital and gained their views. Victor was very mindful of the power that he had in terms of how he wrote the report, what he highlighted and the weight he gave to strengths and risk factors. He set aside sufficient time to enable Kazumi to read the report and spent time with him explaining the content and reasons for the conclusions that he had reached.

Victor's practice sought to empower Kazumi, who was detained on a compulsory order, as he advised Kazumi of his legal rights, and ensured that he received the advocacy service that he was entitled to. Victor listened carefully to Kazumi's views, and researched community options that would enable Kazumi to be safely discharged from hospital. It is always the social worker's responsibility to engage with service users through communicating sensitively (see Chapter 6).

The practice of summation and making recommendations

One criticism that is often made of case recording and report writing is that the writing can be descriptive with little attempt to summarise the key points and make recommendations based on a sound assessment (see Chapter 12). This may be due to defensive practice where the social worker does not have confidence to make clear decisions and recommendations (Chapter 14). It was mentioned earlier that skills are transferable from writing assignments for university, where you are required to use critical analysis and argument. These are the same skills that should become routine in case recording and report writing, so that appropriate action can be taken.

CHAPTER SUMMARY

If we return to the comments made by the social care assessor and director that began this chapter we can now provide clear evidence of how erroneous these comments are. The importance of developing effective and confident writing skills has now been demonstrated. We have considered the different types of writing, and the need for this to be underpinned by the ethical and value base of social work. There are strong linkages between the writing skills and research required for academic work at university, and these skills can be transferred to your practice in placement. Writing, like all aspects of social work, requires personal reflection and self-knowledge. You need to select a method of recording and report writing that provides concise, evidence-based information and recommendations that demonstrate competent and anti-oppressive practice. Writing is a powerful activity and its effective use will enhance your professional practice and personal well-being.

FURTHER READING

Healy, K and Mulholland, J (2007) *Writing skills for social workers.* London: Sage. This is a comprehensive and accessible book for students and qualified social workers.

Thompson, N (2003) *Communication and language.* Basingstoke: Palgrave Macmillan. This book includes all forms of communication and addresses anti-oppressive practice.

REFERENCES

BBC News country profiles (2012) (online) Available from: www.news.bbc.co.uk/2/hi/country-profiles/default/stm (accessed 3 August 2012).

Brown, K and Rutter, L (2008) *Critical thinking for social work.* 2nd edition. Exeter: Learning Matters.

Cottrell, S (2008) *The study skills handbook.* Basingstoke: Palgrave Macmillan.

Department of Health (1999) *Recording with care: inspection of case recording in social services departments.* London: Department of Health.

Healy, K and Mulholland, J (2007) *Writing skills for social workers.* London: Sage.

Lishman, Joyce (2009) *Communication in social work.* 2nd edition. Basingstoke: Macmillan.

Mantell, A and Scragg, T (eds) (2008) *Safeguarding adults in social work.* Exeter: Learning Matters.

Mental Health Review Tribunal (2012) (online) Available from: www.justice.gov.uk/tribunals/mentalhealth (accessed 3 August 2012).

Moon, J (1999) *Learning journals: A handbook for academics, students and professional development.* London: Kogan Page.

Munro, E (1998) Improving social workers' knowledge base in child protection work. *British Journal of Social Work,* 26, 793–808.

Munro, E (2011) *The Munro review of child protection: Final report, a child-centred system.* London: The Stationery Office.

Office of Public Sector Information (1998) Data Protection Act. London: HMSO.

Ofsted (2011) The Voice of the Child (online). Available from: www.ofsted.gov.uk/resources/ voice of the child (accessed 31 July 2012).

Pritchard, J (2007) *Working with adult abuse.* London: Jessica Kingsley Publishers.

Tanner, D and Harris, J (2008) *Working with older people.* London: Routledge.

Thompson, N (2002) *People skills.* 2nd edition. Basingstoke: Palgrave Macmillan.

Thompson, N (2003) *Communication and language.* Basingstoke: Palgrave Macmillan.

Thompson, N (2006) *Anti-discriminatory practice.* 4th edition. Basingstoke: Palgrave Macmillan.

Trevithick, P (2012) *Social work skills.* 3rd edition. Maidenhead: Open University Press.

Chapter 4

Skills for self-management

Barbara Hall

A C H I E V I N G   A   S O C I A L   W O R K   D E G R E E

This chapter will help you to develop the following capabilities from the **Professional Capabilities Framework**.

- **Professionalism.** Identify and behave as a professional social worker, committed to professional development.
- **Contexts and organisations.** Engage with, inform and adapt to changing contexts that shape practice. Operate effectively within own organisational frameworks and contribute to the development of services and organisations. Operate effectively within multi-agency and inter-professional settings.

It will also introduce you to the following standards as set out in the 2008 social work subject benchmark statement.

5.8   Skills in personal and professional development

Introduction

In this chapter we will be considering some of the skills necessary for self-management in the social work environment. Social work is undergoing significant change and for social workers there are some skills which need to be added to their 'survival tool kit'. At the heart of the chapter are the concept and implications of the 'psychological contract' between the employer and the employee, informed by the Social Work Reform Board 'Standards for Employers of Social Workers in England and Supervision Framework' (2010). The chapter also looks at practical approaches to time management, and an exploration of the management of change. Later in this chapter you will be encouraged to explore the use of supervision and to consider the importance of developing a personal development plan. Maintaining personal safety is also explored in this context to emphasise that the well-being of employees is the joint responsibility of the individual social worker and the employer.

The psychological contract

The concept of the psychological contract emerged in the 1960s but became more popular in the 1990s based on the work of Mullins (1996). Guest and Conway (2002) define the psychological contract as *the perceptions of the two parties, employee and employer, of what their mutual obligations are towards each other.*

Unlike the contract of employment, which is a legal contract, the psychological contract deals much more with perceptions. Some of the perceptions may be made explicit at the point of recruitment: they derive from informal discussions about the way we do things around here; from the views of colleagues already in employment and their perceptions concerning whether the employer is a good one or not; and also through the organisation's approach to supervision, performance management and appraisal. The important thing is that these perceptions are believed by the employee to be part of the relationship with the employer. The Chartered Institute of Personnel and Development factsheet (CIPD 2008) concerning psychological contracts states:

> It is the psychological contract that effectively tells employees what they are required to do in order to meet their side of the bargain, and what they can expect from their job . . . Basically the psychological contract offers a metaphor, or representation of what goes on in the workplace . . . It offers a framework for addressing 'soft' issues about managing performance; it focuses on people, rather than technology; and it draws attention to some important shifts in the relationship between people and organisations.

ACTIVITY **4.1**

At the point of beginning a new placement or starting a new job, considering the following questions might help you to engage with your new colleagues and build rapport more quickly.

What unspoken rules do I need to be aware of in this team?

Where does the power lie in this team?

What do people expect of students in this team?

How is the tea fund managed in this team?

Comment

The last question may sound rather flippant, but the state of the tea fund and the way in which it is managed can tell you a lot about the way a team shares or does not share activities.

The CIPD (2008) factsheet also suggests the concept of 'process fairness', which is concerned with people wanting to know that their interests will be taken into account when important decisions are taken: they would like to be treated with respect; they are more likely to be satisfied with their job if they are consulted about change. Underpinning such expectations is the need for managers to be fully committed to communicating with their staff on all aspects of the life of the organisation, which may impact the well-being and expectations of the employee.

The Social Work Reform Board (2010) recommended national standards for the support that social workers should expect from their employers and managers in order to be able to do their jobs effectively. It also recommended a national framework for social worker supervision.

All employers of social workers should:

- have in place a social work accountability framework informed by knowledge of good social work practice and the experience of service users, carers and practitioners;

- use effective workload planning systems to make sure the right number of social workers, with the right skills and experience, are available to meet current and future service demands;

- implement transparent systems to manage workload and case allocation to protect service users and practitioners;

- make sure social workers can do their jobs safely and have the practical tools and resources they need to practise effectively, also assess risks and take action to minimise and prevent these;

- ensure social workers have regular and appropriate social work supervision;

- provide opportunities for continuing professional development, as well as access to research and practice guidance;

- ensure social workers can maintain their professional registration;

- establish effective partnerships with higher education institutions and other organisations to support the delivery of social work education and continuing professional development.

When you are asked at a job interview if you have any questions for the panel, you could reframe some of the above statements into searching questions to help inform your choice of employer.

Social workers by the same token are required to be accountable for the quality of their work and take responsibility for maintaining and improving their knowledge and skills. The IFSW (International Federation of Social Workers) Charter of Rights for Social Workers (2011) states that social workers should have the right to access lifelong learning and *career progression routes, which maintains practice*. It is every social worker's personal and professional responsibility to ensure they have the relevant skills, knowledge and understanding to do their job effectively. Continuous professional development is a registration requirement for every social worker. The Professional Capabilities Framework (PCF) developed by the Social Work Reform Board is the social work CPD framework that informs and links an individual's professional development to the career structure. The Professional Capabilities Framework is owned by the College of Social Work on behalf of the social work profession. The Professional Capabilities Framework has nine domains. These are:

- Professionalism;

- Values and ethics;

- Diversity;

- Rights, justice and economic well-being;

- Knowledge;

- Critical reflection and analysis;

- Intervention and skills;

- Contexts and organisations;

- Professional leadership.

At each developing stage of your career, from student to newly qualified worker to expert practitioner, these nine domains will form the measures of your personal and professional progress.

Starting with your student experience you will be aware of the importance of the quality of relationships you have with your practice assessor and your tutor/s for your learning and development. It cannot be overestimated how important it is for you to also develop trusting and open relationships with your line manager/s, who will be responsible for your supervision and support and for your personal development in the workplace. Similarly it cannot be overestimated how important it is to have effective and supportive relationships with your team colleagues. You will learn from them, be supported by them and be buoyed by their friendship and concern.

CASE STUDY

Libby qualified a year ago and has successfully completed the NQSW (Newly Qualified Social Worker Programme). She is now finding the demands of her full-time job very difficult to manage. Libby really enjoyed her social work degree and the NQSW programme and knew all the way through her qualifying training that she wanted to specialise in work with children and families. Libby is working in a Children's Assessment Team, where she is one of two recently qualified social workers, but she has been taken under the wing of some of the other more established team members who seem very experienced and confident. The Team Manager supervises Libby once a month and is encouraging and supportive.

Libby has been feeling quite stressed lately: her caseload includes two young single-parent families presenting with very challenging and intimidating behaviour, to the extent that she has felt quite frightened when visiting them in their homes. The two mums are neighbours and friends. Libby and her colleagues suspect that alcohol and drug misuse are contributing to concerns about the three under-fives involved. Libby has not mentioned her feelings of anxiety to anyone at work as she fears it might reinforce people's views about her lack of experience.

Libby has had a real run of bad luck lately. She backed her car into a bollard when parking two weeks ago and, although she was unhurt, her car needs about £600 spent on it. A few days ago she lost her purse containing all her bank cards, and yesterday, to cap it all, she ended up weeping with the mother of a two-week-old baby recently diagnosed with a life-threatening illness. Libby fears she is not coping very well in her first job. However, she finds it very difficult to talk to anyone about how she is feeling, as she is worried they might think she is not up to the job.

ACTIVITY 4.2

Write down some of your initial thoughts about what is happening to Libby and why.

How might the psychological contract and the Standards for Employers of Social Workers be used to support her?

Comment

There are occasions when even very experienced workers feel intimidated and afraid. Such feelings, however experienced or inexperienced a worker you are, should never be kept to yourself. It is incumbent on you, your line manager and your organisation to ensure your safety, both physical and psychological. The situation Libby is in with the two mums whom she finds very intimidating must not be minimised.

The other side of this coin is about becoming over-confident and not spotting the signals that potentially could put you at risk.

RESEARCH SUMMARY

Highlights from the National Task Force

The research overview of the work of the National Task Force on Violence (DoH 2007) highlights that violence and abuse in social care are significantly under-reported. They comment that the factors influencing the low levels of reporting are: believing that management will not support staff; believing that you are to blame; believing that you will be seen as incompetent because you cannot handle violence and abuse; and the belief that verbal abuse and threats are part of the job.

> *The consistent message from staff, service users and the research is that violence and abuse should not be seen as part of the job.*

Where social workers have any concerns about their safety, this must be shared with the line manager and colleagues immediately and the operational procedures in place must be followed.

Work-related stress

In Chapter 2 we considered how our thoughts, values and belief systems impact on our behaviour. This chapter takes a look at the symptoms of stress and the impact the organisation can have on relieving workplace stress.

Work-related stress is defined as:

> *a pattern of emotional, cognitive, behavioural and physiological reactions to adverse and harmful aspects of work content, work organisation and the working environment. It is a state characterised by high levels of agitation and distress and often feelings of not coping.*

> (Diamantopoulou 2002, p3)

Diamantopoulou goes on to note that: *It is clear that work related stress is one of the most important threats to workers' wellbeing.*

Cox and Rial-Gonzalez (2002, p5) consider that:

> *People experience stress when they feel an imbalance between the demands placed on them and the personal and environmental resources that they have to cope with these demands. This relationship between demands and resources can be strongly moderated by factors such as social support – both at work and outside work – and control over work.*

Table 4.1 (Cox and Rial-Gonzalez 2002) shows the known stress-related work factors grouped into ten categories. These different categories, suggest the authors, relate to either work context or work content.

Table 4.1 Factors associated with work-related stress (adapted from Cox et al., 2000, cited in Cox and Rial-Gonzales 2002)

Category	Hazards
	Work context
Organisational culture and function	Poor communication, low levels of support for problem-solving and personal development, lack of definition of organisational objectives
Role in organisation	Role ambiguity and role conflict, responsibility for people
Career development	Career stagnation and uncertainty, under- or over-promotion, poor pay, job insecurity, low social value to work
Decision 'latitude' control	Low participation in decision-making, lack of control over work. (Control, particularly in the form of participation, is also a context and wider organisational issue)
Interpersonal relationships at work	Social or physical isolation, poor relationships with superiors, interpersonal conflict, lack of social support
Home–work interface	Conflicting demands of work and home, low support at home, dual career problems
	Work content
Work environment and work equipment	Problems regarding the reliability, availability, suitability and maintenance or repair of both equipment and facilities
Task design	Lack of variety or short work cycles, fragmented or meaningless work, under-use of skills, high level of uncertainty
Workload/ work pace	Work overload or underload, lack of control over pacing, high levels of time pressure
Work schedule	Shift working, inflexible work schedules, unpredictable hours, long or unsocial hours

CASE STUDY

On reflection Paul can now see how he had ignored the symptoms of stress he had been experiencing for a long time. It was precisely because he had been feeling so low for such a long time that it had come to seem normal for him. He had begun to feel trapped by his job, and knew that he had changed from being an empathic person to someone very detached and rather cynical. His partner had complained frequently about his irritability and apathy and about how insular he had become. It was not until Paul started to have physical symptoms that he eventually went to see his GP. He had been having palpitations, which the doctor described as symptoms of anxiety. He also told Paul he was suffering from high blood pressure and that his lifestyle would need to change. The doctor insisted that Paul take sick leave and he was away from work for five months.

Paul recently shared his experience with colleagues in a team meeting. He has been back at work now for three months. He highlighted three key things that had triggered his feelings of stress.

(Continued)

(Continued)

- Feeling he had to live up to impossible goals he had set himself, which rendered him very susceptible to being asked to take on extra cases at allocation meetings.
- Being expected to be too many things to too many people.
- Having to undertake work that frequently was at odds with his value base and the very reasons he had come into social work.

ACTIVITY 4.3

As part of the team meeting, Paul asked his colleagues to consider the following questions. Answer the questions for yourself.

- Do you know when to say no, and how to say no without feeling you are letting people down?
- How frequently do you take a proper lunch break?
- How frequently do you actually leave the building to have your lunch?
- What mechanisms do you employ at work to enable you to switch off from work for a while?
- How often do you have a laugh with colleagues at work?
- Where does your support come from; who is in your support network?
- Do you have a hobby, pastime that you enjoy, can get absorbed in?
- Do you exercise daily; do you eat healthily?

Paul feels he could have avoided the build-up of stress if he had considered some of the above issues, but he also feels his line manager could have been more proactive and perhaps thought about providing him with more support at work: a transfer, a secondment, or simply not asking him to take on more cases. Paul was also not aware that the organisation had a confidential counselling service. He would have contacted the service if he had known about it.

Comment

The one thing Paul has learned is that he has to assume responsibility for his own health and not wait for other people to rescue him. Paul realises his health and well-being have been seriously affected, but he is also aware that the organisation continued to function during the time he was on sick leave.

The concept of 'Me & Co' at work (Sercombe , 2001, p48) is useful in conceptualising a healthy view of the working transaction:

Your boss may be your boss but he is also a customer of yours! When you give good service, keep up to date and work well, if he is a good customer he will pay well in expressed appreciation, good pay, and more opportunities for you when they are available to him. If you do not provide what he wants, or he does not provide what you want in return for your resources, you will eventually find another job.

Time management

Managing time is an interesting and debated concept (can you really *manage* time?), but we do know that time passes quickly and sometimes we do not use the time available to us to best effect. The use of time only becomes problematic when we are not delivering on deadlines, when we are letting people down by not keeping appointments or we are causing ourselves unnecessary anxiety because we are procrastinating, or we are unable to find the time to be with loved ones.

Williams (2008, p2) identifies three approaches to effective time management.

- Develop ways of working in the same way but working more quickly (scan reading, for example).

- Develop ways of doing the same job differently (for example, having a relevant agenda instead of having an unstructured and unprepared meeting).

- Reconsider how we think about time, our approach to it and what we value.

Williams (2008, p2) argues that most time management training focuses on the first two points, tending to focus on tools and techniques, software and electronic reminders. However, she states:

I believe that what underpins effective management of time is a suitable attitude, approach or belief system in relation to time. This influences what is regarded as important, and inspires creative ways of dealing with 'time stealers'. . . It helps you to make decisions about what to do, or what not to do, and the way in which you might do it.

Some of you will have seen the YouTube video of the late Professor Randy Pausch's last lecture on time management (Pausch 2007). At the time of the lecture Professor Pausch was terminally ill, hence the urgency of his messages. He provided some hard-hitting messages about our use of time and some memorable quotes. He talked about the *time famine* and bad time management leading to stress. He suggested doing the *ugliest* thing on your 'to do' list first. He suggested that each of us have creative and less creative parts of the day and that we need to schedule our days to use the creative times effectively. All of us will be aware of the exhortation to touch each piece of paper only once (an impossibly difficult rule to follow!) but I was taken with his suggestion not to use our email inbox as our 'to do' list, and to turn off the ping on the email system which signals when a new email has arrived. As noted above in the section on stress, Professor Pausch emphasises the importance of learning to say no.

Pausch cites Covey's four-quadrant approach to work that needs to be done and suggests the prioritisation of work accordingly (Covey, 1989).

	Due soon	Not due soon
Important	1	2
Not important	3	4

Covey (1989) suggests, *deadlines are important, establish them yourself.*

Williams (2008) suggests that changing one's approach to the use of time is fundamentally about wanting to change and being committed to doing so. She suggests asking yourself the following questions to ascertain your motivation for change.

ACTIVITY 4.4

Are you happy with your current use of time?

Are others less happy with your use of time?

If the answer to the second question is yes, do you feel concerned about this?

Are you really interested in changing how you manage and use your time? Why?

Do you believe that the change is worth the effort?

Williams also suggests individuals or groups could focus on 'time stealers'. She breaks down 'time stealers' into three categories for consideration. These are:

- time stealers that you generate yourself;
- time stealers that others inflict on you which you allow to continue;
- time stealers that affect you which are caused by others and over which you believe you have little or no control.

Comment

There is a range of approaches to the management of time, but fundamentally we need to be motivated to change the way we prioritise and undertake our activities. That means reflecting on how we use our time well, and how and why we sometimes succumb to the time stealers. A good starting point is a daily 'to do' list. Make a list of all the things you intend accomplishing each day. Tick them off when you have done them. Start with those things which will not be too time-consuming; a few ticks on your to do list will motivate you to do more.

Also, make a note of the things you have done each day that were not on your original list and ask yourself how and why they crept in. Big pieces of work can be very daunting; make them more manageable by chunking them up. If, for example, you are writing a report for a panel, do it in stages rather than trying to do the whole report in one go. Sometimes, taking a step back from a report you have started and are struggling with is really helpful in enabling you to see the wood for the trees. Also, remember that things always take more time than you anticipate, so add at least a further 20 per cent to your first estimate.

Coping with change: getting a grip

In this part of the chapter we are going to focus on coping with change.

At times of organisational change, as well as coping with the change programme impacting the wider organisation, individuals are also required to deliver the day-to-day work of the organisation.

> *Doing something and changing how you do it at the same time is no mean feat and should not be underestimated.*

> *This requirement can be incredibly demanding on individuals and, if not recognised, can lead to severe morale and motivation problems.*

> (CIPD Toolkit 2006, p11)

The toolkit presents the following explanation of the change cycle which individuals will typically experience: *the timing and depth of the experiences varies between individuals but tends to follow the same pattern.*

- **Immobilisation** *This is the initial feeling of being 'stunned' and may last for just a moment or continue for some time.*

- **Denial** *People who disagree with any aspect of the change will spend longer in denial than those who see change as positive. Typically those in denial will behave as if nothing has changed or is going to change.*

- **Anger** *Although anger can be expressed in a number of ways, in the context of the change cycle, it signifies that people have acknowledged the change.*

- **Bargaining** *Impacts of the change have been recognised and people begin to consider alternatives.*

- **Depression** *Nostalgia for the old ways of doing things and old relationships takes hold. Where radical change has taken place, this phase may take a long time to pass.*

- **Testing** *People buy into the change and start challenging and testing the change under different scenarios.*

Individuals will take differing lengths of time to progress through the different stages of the cycle. It will be much harder, and take much longer, for people who resist or disagree with the value base underpinning the organisational change to progress through this cycle, and many will take the options on offer for leaving the organisation. This creates difficulties for the organisation as layers of experience and expertise are lost.

It is important for social work students to be aware that most, if not all, statutory social work agencies will either be starting, in the middle of, or concluding major change programmes and reorganisations of service.

CASE STUDY

Charlie is the team manager of a safeguarding children team which, as well as being subsumed into a new Children and Families Directorate, is also being relocated to a new building in the town, which they will be sharing with Education. The impact of this is that the team will no longer be sharing the building with their adult services colleagues, or be part of the same department. The team is very apprehensive about the changes.

ACTIVITY 4.5

- *Put yourself in the shoes of one of Charlie's team. What would you want to ask Charlie about what is happening?*
- *If you were Charlie, the team manager, what would you be doing to support your team?*
- *Thinking back to the earlier discussion concerning the psychological contract, how might change of this magnitude affect the employer–employee relationship?*
- *What have been the major changes you have experienced and how did you cope?*

Sercombe (2001, p53) rather descriptively suggests that:

> *We have been thrown into a fast flowing river, and the current is increasing. To hold onto the riverbank will easily tear us apart. How can we survive the trip? By understanding the river of change, learning how to use its opportunities, and adjusting. Trying to argue with the river does not work.*

Taking control: using your supervision to best effect

The final part of this chapter considers issues around the use of supervision. It considers the ways in which taking control of your learning and development can help you cope with constant change, and help you to find a way forward for yourself, by getting the most from the organisation.

Regardless of the enormous changes experienced within social work, supervision remains one of the key constants associated with good social work practice. Morrison (1996) provides a succinct and enduring definition of supervision.

> *Supervision is a process in which one worker is given responsibility to work with another worker in order to meet organisational, professional and personal objectives. These are competence, performance which is accountable, continuing professional development and personal support.*

Morrison (1996) goes on to define the purpose of supervision, which is to:

- ensure the worker is clear about roles and responsibilities;
- ensure the worker meets the agency's objectives;
- ensure quality of service to users and carers;
- support a suitable climate for practice;
- support professional development;
- reduce stress;
- ensure the worker has the resources to do the job.

The Social Work Reform Board (2010) states that supervision should:

- improve the quality of decision-making and interventions;
- enable effective line management and organisational accountability;
- identify and address issues related to caseloads and workload management;
- help identify and achieve personal learning, career and development opportunities.

Care and feeding of bosses

The following are some suggestions about how you can get the best out of your supervision with your line manager. Professor Pausch calls this approach *care and feeding of bosses.*

- Make notes before supervision covering the areas of work you need to discuss with your supervisor and the outcomes you are seeking to achieve. Share this agenda with your supervisor prior to your supervision where possible.
- Ask if you can make your own supervision notes (your supervisor will almost certainly take notes, particularly noting key activities agreed between you).
- Ask your supervisor if it is possible to meet somewhere other than their office. If it has to be their office, ask your supervisor if they would mind switching off their phones.
- Make sure you convey to your supervisor how much you value your time with them; this will help to make the supervisor think again about how to manage interruptions to your supervision time.

- Never allow your supervisor to feel it is OK to cancel your supervision. This is not about making your supervisor feel bad; it is about you conveying that you, and your supervision time, are precious.

- Ensure that discussion about your personal and professional development does not drop off the supervision agenda because of all the other things that need to be discussed. Alternatively, book a special supervision with your supervisor just to consider your development.

> *Employers must enable their employees to meet the standards . . . They must provide training and development opportunities to enable staff to strengthen and develop their skills and knowledge. Thus both social (care) workers and their managers are held accountable for the currency of their applied knowledge and skills and for whether the learning culture provides opportunities for individual and collective growth into job roles.*
>
> (Preston-Shoot, 2007, p20)

CASE STUDY

When Rakesh was on placement during his social work degree, his practice teacher was undertaking a master's degree in Leadership in Social Work. As part of the MA course she had been asked to develop a personal and professional development plan, which was to form the basis of her learning, and help to identify the gaps in her learning. The practice teacher asked Rakesh to undertake the same exercise as she felt it would help him to shape his learning programme for the future, and also help him to articulate a career plan for his future. The practice teacher explained to Rakesh that developing her own personal and professional development plan had helped her feel in control of her learning and had assisted her to see her progression as a social worker over the years, and also understand better the periods of her life when she had felt stressed and out of control. Rakesh gained much from developing his personal development plan and now uses it as a work in progress in his supervision. He is using it to shape his future.

ACTIVITY 4.6

This activity is based on the assumption that people undertaking the development of a personal and professional development plan will build a picture of their qualities, capabilities, strengths and weaknesses both as a person and in relation to work tasks, roles and challenges. The individual's increased self-awareness will help assist personal development and career planning. Additionally, the approach will assist in articulating and overcoming emotional and professional blockages, and assist in career development and hopefully progression. It will also help to meet the Health and Care Professions Council requirements for continuous professional development. Self-awareness is essential for us as social workers, and most of us find reflecting on ourselves a fascinating activity.

Seven questions are posed to underpin the personal and professional development planning process. These are listed below. You are invited to undertake the activity, as Rakesh did, and start to build your portfolio.

- *Who am I?*
- *What have I done?*
- *What are my current challenges?*
- *How do I learn?*
- *How do others see me?*
- *Where am I going?*
- *How will I know when I get there?*

Comment

A nurses' leadership paper (RCN 1996) provides some helpful pointers on areas of personal development which can promote your career development. It emphasises a range of characteristics, over and above the expected empathy and technical aspects of nursing, as indicating a person with leadership potential. Personal characteristics include:

- the desire to influence (sometimes they may be angry);
- acting with bravery and taking risks;
- self-motivation;
- recognition of personal limitations;
- acting with confidence.

Interpersonal skills include:

- the ability to facilitate and enthuse others;
- working in a supportive style;
- using authority with discretion;
- the ability to say no;
- allowing others to take the praise.

These are good measures that can be used for spotting and developing potential in oneself and in others.

CHAPTER SUMMARY

This chapter has taken a practical approach to issues of self-management and has developed the theme that the employer and the individual have a shared responsibility for well-being and safety at work. You have been taken through activities which may help you to maintain your well-being and enable you to feel in control of the present and your future. As in Chapter 2, self-development and learning are central as mechanisms for maintaining well-being and equilibrium at work.

FURTHER READING

Cottrell, S (2003) *Skills for success: The personal development planning guide.* Basingstoke: Palgrave Macmillan.

Johnson, S (1999) *Who moved my cheese?* London: Vermilion Press.

This is a simple story that takes about an hour to read, and uses cheese as a metaphor for dealing with change.

REFERENCES

CIPD (2006) *Approaches to change. Key issues and challenges.* Available from: www.cipd.co.uk (accessed 25 June 2013).

CIPD (2008) (Revised) *Factsheet: The psychosocial contract.* London: CIPD.

Covey, S (1989) *The seven habits of highly effective people.* New York: Simon and Schuster.

Cox, T and Rial-Gonzalez, E (2002) *Work-related stress: The European picture.* European Agency for Safety and Health at Work, Magazine 5.

Department of Health (2007) *National taskforce on violence.* London: Department of Health.

Diamantopoulou, A (2002) *Europe under stress.* European Agency for Safety and Health at Work, Magazine 5.

Guest, DE and Conway, N (2002) *Pressure at work and the psychological contract.* London: CIPD.

IFSW Charter of the Rights for Social Workers (2011) Available from: www.ifsw.org/europe (accessed 22 December 2012).

Morrison, T (1996) *Staff supervision in social care.* Brighton: Pavilion.

Mullins, L (1996) *Management and organisational behaviour.* 4th edition. London: Pitman Publishing.

Pausch, Randy (2007) *Last lecture.* Google: YouTube.

Preston-Shoot, M (2007) Engaging with continuing professional development: With or without qualifications. In W Tovey (ed.) *The post qualifying handbook for social workers.* London: Jessica Kingsley.

Royal College of Nursing (1996) *Developing leaders: A guide to good practice.* London: RCN.

Sercombe, A (2001) *Fifty ways to a better life.* Brighton: Word Publishing.

Social Work Reform Board (2010) Building a safe and confident future: One year on – detailed proposals from the Social Work Reform Board.

Williams, T (2008) CIPD member resource, *Time management activities.* London: CIPD.

Part 2
Building relationships

Chapter 5

Skills for empowerment, participation and advocacy

Colin Goble and Jane Donson

ACHIEVING A SOCIAL WORK DEGREE

This chapter will help you to develop the following capabilities from the **Professional Capabilities Framework**.

- **Professionalism.** Identify and behave as a professional social worker, committed to professional development.
- **Values and ethics.** Apply social work ethical principles and values to guide professional practice.
- **Diversity.** Recognise diversity and apply anti-discriminatory and anti-oppressive principles in practice.
- **Knowledge.** Value and take into account the expertise of service users.
- **Intervention and skills.** Be able to communicate information, advise instruction and professional opinion so as to advocate, influence and persuade.

It will also introduce you to the following standards as set out in the 2008 social work subject benchmark statement.

5.7   Skills in working with others

Introduction

In this chapter we will look at the knowledge and skills that underpin the promotion of service user empowerment, participation and advocacy in social work and social care in line with current government policy for both vulnerable adults and children (e.g. DoH 2001a, DoH 2001b, DoH 2006, DCSF 2007, DfES 2007a and DfES 2007b). The idea of service user empowerment is central to the values that underpin professionalism in social work and social care, where a strong emphasis is placed on participatory practice and strategies of professional advocacy (Banks, 2006). Putting these values into practice requires both understanding and commitment to move beyond well-meaning sentiment and rhetoric, and it is the aim of this chapter to help develop both.

Increasing service user participation in decisions about care and service development is at the heart of any intervention in social work, and over the last decade there has been a positive shift in the legislative and policy framework relating to participation. Changing attitudes and developing an understanding of the importance of service user participation in delivering positive outcomes is a key aspect of good practice.

We will begin by identifying four different theoretical models of empowerment in order to develop an understanding of the concept, from which we can go on to shape an approach to practice. We will focus mainly on working with children and adults with learning difficulties, partly because that is where our knowledge and experience lie, but also because lessons learned in relation to this particular group can be of universal value when applied to other client groups. We would argue that if we can get it right for people with learning difficulties then we can improve practice for all. Also, people with learning difficulties have historically been among the most disempowered and oppressed social groups and their struggle for empowerment is both instructive and inspirational. So let us begin by looking at the concept of empowerment, and examine why it is so important in the social care field.

Empowerment

To understand why empowerment is such an important issue in social work we need to appreciate that the experience of many of its main client groups – children, young people, and adults with learning difficulties, for example – has often been one of extreme disempowerment. The reasons for this are many and varied, but the end result has been a common experience of a significantly devalued identity, and a voice that has rarely been listened to or taken seriously. To explore the impact of this, think about the following activity.

ACTIVITY **5.1**

Think of an incident or occasion when you had something of great importance that you wanted to say, but you didn't know how to express it, or those with power over you either would not listen or would not take what you had to say seriously. How did this make you feel?

Comment

Many of us have experiences like this that we can remember – often from childhood. They tend to stay with us for years, burning and niggling away inside us because of their deep emotional impact. Do you remember perhaps feelings of anger, rage, frustration and a deep sense of injustice? Now think about what might have happened if this kind of experience had occurred over and over again, perhaps on a daily basis, for most of your life. If, for example, you had little or no choice over where you live, who with, when and what you eat or drink, how you spend your days, what time you get up or go to bed, what clothes you wear, etc.

What kind of impact do you think this might have had on your understanding of who you are, how valued your voice or opinion is, and how you might feel about, and behave towards, those who control your life?

Sadly, we have a very good understanding of the impact of a life lived with this degree of powerlessness because we have frequently seen the effects in the behaviour of adults and children who have been forced to live such lives because the dominant view of powerful professional and social elites has been that they are unable to live in any other way. The effects range from a passive, learned helplessness, to bizarre, disturbed and aggressive forms of challenging behaviour, often directed at themselves; all symptomatic of a deeply devalued identity and low self-esteem. There have been some famous studies of oppressive and restrictive regimes in large institutional settings, some of which were highly influential in helping to create the case for deinstitutionalisation and community care (Goffman, 1961; Wolfensberger, 1975).

The shift towards community-based care in the 1980s led to a widespread improvement in the standard of services. On its own, however, it failed to address the fundamental imbalance of power between professionals, staff and service users that perpetuates the disempowerment of the latter.

ACTIVITY **5.2**

Can you suggest why adults, children and young people with learning difficulties are still less likely to be involved in decisions affecting their lives? What are the barriers and challenges, and how might these issues be addressed?

Comment

Barriers and challenges are likely to sit within the areas of:

- training, support and resources;
- knowledge, understanding and beliefs about disabled people;
- structures, processes and service systems.

Consideration also needs to be given to the person's communication skills, and whether professionals have invested sufficient time to develop a meaningful relationship and gained a real understanding of their wishes and needs.

Having looked at the impact of disempowerment, we will now look at some theoretical models of empowerment.

Theoretical models of empowerment

In relation to social care four main theoretical perspectives have been influential.

The consumerist model

Derived from neo-liberal economic theory, the consumerist model sees the problem as a lack of choice in services and support for service users. The solution is seen as using 'market forces' by opening up state-dominated systems to allow more service providers to operate – particularly from the private and voluntary sector – thus, theoretically at least, creating more choice. This model was pursued by Conservative governments in the 1980s and early 1990s in their community care reforms, which introduced a 'market' style system in which a variety of providers would compete to provide the services needed by service-user groups, who were defined as 'consumers'. New Labour adapted this approach further by promoting greater service user control over budgets – via 'direct payments', for example – which they can then use to buy the services and support they need (Wall and Owen, 2002).

The political model

Influenced by neo-Marxist ideas and social movement politics, this approach sees the problem as oppressive discrimination against marginalised social groups. The solution is seen as collective action to pursue a rights-based agenda by groups such as the disability movement, the self-advocacy movement for people with learning difficulties, and the survivors' movement for people with mental health problems. A strong influence on this approach has been the social model of disability, which argues that services and professions who work with disabled people often act in an oppressive way in their lives because their understanding of disability comes not from disabled people themselves, but from powerful elites, particularly the medical profession. This medical model of disability focuses on pathology in the individual and is preoccupied with the need to diagnose, treat and provide lifelong, medically dominated care. In contrast, the social model redefines disability as a form of oppression imposed on people who experience various kinds of 'impairment', or functional difficulty – physical, sensory or intellectual (Oliver, 1996).

The personal/cultural model

This model is influenced by feminist and post-modern ideas. From this perspective empowerment involves reconstructing identity as a basis for political and economic action. Strategies involve forming groups and organisations, and/or undertaking cultural activities (including in art, literature, music, etc.) in which oppressed groups can create and affirm their own identity and voice, rather than letting these be created for them by dominant groups and professions. This is a strategy that has also been followed with some success in the disability movement, with some arguing that society in general needs to embrace and celebrate a much wider diversity of human capacity and experience, moving towards an affirmative model of disability (French and Swain, 2008).

The professional model

This is arguably the most contentious model of empowerment in that it has been argued by some that professionals are usually part of the problem rather than part of the solution (French and Swain, 2001). Professional models of empowerment are often based on a rehabilitative, or 'adjustment' approach which has emphasised getting service users to 'do things for themselves', focusing on issues such as self-care, feeding and mobility, for example. Oliver (1996) has criticised this approach, arguing that this is a very limited conceptualisation of empowerment. Genuine empowerment, he argues, lies rather in giving disabled people legal rights, control of budgets and service systems, and the autonomy to choose where they live, who they are supported by, and how, when and what type of support is provided. This kind of approach has gained increasing influence over government policy in the last decade through the 'personalisation agenda' (Carr, 2008). Though still in its early stages, this agenda has created a challenge to traditional power relationships in social care, and will inevitably lead to a reshaping of professional roles, identities, knowledge and skills in the process. It should be remembered, however, that, in practice, these models are not necessarily implemented in a mutually exclusive way. The policy agenda of the New Labour governments, for example, mixed elements from all these models to some extent, although the 'consumerist' model has dominated government policy since the 1980s, up to and including the current personalisation agenda.

RESEARCH SUMMARY

Sutcliffe and Simons (1995), in an evidence-based approach to promoting empowerment involving extensive qualitative research with adults with learning difficulties, identified nine main themes emerging from research into promoting empowerment in practice.

1. Professionals must be willing to learn from the experience of people with learning difficulties themselves and their significant others. *Central to this is recognising the value of the* lived experience *of disability rather than just professional expertise* about *disability.*
2. It will take time for staff and people with learning difficulties to develop the necessary skills and confidence. *People with learning difficulties may require significant amounts of training and personal support to develop the skills and confidence necessary to self-advocate, and/or participate in taking a greater degree of control over their lives. This will take time and require a long-term commitment from individual professionals and their service organisations.*

(Continued)

(Continued)

3. The amount of control and autonomy an individual can exercise will vary. *An important principle in working with people with learning difficulties, and other vulnerable client groups, is the idea of maintaining a 'person-centred' focus (Gates, 2005). This recognises that, whatever 'condition' a person may be affected by, an empowering practice needs to focus on individuals and the outcomes they want, rather than on 'conditions' or 'syndromes' (see the personal outcome approach discussed in Chapter 5). Empowerment is about choice, including the choice not to participate. Even where an individual shows a preference not to be involved in formal processes and procedures of participation, however, a commitment should still be made to organise their care and support in line with their known wishes and preferences.*

4. We need to adapt structures, not people. *Carr (2004), in a review of the promotion of service user participation by local authorities in the UK, identified the way that it can be undermined and turned into a tokenistic exercise by a failure to recognise that it requires organisations to transform their systems, practices and processes to make them accessible to, and usable for, service user groups and individuals.*

5. We need to change the culture from one where we talk about people to one where we talk in dialogue with them about their lives and aspirations. *Beresford and Trevillion (1995) argued for the creation of a collaborative culture in care and support services. At the core of this lies the development of trust and good relationships between professionals, staff and service users themselves, and also their families, relatives and other carers (see Chapters 6 and 7). In particular, they place commitment to the involvement of service users at the centre of their strategy for creating collaborative culture and practice.*

6. We need to celebrate diversity in people and solutions to their problems. *A dialogue-based, person-centred approach will inevitably move us away from the kind of 'one-size-fits-all', resource-led solutions which have tended to dominate service delivery in the past. An approach that emphasises dialogue with individual service users and/or their representatives to identify their needs and aspirations, and the problems they face in meeting and achieving them, is central.*

7. We need to face up to tensions over who speaks for whom, and recognise that different stakeholders (service users, informal carers, staff and professionals) have different agendas. *For people with intellectual impairments in particular – learning difficulties, brain damage, stroke and dementia – the issue of whose voice is dominant is often crucial in deciding the extent to which their wishes, desires and preferences are met in designing and delivering care and support, particularly if that person has either never developed, or has lost, their actual voice. For people in this situation the presence of others who can speak for them is vital. This role is often taken up automatically by parents and other*

relatives, or – where these are absent or not accessible on a day-to-day basis – the care staff or professionals who work with them. It is important, however, to remember that each of these stakeholders has interests that are different and distinct from the individual service user themselves.

8. We need to put service users at the centre of our thinking, processes and actions. *A person-centred approach to working with service users will necessarily mean that we focus on promoting the needs, desires and aspirations of the person themselves. Care systems are often organised around standard processes. This can lead us down bureaucratic pathways where service users are seen purely as 'cases' to be dealt with, instead of being seen as people with their own life history and story, of which we are only a part.*

9. We need to accept and actively promote the idea that service-user-led organisations can represent the people we support. *Carr (2004) reminds us that, for empowerment and participation to be effective rather than tokenistic, we need to address issues of representation. The self-advocacy movement for people with learning difficulties, like the survivors' movement for people with mental health problems, and the wider disability movement, have all identified the need for collective representation in order to give weight and strength to their voice. This can sometimes be seen as threatening by service organisations, staff and professionals, however, who have often become adept at disarming or ignoring it. Adopting a person-centred service should not become a substitute for independent and/or group representation, however. It takes courage and tenacity to take on entrenched professional and organisational power; even more so if you lack the confidence, knowledge and skills necessary. This is what collective representation provides, and history has shown that it is an important part of the struggle of any oppressed group in gaining empowerment.*

Implications for practice

As the research review above illustrates, learning from the experience of disabled people includes the development of research and networking skills designed to identify and access sources of service-user knowledge and expertise – via the internet, academic library resources and self-help/self-advocacy groups, for example, and the growing wealth of literary sources written and informed by disabled people and their allies.

It also involves listening and communicating in ways that allow the voice and perspective of service users to emerge, and to inform your own, and your organisation's, thinking and practice, valuing this perspective and expertise as primary, over the secondary 'technical' and theoretical knowledge of human science experts.

Good communication skills are also needed to enable people with learning difficulties to develop the necessary skills and confidence to speak out. This should involve negotiation and collaboration with service user groups and organisations, to help identify and meet development needs. It will also help to promote the development of a collaborative culture, as outlined below in relation to theme 5, above (p 76), and underpins the development of person-centred assessment skills that focus on the needs and wishes of individuals. This should not just mean familiarity with forms and procedures, but also with empathic and sensitive forms of communication needed to build trusting relationships with service users and/or their carer/advocate.

Collaboration with 'important others' in the person's life, as well as inter-professional and multi-agency working across various services and agencies, is also an important aspect of this, as is developing a knowledge of actual and potential sources of help and support – services, professions, agencies, and community resources – to meet the person's needs and desired goals.

Networking and building relationships with appropriate service-user-led organisations is also important, as is the use of communication systems and procedures which are 'user friendly', open and accessible to service users, carers and advocates. Using plain spoken and written language and developing skills in the use of signing and audio/visual systems are essential. These issues were highlighted by Beresford and Trevillion (1995) who identified the following elements in creating a collaborative culture.

- Allowing space and time for involvement, at whatever level the service user is able or willing to be involved.

- A commitment to including the service user, their advocate or representative in decision-making at all levels, including important life choices.

- Keeping the use of technical language in its appropriate context.

- Not sacrificing service user interests to inter-professional power play or disputes; being led by the needs of the service user; and keeping areas of potential conflict – such as what constitutes a health rather than a social care need – out of meetings involving the service user or their supporters.

Ultimately, the building of warm human relationships with service users will help us to ensure that our thinking and actions stay focused on their, rather than our, needs.

We will now go on to look at the concept of advocacy.

Advocacy

Advocacy is about speaking up for yourself, or others. The concept has its origins in the legal system, and in Western societies there is a strong tradition of professionalised legal advocacy. This is a very powerful and high-profile form of advocacy, but it is only one kind. The other main forms include the following.

- **Political advocacy** This includes the rights-based advocacy of the 'disability movement', which focuses mainly on campaigning and lobbying activity.

- **Self-advocacy** This has some crossover with political advocacy, but centre specifically on service users speaking up for themselves, either individually or collectively, and at all levels, from major political issues to day-to-day choices about their lives.

- **Citizen advocacy** This is where a person independent from services takes on the role of speaking up for the interests of the person.

- **Issue advocacy** This is similar to, and perhaps involves, legal advocacy, where trained advocates will take on specific issues for an individual or group of service users as they arise (Gray and Jackson, 1998).

- **Professional advocacy** This is where a service professional, such as a nurse or social worker, takes on the advocacy role. This can be an important and even vital role, although it does have its dangers. It is important to remember that effective advocacy may require the absence rather than the intervention of professionals, no matter how well meaning. A social worker, for example, is inevitably a representative of the local authority, private or voluntary sector organisation they work for. This is an interest that can potentially conflict with the interests of service users. For example, the organisation may be under pressure to reduce costs, which may lead to pressure to restrict spending to meeting only those needs regarded as essential rather than desirable. Views on what is regarded as essential and what is considered desirable may well vary, however, depending on the perspective of different stakeholders. The first stage of planning any advocacy intervention, therefore, is to ask the question, *Am I the right person to do it?* A person-centred focus may require us to accept that our client's interests are better served by an advocate who is independent of organisational and professional interests that may constrain us – a 'citizen' or 'issue' advocate, for example. This is illustrated further in the following case study.

CASE STUDY

Angela

Angela is 45 years old. For 20 years she lived in an NHS mental subnormality hospital where she was admitted at the age of five, spending a further 20 years in a number of NHS, social service and private-sector residential homes. She has a mild learning difficulty, can read and write, is quite articulate and physically able, if very overweight. She frequently flew into rages, crying out for her parents. She was prescribed antipsychotic medication and anti-depressants, and was put on repeated behavioural programmes to help control her temper. When calm and lucid, Angela repeatedly expressed her desire to live on her own, near enough to her mother to visit, get a job, and learn to look after herself.

The big change came when a community learning disability nurse working with Angela successfully advocated to her service manager that Angela's behaviour

(Continued)

(Continued)

should be seen as communicative rather than psychotic. The nurse contacted a social worker, who undertook an assessment which led to a plan being agreed to move Angela to a halfway home where she would learn the skills to help her live independently. However, there was still some resistance from her consultant psychiatrist and from the owners of the privately run home where she lived. To strengthen the case the social worker referred Angela to a local independent advocacy organisation. They appointed an advocate who took up and success-fully argued Angela's case to live independently, with an appropriate support package from a local housing association.

Angela spent three months in a halfway house, finally moving out of residential care altogether. She has now been living independently, with support, for two years. She has a part-time job at a local Co-op, regularly visits her mother, who lives within walking distance, and has joined a local self-advocacy group. This group runs a variety of social activities, as well as helping Angela gain the knowledge and confidence to speak up for herself.

Comment

We can see that various forms of advocacy played a crucial part in the success of Angela's move from a restricted life, organised and run for her by professional experts, to a life of supported independence, where she earns her own living, has contact with her family, and has her own circle of friends and support. First there was the learning disability nurse, who understood the communicative rather than psychotic nature of Angela's behaviour. She was able to present an evidence-based case to key decision-makers, and collaborate with a social worker to assess Angela's needs and advocate further for a change of approach. Crucially, Angela's social worker was able to appreciate his own limitations, and involved independ-ent advocates who were able to make the final case to develop a new support package for Angela. They did not stop there, however, realising that for Angela to achieve real empowerment in her life she needed help from a self-advocacy organ-isation that can encourage her to achieve further autonomy.

We are not arguing that a professional cannot advocate for the interests of his or her clients; this is in fact a key part of the role. In most cases, however, pro-fessional advocacy is probably best restricted to service-level advocacy – that is, advocating for access to the skills and expertise of other professionals within or across different services. This requires a good level of knowledge about other professional roles, referral systems, finance issues, and about one's own position within the service context, combined with an informed and up-to-date knowl-edge of interventions and services which may help services users to meet their assessed needs.

The importance of advocacy for children and young people

There is a growing recognition of the importance of advocacy for children and young people in need, and those who are looked after; particularly when plans are being made for their future, but also in their day-to-day lives. Understanding and appreciating their views and feelings helps them feel involved and assists with decision-making.

Many young people require support to articulate their wishes and views, particularly when there is conflict or disagreement, and may find it extremely difficult to express themselves to a professional or in the range of forums where major decisions are made. Respect and independence are requirements of successful advocacy, as is the importance of developing a trusting and honest relationship with the young person (NSPCC, 2005). Independent advocates can support children and young people to ensure that their rights are respected and their views and wishes are heard. This enables the promotion of young people's views in a range of situations including child protection conferences, planning meetings, and if they are placed away from home in a residential placement. It provides an opportunity for their views to be listened to and properly considered with a greater degree of objectivity and independence.

Within court proceedings the child or young person will have independent representation from a Cafcass officer (Children and Family Court Advisory and Support Service) who looks after their interests in family proceedings. They will advise the court on what is considered to be in the best interests of the individual child or young person.

CASE STUDY

Permanency planning is under way for a sibling group of children (aged two, three and eleven years). The eldest child exhibits very challenging behaviour and has already experienced a foster placement breakdown. He is no longer placed with his siblings but has regular contact with them and with his birth mother. He is expressing a wish to maintain contact with his birth mother and continue to live with his younger siblings. Adoption is thought to be in the younger children's best long-term interests. Due to the differing needs of the siblings it is likely that they will not be placed together.

ACTIVITY 5.3

How would you obtain the views, feelings and wishes of the children?

How will you ensure the eldest child's voice is heard and his needs met alongside those of his younger siblings?

How will you enable him to participate in decisions made about his future?

Comment

It is important to consider each child individually, remembering each one's stage of development and level of understanding, their individual needs and how these might be best met. You would also need to consider if the children should be placed together; the arguments for and against this, and how the issues around contact would be managed. Given each child's level of understanding and developmental stage, a range of techniques may be required, such as observation, the use of art or play to ascertain their feelings and wishes, as well as working closely with other people who know the children well.

Degrees of participation in children and young people

Children and young people's participation and involvement in decision-making will develop as they mature, and may be influenced by their relationship with parents, care-givers and professionals supporting them. There will be occasions where young people are given greater responsibility and enabled to be involved to a greater or lesser degree in decisions relating to their lives. Working in partnership with all parties to gain their involvement is a key policy priority and good practice.

Local authorities are expected to consult children and young people about issues that impact on them individually and to support service development. Examples of this include the development of Children and Young People's Plans (Children Act 2004), leisure activities, commissioning services such as youth and short break services for children with disabilities.

Two models of participation for children

A number of models have been developed to indicate the level of participation a young person actually has in decision-making. This will vary depending upon the issue and level of involvement. Decisions about when parents and professionals should step back can be contentious.

The 'ladder of participation' model developed by Arnstein (1969) was an attempt to show how participation can affect social change. It was adapted by Hart in 1992 to focus on the participation of young people in education. Hart suggested eight levels, each one representing an increasing degree of participation and active involvement. At the lowest level, at the bottom of the ladder, children and young people have very little influence on decisions. Rising through the levels there are incremental increases in participation until at the top level true involvement is demonstrated. This model can assist individual workers or organisations to determine the current level of participation, and help improve their approach (see Table 5.1).

An alternative model of participation was developed by Treseder (1997) to explain the level of control young people might exercise over decisions affecting

Table 5.1 Degrees (ladder) of participation (Hart, 1992)

User-initiated, decisions shared with adults

Projects empower service users; enable learning and access

User-initiated and directed

Service users initiate but are supported

Adult-initiated, decisions shared with users

Decision-making is shared

Consulted and informed

Service users give advice on projects or programmes designed and run by adults

Assigned but informed

Service users are assigned a specific role and informed about how and why they are being involved

Tokenism

Service users appear to be given a voice, but in fact have little or no choice about how they participate

Decoration

Service users are used to help or 'bolster' a cause in a relatively indirect way

Manipulation

Pretence that the causes are inspired by service users or young people

Adapted from Hart (1992) Children's participation from tokenism to citizenship.

activities they are involved in. It is neither better nor worse than Hart's and can be used interchangeably as required for the particular circumstance. Based on Hodgson's (1996) five conditions for empowerment, Treseder's model similarly suggests five equal but different degrees of participation.

Consulted and informed The project is designed and run by adults, but children are consulted. They have a full understanding of the process and their opinions are taken seriously.

Assigned but informed Adults decide on the project and children volunteer for it. The children understand the project, they know who decided to involve them and why. Adults respect young people's views.

Adult-initiated, decisions shared with children Adults have the initial idea, but young people are involved in every step of the planning and implementation. Not only are their views considered, but children are also involved in taking the decisions.

Child-initiated and directed Young people have the initial idea and decide how the project is to be carried out. Adults are available but do not take charge.

Child-initiated, decisions shared with adults Children have ideas, set up projects and come to adults for advice, discussion and support. The adults do not direct, but offer their expertise for young people to consider.

Skills for promoting empowerment, participation and advocacy

We have already identified that the key skills for promoting empowerment, participation and advocacy centre on communication. They include the following.

- *Assertiveness skills* These include the ability to express your own point of view or perspective in a way that is perceived by others as confident, rather than passive and/or aggressive (See Chapters 6 and 7).

- *Negotiation skills* Social work often involves negotiating who will do what, how, by when, and who will pay for it (see Chapter 10). It is important here to work constructively, knowing when and when not to compromise, and to try and achieve 'win–win' solutions where possible. A principled and value-based approach can be of particular value in helping to set the parameters for negotiation.

- *Encouraging information gathering and sharing* Control of information and its dissemination is one of the ways in which professions have sometimes engaged in oppressive and disempowering practices. The development of a collaborative culture requires a commitment to ensuring that accurate information is gathered and shared at the right time, in the right place, and in the right format; primarily with service users, but also with those people who need to know in order to achieve the best outcomes for service users (see Chapter 3). It may also require the use of alternative and/or augmented communication systems, the accessing of which may be a number one priority for service users with communication difficulties.

- *Constructive advice, supervision and reflection* Social work can be complex and demanding, and good support, supervision and governance systems are important to make it work successfully (see Chapters 1 and 4).

- *Active listening* To promote empowerment and participation, practitioners acknowledge the importance of listening to vulnerable adults, children and young people. Children will learn the skills of listening to others, compromise and negotiation through being listened to. In doing so they will increase their self-esteem, independence and confidence. The UN Convention on the Rights of the Child states that all children have a right to be heard and to participate in decisions that affect their lives; both in the private and public arena. Article 12 requires that *every child has the right to express his or her views and these views must be taken seriously*. This right is supported by legislation, policy and guidance. Examples of this include the Children Act 1989 (Section 22), the Children Act 2004 and *Every Child Matters* 2003. A particular emphasis is given to those whose voices are least likely to be heard. The current statutory framework and rights, which have been strengthened over the past decade to enhance the participation of children and young people, will not alone ensure good practice in effective consultation and participation. This requires commitment and the continuing development of good practice and systems to enable young people to be involved.

- *Acting and working in a businesslike manner* All of the above will be greatly helped if your own approach is grounded in behaviour associated with professionalism (see Chapters 4, 8 and 14).

As Beresford and Trevillion (1995) pointed out, making participation a reality often requires a cultural shift and commitment, both strategically and operationally, within organisations. It also requires individual practitioners to understand and develop the skills identified above to engage positively with vulnerable adults, children and young people, to facilitate an increase in the level of control they can assert in decision-making relating to their lives, and in making empowerment a reality.

CHAPTER SUMMARY

Least heard are the voices of the people who experience social work directly, either as users of the services or as the carers *(Doel and Best, 2009, p1)*. In this chapter we have looked at the knowledge and skills that underpin the promotion of service user empowerment, participation and advocacy in social work and social care. We have explored the idea of service user empowerment and located it in relation to the values that underpin professionalism in social work and social care. We have seen that putting these values into practice requires knowledge, skills and commitment, and we have looked at some different models of empowerment and the theoretical perspectives that influence them.

We have also discussed lessons drawn from research about the strategies and skills required to put our understanding of empowerment and participation into practice, before going on to look specifically at advocacy as a strategy to achieve both. The central message is that we need to develop a 'shared expertise' with service users, based on a dialogue with them about their needs, desires and aspirations, and that we should always strive to ensure we work in ways which promote, rather than hinder, their struggle for empowerment.

REFERENCES

Arnstein, S (1969) A ladder of participation. *Journal of American Institute of Planners*, 35, 216–24.

Banks, S (2006) *Ethics and values in social work.* 3rd edition. Basingstoke: Palgrave Macmillan.

Beresford, P and Trevillion, S (1995) *Developing skills for community care: A collaborative approach.* London: Arena.

Carr, S (2004) *Has service user participation made a difference to social care services? SCIE Position Paper 3.* London: Social Care Institute for Excellence/The Policy Press.

Carr, S (2008) *Personalisation: A rough guide.* London: Social Care Institute for Excellence.

Children Act (1989) London: Her Majesty's Stationery Office.

Children Act (2004) London: The Stationery Office.

DCSF (2007) *Aiming high for young people: A ten year strategy for positive activities.* London: HMSO.

DfE (2003) *Every child matters.* London: The Stationery Office.

DfES (2007a) *Aiming high for disabled children: Better support for families.* London: The Stationery Office.

DfES (2007b) *Care matters: Time for change.* London: The Stationery Office.

Doel, M and Best, L (2009) *Experiencing social work.* London: Sage.

DoH (2001a) *National service framework for older people.* London: The Stationery Office.

DoH (2001b) *Nothing about us without us: The service users advisory group report.* London: HMSO.

DoH (2005) *Improving the life chances of disabled people.* London: HMSO.

DoH (2006) *Our health, our care, our say.* London: HMSO.

Ferris-Taylor, R (2003) Communication. In Gates, B (ed.) *Learning disability: Towards integration.* London: Churchill Livingstone.

French, S and Swain, J (2001) The relationship between disabled people and health professionals. In Albrecht, G, Seelman, K and Bury, M (eds) *Handbook of disability studies.* London: Sage.

French, S and Swain, J (eds) (2008) *Disability on equal terms.* London: Sage.

Gates, B (ed.) (2005) *Care planning and delivery in intellectual disability nursing.* Oxford: Blackwell Publishing.

Goffman, E (1961) *Asylums: Essays on the social situation of mental patients and other inmates.* Harmondsworth: Pelican.

Gray, B and Jackson, R (eds) (1998) *Advocacy and learning disability.* London: Jessica Kingsley.

Hart, R (1992) *Children's participation: From tokenism to citizenship.* Florence: UNICEF International Child Development Centre.

Hodgson, D (1996) *Young people's participation in social work planning: A resource pack.* London: NCB.

NSPCC (2005) *Speaking out. A guide for advocates with children and young people with disabilities.* Available at: www.nspcc.org.uk/Inform/publications/downloads/speakingout_wdf48015.pdf (accessed 20 November 2012).

O'Brien, J and Tyne, A (1981) *The principle of normalisation: A foundation for effective services.* London: The Campaign for Mentally Handicapped People.

Oliver, M (1996) *Understanding disability: From theory to practice.* Basingstoke: Macmillan.

Participation Works (2010) *Listen and change: A guide to children and young people's participation rights.* London: Participation Works.

Ryan, J with Thomas, F (1987) *The politics of mental handicap.* London: The Free Press.

Sutcliffe, J and Simons, K (1995) *Self advocacy and adults with learning difficulties: Contexts and debates.* Leicester: The National Institute for Adult Education.

Souza, A with Ramcharan, P (1997) Everything you wanted to know about Down's syndrome but never bothered to ask. In Ramcharan, P (ed.) *Empowerment in everyday life.* London: Jessica Kingsley.

Treseder, P (1997) *Empowering children and young people: Promoting involvement in decision-making.* Available at: www.nonformality.org/wpcontent/uploads/2011/07/Participation-Models (accessed 13 November 2012).

Wall, A and Owen, B (2002) *Health policy.* 2nd edition. London: Routledge.

Wolfensberger, W (1972) *The principle of normalisation in human services.* Toronto: National Institute on Mental Retardation.

Wolfensberger, W (1975) *The nature and origins of our institutional models.* Syracuse: Human Polity Press.

Chapter 6

Skills for engagement

Andy Mantell

A C H I E V I N G   A   S O C I A L   W O R K   D E G R E E

This chapter will help you to develop the following capabilities from the **Professional Capabilities Framework**.

- **Diversity.** Recognise diversity and apply anti-discriminatory and anti-oppressive principles in practice.
- **Knowledge.** Apply knowledge of social sciences, law and social work practice theory.
- **Critical reflection and analysis.** Apply critical reflection and analysis to inform and provide a rationale for professional decision-making.
- **Intervention and skills.** Use judgment and authority to intervene with individuals, families and communities to promote independence, provide support and prevent harm, neglect and abuse.

It will also introduce you to the following standards as set out in the 2008 social work subject benchmark statement.

5.5.4 Intervention and evaluation
5.6   Communication

Introduction

At the heart of social work is the quality of the relationships that we establish with service users, carers, colleagues and other professionals. This chapter will explore how we develop relationships with people; how we engage with them. The nature of these relationships and their significance to practice then provides the context for exploring skills in engaging with people. After clarifying the meaning and media for engaging, the process for developing good relationships will be explored in more detail. Communication (see Chapter 7) can be seen as critical for developing and sustaining relationships and is at the core of the subsequent chapters. Engagement, however, provides the social lubricant for effective communication.

Building relationships

We live in a social work climate increasingly concerned with outcomes and the evidence base to produce those outcomes. In such an atmosphere it is easy for the humble relationship to be overlooked. The managerial concern with resources, throughput and output has led to a focus on the outcomes for the organisation, producing service-led procedures that inhibit rather than nurture relationships. Recently, however, there has been a renewed emphasis on the outcomes that service users and carers wish to achieve (Cook and Miller, 2012). Establishing a relationship is crucial for engaging with carers and service users about the outcomes that are important to them (Cook and Miller, 2012) and consequently for empowering practice (see Chapter 5). It does not matter if you have the most effective tools to hand, if you do not build good relationships with your clients, your colleagues and other agencies, the experience and outcome of your interactions are likely to be less successful. Failing to engage with people will inhibit the exchange of information (Smale *et al.*, 1993), undermine our assessments and hamper negotiations towards consensus outcomes and subsequent decision-making (see Chapters 11, 12, 13 and 14).

RESEARCH SUMMARY

Lessons from counselling

Boisvert and Faust (2003), in an interesting analysis of studies into the effectiveness of counselling, found that people change more due to common factors than to specific factors associated with therapies and that 10 per cent of people will actually get worse as a result of therapy. Crucially, the relationship between the therapist and the client is the best predictor of treatment outcome and is more important than the approach selected (Boisvert and Faust 2003, p511).

Comment

Considering these findings in relation to social work raises some interesting points. You are unlikely ever to find a method of practice that will always work. Instead you will need to be eclectic, assembling a tool box of well-practised methods that you can apply in different situations (Trevithick, 2005).

Most significantly, your relationship with the person, rather than the method you adopt, will be the better determinant of the outcome of your intervention. Cook and Miller (2012) contend that the process of working with someone is a central tenet of social work practice. Emphasising the therapeutic importance of relationships marks a revisiting of social work's psycho-dynamic roots. However, as Lefevre (2008) points out, contemporary practitioners consider the person in a wider social context, incorporating an understanding of anti-oppressive practice and empowerment.

While interventions have great potential to help carers and service users, contact with social services departments can be stigmatised as well as stigmatising, making service users and carers reluctant or defensive in their contact. Social workers who are focused entirely on gathering facts, rather than on how and when we explore people's often traumatic experiences, are likely to be viewed by carers and service users as intrusive and insensitive. Thus, this approach can reinforce the perception of services as uncaring bureaucracies, perpetuating mistrust, increasing the psychological distance and decreasing empathy between parents and workers (Howe, 2010). While we will always need to gather data in order to audit and create the evidence base for our practice, this 'proving agenda' should not be allowed to supersede the 'improving agenda'; concern for the personal outcomes of those with whom we work (Miller, 2012).

ACTIVITY *6.1*

Admirable qualities

Write down the five most important attributes or qualities you appreciate in others.

Comment

The points that you identified may have included openness, respect, honesty, reliability and being non-judgemental. Unsurprisingly, carers and service users also value these qualities as well as attributes such as warmth and humour that display the *human aspect* of the professional (Lefevre, 2008, p90). However, while we appreciate these behaviours we can have a high degree of tolerance depending on our expectations of a particular relationship. You may, for example, consider reliability as an absolute in a partner, but not in a casual acquaintance. In our interventions with carers and service users we understand how they may have limited experience of receiving or giving these attributes that nurture positive relationships. This can be particularly true of young people in abusive situations. However, our tolerance of the lack of such qualities will depend on factors such as the nature and stage of our intervention and the needs of the individual. For example, in working with Paul, a 24-year-old man who misused substances, his respect had to be earned over time and his level of honesty and reliability gradually followed.

Changing roles, changing relationships?

In the same way that we require different methods to suit different situations we also need to employ a range of relationship styles to suit the situation and the role we are undertaking. Howe (1994, p518) summarised social workers' roles in terms of care, control and cure. However, there has been a continued shift towards a less paternalistic position, with people managing their own care (DoH, 2006, 2007, 2008, 2012). This has been accompanied by an increasing tension between a culture of rights and risk aversion (see Chapters 5 and 13). Since then the language and corresponding emphasis in practice has shifted in adult social work so that 'care' has translated to the more detached 'care management', 'control' has become 'protection' through risk assessment and management (see Chapter 4) and cure has transformed into 'change' through empowerment. Braye and Preston-Shoot (1995) have argued that to achieve empowering practice, social worker relationships should be based on consultation, i.e. clients influencing the decision-making process; participation, i.e. clients' active involvement; partnership, i.e. power and responsibility sharing; and control, i.e. respecting the autonomy of the individual. Cook and Miller (2012) argue for a fundamental shift to a personal outcomes approach (POA). Rather than being preoccupied with needs and risks and the services to address them, the focus shifts to the outcomes for the service users and carers and how to achieve them. This obviously requires a frank exchange of information and negotiation where their concerns may be at odds with the wider society. The nature of the relationship with them can be crucial to this process.

CASE STUDY

The nature of empowerment?

Sharon Day is a 42-year-old Afro-Caribbean woman who suffers from bipolar affective disorder (manic depression). She is married to Raymond (47), who also suffers from mania and they have a six-year-old daughter, Faye. Ms Day became suicidal following a long period of depression. Mr Day struggled to support her and look after Faye. Ms Day was compulsorily admitted to a psychiatric unit under the Mental Health Act 2007 and given electroconvulsive therapy (ECT).

Comment

You may be surprised to hear that Ms Day was pleased that she was detained and received ECT. At that point she felt out of control and unable to manage and was grateful to services for 'taking over'. However, following the course of ECT she wanted to regain control and return to her family with minimal support.

If Ms Day had received support at a much earlier point she might never have required such extreme reactive intervention. Her situation consequently demonstrates how simply targeting services at those in greatest need without also being proactive can be disempowering.

This is an extreme situation, but it is important to recognise that at different points in our relationships with carers and service users we may need to be more or less directive. Often, in short-term interventions this follows a progressive pattern but it is not always the case. Such situations also require great sensitivity to the individual's situation and our interaction with them – it is easy to become paternalistic (see Chapter 2 for a discussion of how we can interact as a parent to a child) or rigid enforcers of our organisation's policies.

Mind the gap

While empowerment is a key social work value, operational exigencies such as managing limited resources can encourage directive crisis interventions. Unfortunately, *a gap exists between the rhetoric of government policy and the reality of practice* (Cree and Myers, 2008, p134). This is graphically demonstrated by the case of Mrs McDonald (*R v. Royal Borough of Kensington* ex parte *McDonald* [2011] UKSC), who wanted to have assistance to go to the toilet at night but whose local authority redefined her needs as the ability to urinate safely and provided incontinence pads instead. Duffy (2011, p192) has cautioned that while *for some personalisation is about entitlements and citizenship, for others it is merely a new technique for delivering services.* If cash-strapped Local Authorities shift to meeting only substantial and critical needs in their application of the *Prioritising need: Putting people first* guidance (DoH, 2010), then the *vaunted flexibility of direct payments may be chimeric* (Thornton, 2011, p220). The new Care and Support Bill (2012) promises much, but does not address the underlying issue of funding; consequently the disparity between intent and impact is likely to increase. Reflective practice not only enables us to keep a critical eye on how we are interacting but also how organisations can restrict our interventions (see Mantell, 2013).

The prevailing ethos of managerialism means that practitioners have actually been spending less time in face-to-face work with carers and service users (Leveridge 2002) and losing sight of the centrality of relationships to practice (Howe, 2010). Yet service users consistently state that the quality of relationships matters (Maiter *et al.*, 2006). If practitioners do not have the time to engage with people then it is difficult to see how they can be attentive to their concerns and develop empowering practice (see Chapter 5). Stevenson (*The Guardian*, 2008) observed that risk-averse organisations tend to respond to their own anxieties (for example, negative media coverage and political criticism) by increasing their procedures, but this is at the cost of the organisation's humanity and undermines the development of therapeutic relationships.

It will be interesting to see, as the lexicon of adult social work discussed above continues to shift towards 'care navigation', 'safeguarding' and 'empowerment' respectively, if social workers will become more engaged with face-to-face practice once more. Certainly, Cook and Miller's (2012) POA has the potential to recalibrate services in a way which will be much more sensitive to meeting carers' and service users' needs, while addressing the managerial concerns of agencies and re-energising practitioners *by restoring the values and principles of professional practice, which were described as having been diminished through care management and bureaucracy* (Miller, 2010, p120).

91

Working alliances

While it is necessary to employ a range of relationship styles in social work, a preferred model remains the working alliance (Greenson, 1967). The relationship is based solely on the role that we are performing for its existence, but it can be more than a *relationship-as-means-to-achieving-desired-outcomes* (Egan, 2007, p49). It can provide a space where a person feels safe, valued and able to reflect on their situation. This space can be particularly useful for children to be able to *regulate, recognise and contain their otherwise overwhelming feelings* (Howe, 2010, p334). The social worker can hold both the parent's feelings and the child in mind and help the parent to understand how our mental states affect our and other people's behaviours. This mentalisation (Howe, 2010) in combination with mindfulness, i.e. paying attention to how children think about things, can empower parents by making the world a less confusing place. Just the process of the parent thinking about their child's thoughts and feelings could make the child safer. This process requires emotional intelligence on the part of the practitioner:

> being able to motivate one's self and persist in the face of frustrations: to control impulse and delay gratification; to regulate one's moods and keep distress from swamping the ability to think; to empathise and to hope.

> (Goleman, 1996, p34)

Rogers (1951), in his client-centred approach, developed the notion of the therapeutic relationship in which the person can be supported to reach their full potential. He considered such relationships to require unconditional positive regard, i.e. valuing the person regardless of their actions; congruence, i.e. genuineness; and empathy (see below). Client-centred practice is an example of a non-directive approach in which the *relationship-in-itself* (Egan, 2007, p49) has intrinsic value.

While social work has been more directive than Rogers' therapeutic approach, an effective working alliance can combine the values of therapeutic relationships (see the research summary below) and the benefits of the relationship as a vehicle for achieving outcomes. As Hudson and Sheldon (2000) observed: *A good working relationship is a necessary but not sufficient condition for being an effective helper* (Hudson and Sheldon, 2000, p65).

RESEARCH SUMMARY

The values of effective relationships

Egan (2007, p56), in his well-respected guide to helping people, expanded Rogers' core values to identify five key elements in helping relationships.

- ***Respect*** *This includes respecting and taking seriously their views and, in social work, often advocating for those views to be heard. This does not mean collusion, and may necessitate challenging the carer or service user.*

In working with people we should not manipulate, exploit or coerce carers or service users. Respect for those we work with also places a responsibility upon us to continue to develop as a competent practitioner. Being competent and committed, Egan (2007, p56) noted, is not completed at graduation; it is an ongoing process, which is reflected in the Professional Capabilities Framework.

- *Empathy Sensing and responding to a person's inner world (Rogers, 1975).*
- *Genuineness The congruent practitioner should be present in the moment, open, spontaneous and not defensive. They should listen and communicate without distortion (Egan, 2007, p56). They should be striving towards a relationship that is not based on dependence or counter dependence (Egan, 2007, p56, after Gibb, 1968 and 1978).*
- *Empowerment Enabling clients to identify, develop and harness their resources to change their lives (Egan, 2007, p57, after Strong, Yoder and Corcoran, 1995).*
- *A bias for action Egan argues that successful intervention should aim to produce an outcome in which the clients become doers rather than mere reactors; preventers rather than fixers; initiators rather than followers (Egan, 2007, p61).*

Comment

While you may view these values as more relevant to therapy than to social work, they nevertheless have considerable merit. If we take Egan's (2007, p61) *bias for action*, the quote included could be a sound bite for the new agenda for change within health and social care.

One of the significant differences between Egan's (2007) model and social work is that in applying the biopsychosocial model (Golightley, 2011), i.e. working in a holistic way, we have a particular concern with the person in their ecological system (Bronfenbrenner, 1979); for example, the framework for the assessment of children in need considers the child's developmental needs, the parenting capacity and family and environmental factors (Department of Health 2000). This means building relationships with members of their micro system (their immediate setting) who may have competing interests; for example, a disabled child's wish to take risks opposed to their parents' wish to protect them. It may mean developing their micro system, for example, enlisting support from the extended family or expanding their social capital, through circles of support (Neville *et al.*, 1995). Support may be facilitated from the meso level (the links between settings in which the person participates), by smoother coordination between schools, social services, health and home. Or the service user may need to hear alternative perspectives to combat discrimination permeating down from the macro level; for example, CBeebies' engaging rendition of *Winnie the Witch* (Thomas, 2006) uses the social model to demonstrate to children how people with disabilities should not be pathologised.

What do we mean by engagement?

You will have a relationship, good or bad, with everyone you work with, but some relationships will be much better than others; you will feel more connected. You will have rapport. Rapport is *the state of harmony, compatibility and empathy that permits mutual understanding and a working relationship between the client and the social worker* (Barker, 2003, p359). Engaging is about developing rapport. Engaging continues throughout a relationship, but is most essential in the early stages, as the old adage points out: *You never get a second chance to make a first impression.*

Some elements of rapport are thought to be unconscious. Transference, for example, is where a person's way of relating to someone in their past is replayed with another person. As Lefevre (2008, p84) notes: *it may feel at times as if there is a real dissonance between who you are intending to be and who the client experiences you as.* As practitioners we also bring our own counter-transference to relationships with carers and service user. This may be an emotional and psychological response to their behaviour or it may be derived from our own relationship history. Transference and counter-transference are not necessarily negative emotions but unwarranted positive responses can also become damaging when expectations cannot be fulfilled (Lefevre, 2008).

Our ability to establish rapport can also be inhibited by our mandate; for example, a child protection investigation may produce superficial co-operation or resistance. We then need to consider our own role in the emotional climate that evolves. If practitioners respond with *defensive, bureaucratic and impersonal practice, they are not going to create an open, constructive and collaborative environment* (Howe, 2010, p331). Howe (2010) contends that in such threatening environments reflexion increases and reflection decreases; that is, we feel more and think less. Preventing this downward spiral is important because not only does it encourage a working relationship that is focused on the child, but also a less stressed parent is less risk to, and more able to safeguard, their child.

Rapport may also suffer due to your making a mistake. In extreme situations failing to engage may result in the carer or service user requesting a change in practitioner. Each intervention adds to our learning and ways of managing difficult situations. Mistakes can happen, but the competent practitioner reflects and learns so that they do not recur (see Chapter 1).

ACTIVITY **6.2**

Ways of engaging

List the different means of communicating by which you engage with people; for example, face-to-face conversation.

Comment

Any means of communicating with other people benefits from the degree to which we engage with the recipient. This includes via communication aids, using an intermediary, by phone or in writing. This chapter will focus on one-to-one involvement, because the skills required are generally transferable to other situations. However, a few points are worth noting.

When you engage people by telephone, the non-verbal cues to your attitude and feelings (after Lishman, 1994) that can facilitate engagement are missing, making you more reliant on your speed of speech, tone of voice and use of language. Written communication, in an email, text or letter, denies tone and consequently requires even more careful consideration of language. A sentence that is softened by your intonation can appear harsh on the page. When you are writing letters or reports, think about the purpose of your communication and ensure you adopt the appropriate level of formality. Always remember that these documents still need to engage the reader to hold their attention (see Chapter 3).

When working with someone who uses a communication aid – for example, an alphabet board or a light writer – try to ensure that you have gained some familiarity with this form of communication prior to meeting the person; it may be necessary to have someone accompany you who is familiar with the system. Interacting via a communication system can easily become a barrier between you; alternatively, it could become a shared activity in which you are engaged towards a common purpose. It is easy for such experiences to be disempowering for the service user and for the carer. It can, for example, be tempting to finish what a person is trying to communicate, but this can deny their voice (see Chapter 5). The same applies to people whose speech is impaired.

If you have to communicate via an interpreter, this creates an immediate barrier to you engaging with the carer or service user. For example, when working with a deaf man with mental health problems, I found that my body language was ignored as he focused on the professional interpreter, who was completely neutral and failed entirely to engage him. Keeping your speech brief will increase the interaction between the three of you and reduce the possibility of mistranslation. Wherever possible, avoid asking family members or members of the community to interpret, as this can inhibit open communication, or alter the conversation towards their agenda, or worse. Working with an African child, we went to considerable lengths to find someone who spoke his dialect. However, during the interview I became concerned that the interpreter's body language towards the child seemed to be hostile. We had a break and I asked her if there was a problem. It transpired that, in her culture, if a child had been sexually abused they were deemed to have become a witch. She had thought she could manage her feelings but was petrified of him.

When you are working with children and families it can be easier to ascertain information from the parents than from the child, but this can lead to the child's views being sidelined (Lefevre, 2010). Activities, such as games, are excellent vehicles for engaging with young – and, indeed, not so young – people. Munro (2011) illustrated how Weld's (2008) Three Houses tool can enable children to present their experiences through writing and drawing. After all, if children do not feel valued and understood, how will they develop trust?

Preparation for developing one-to-one relationships

Successful engagement with anyone can be facilitated by planning and preparation. The more you know about a person the better placed you are to plan for the most likely eventualities and prepare for meeting them. Reading the file notes can provide invaluable background information, such as the person's social history and previous experiences of social work intervention. It is consequently essential that these records are clear, concise, coherent and above all accurate (see Chapter 3). When working on a hospital ward I would always check with the charge nurse before seeing a patient, even if I had been working with the patient for months. As well as being a courtesy and promoting multi-disciplinary working (see Chapter 8), this ensured that I had the most up-to-date information.

CASE STUDY

Credible assessments

Rita Brown was a 44-year-old woman with Huntington's disease (a rare, degenerative neurological condition) whose case records stated that she was aggressive and non-co-operative. She lived in a one-bedroom flat, the floor of which was covered in magazines to a depth of about eight inches. At our first meeting, she lurched up to me so that she stood very close and spoke in a slurred voice while waving her arms at me.

Comment

From the information I had received I decided it would be prudent to visit Rita accompanied by a colleague and on entering her flat I was careful to ensure that my path to the exit was clear. However, it is important to caution against over-reliance on what you are told and have read before you meet someone. Rita's slurred speech, her arm movements and her inability to judge appropriate proximity were all symptomatic of her Huntington's disease. Nevertheless, I did need to be aware that her arm movements were involuntary and that she might hit me accidentally. She obsessively bought cookery magazines and as she found herself becoming unsteady she had put them on the floor to provide cushioning in case she fell. Her reputation for 'unco-operativeness' was due to her not wanting a care worker to remove them, and to her tendency to go out if the care worker was late. I explained to the care agency that people with Huntington's disease can develop rigid thinking, which in Rita's case meant that if a person said they would visit her at 8 a.m. they had better be there then, not 20 minutes later.

This case study demonstrates how a lack of understanding of and respect for a person's situation, as well as failings in services, such as poor punctuality, can wrongly lead to service users being labelled negatively. This is not to say that information should be ignored or not sought, but that we should approach people with an open mind rather than an empty one (after Strauss and Corbin, 1994). The more perspectives that we can gather, the better our understanding is likely to become.

Introductions

The circumstances, place and manner of our introduction to a person are likely to affect the rapport that we develop. High-stress situations for the carer and the service user can intensify their response to you. This may be a positive or negative effect depending on whether you are identified as an ally or a threat.

The environment in which you meet can also have a major influence upon the quality of your subsequent relationship. Meeting in the person's home may inhibit an abused child's ability to talk freely, but enable an adult with learning difficulties to feel safe and empowered. Statutory involvement, such as mental health assessments, can be experienced as an invasion of the privacy and sanctuary that home symbolises. A person with mental health problems once told me that, while he needed interventions at times, he wished they could all occur away from his home.

Environments obviously need to be accessible to disabled people and to people for whom English is not their first language. I once worked for a social services department which provided leaflets explaining how to complain about the service in 12 different languages, but leaflets explaining how to access the service were available only in English.

ACTIVITY **6.3**

Welcome?

Think about the lobby and waiting room where you are working. How welcome would you feel if you were a carer or service user coming to the office for the first time?

Comment

If the reception staff and environment do not appear welcoming and safe, your ability to engage with those who visit has already been compromised. For example,

I once visited a social work office and was waiting in the scruffy waiting room with another person. On the table was one out-of-date gossip magazine that added to the general effect of neglect. A woman came in and, after a brief conversation with the receptionist through the security glass, started shouting and swearing. The receptionist retreated, leaving those of us in the reception area to fend for ourselves.

The manner in which we are greeted discloses a significant amount about the expected nature of the relationship, from the person whose first words to me were *F*** off!* to the offer of tea and cake. As Lishman observed: *They frequently arrive at a social work agency with a sense of stigma or shame and suspicious, hostile or fearful expectation* (Lishman, 1994, p6).

Remember that greeting rituals vary from culture to culture, so try to ensure that you are informed about the cultural and religious practices of the person you are meeting. Simple acts like shaking hands can create or remove boundaries. Similarly, the inappropriate use of someone's first or surname can be a considerable cause of offence, particularly if you get their name or the pronunciation wrong. Older people may be offended by the informality of first names, or younger people uncomfortable with the formality of surnames; as a general rule, ask rather than assume. It is, however, essential to confirm who they are, who you are, and why you are meeting them.

Use of self

When someone meets you they are not just meeting a professional, they are also meeting you, a person. Feeling that they are meeting a real person, not merely a professional persona, is crucial to carers and service users engaging with social workers (after Clarkson, 1990). Lefevre (2008) argues that detached objectivity is a fallacy; we cannot help but bring ourselves to the relationship. However, use of self needs to be carefully monitored to ensure that the purpose of the relationship is not shifted towards meeting our needs rather than theirs.

Who we are has a significant impact on how people will respond to us. It is important that we understand not just how we view ourselves but also how others view us. We must remain aware of how factors such as our profession, gender, sexuality, age, ethnicity, religion, class and accent can instantly endear or alienate us to another person. Sometimes it can be important to acknowledge such factors; however, sometimes we have to recognise the vagaries of interactions. For example, on my first visit to a 19-year-old man with learning difficulties, he ran to me and threw his arms around me. His mother had stood frozen to the spot and then relaxed and said, *Oh, that's good! He bit the last social worker.* I never did find out why he decided to hug rather than bite me.

We can have more control over other factors, such as our dress, but our cultural backgrounds may still determine the level of freedom that we experience in our dress codes. What you wear may have a strong link to your sense of identity;

however, it is important to weigh your individuality against the role you are performing and the context. If you are representing a person in court, it is important that you engage with the court as a credible professional. If you present yourself in a casual manner your evidence may be undermined (see Chapter 2). However, in less formal settings, wearing a suit may create a barrier between you and the service user and limit your ability to play with children. A sensible choice of clothing can also significantly reduce your risk of injury in difficult situations; for example, ties and dangling jewellery can easily be grabbed accidentally or on purpose.

In considering ourselves we need to explore how we feel about the emotive events in life which are often the precursor to our involvement in people's lives. For example, cancer, dementia, AIDS and death remain for some people taboo subjects. Those we work with may be trying to make sense of their situation, while facing ignorance or stigma and discrimination from those around them. We need to explore and become aware of our own feelings and thoughts prior to being confronted by them when we meet those we are supposed to help. We must also be careful to go at their pace, not our own, when exploring such issues and at times recognise that such discussions may be 'off limits'. At other times we need to have the resolve to investigate those taboos that the service user, carer, wider society and our own sensibilities would rather shy away from, such as female sexual abuse of children.

Your knowledge base plays a significant role in your understanding of situations and in the confidence that people then develop in you. Carers and service users often feel isolated, but knowing that you have an understanding of some of the challenges that they face when, for example, a family member has an acquired brain injury, can help to reduce the sense of being alone, facing the unknown. However, it is essential that we acknowledge when we do not know, but make it clear that we will find out, rather than making assumptions.

Body language, or non-verbal communication (NVC), is important as it may convey our thoughts, feelings or mood to others. While this may not always be conscious, with practice and self-awareness you can identify and avoid habitual patterns, such as drumming fingers, which can imply boredom (see Chapter 2). Ideally your body language will be open and receptive, relaxed but attentive, not casual. Awareness of NVC can sometimes help you to identify the mood of a carer or service user far more effectively than their verbal communication. If you are working with someone who has difficulty or is unable to communicate verbally, reading their NVC is essential. Sensitivity to NVC can also help you to realise when you are mirroring the body language of others. Used expertly and judiciously, mirroring can become a deliberate act to create a sense of connection between you; it can also be used to modify behaviour. For example, if you are both tense and you start to relax, the other person may mirror that behaviour. However, it is also important to note that body language is culture-specific and consequently highly susceptible to misinterpretation. The person may, for example, view your body language as showing you are not interested or not taking them seriously, or interpret your mirrored tension as an aggressive response.

It is important to remain sensitive to the other person's body language but also to the instinctive responses of your own body and autonomic nervous system. If a carer or service user is aggressive towards you, your body will react. Your fight-or-flight impulse will be triggered and your body will release adrenaline, your pulse will increase and your breathing is likely to become shallower. It is therefore very important to consciously relax and breathe more deeply; this will help reduce your anxiety and fear. At the same time this projects the message that you are not scared and you are not being aggressive, both of which can trigger violence (see Chapter 7). Such NVC is picked up and responded to far more readily than your verbal communication in conflict situations.

Hearing their story

The purpose of our intervention will influence the relationship that we are likely to develop. However, in engaging with people we need to have an openness which goes beyond that purpose, as the intervention may change as our assessment goes beyond the presenting problem. While understanding needs (Chapter 12) and risks (Chapter13) is essential, it is also paramount that we do not become blinkered by these concerns, potentially pathologising the individual and promoting paternalism in the practitioner. There is an irony in the fact that parents tend to focus on their child's bad behaviours and practitioners tend to focus on the parents' bad behaviours, rather than exploring the psychology behind those behaviours (Howe, 2010). We need to ensure that we recognise and promote their strengths (Saleebey, 2012) and the outcomes they wish to achieve (Miller, 2012) so that, where possible, it is a relationship based on partnership. The quality of our relationship will dictate how much information a person will disclose. Open, active listening to their concerns will ensure that you gain the most from the information that is shared. Yet Forrester *et al.* (2008) found in a study of 40 social workers that there was a tendency for them to adopt confrontational and aggressive styles towards provided case studies. Forrester *et al.* (2008) considered that the lack of empathy and listening observed was indicative of systemic rather than individual failings.

RESEARCH SUMMARY

Are you listening?

McKay et al. (1995, p16) identified 12 inhibitors to active listening.

- ***Comparing*** *Comparing yourself to the other person, which distracts from actually listening to what they are saying.*
- ***Mind reading*** *Second guessing what the person means.*
- ***Rehearsing*** *Attending to what you will say next rather than what they are saying.*

- **Filtering** *Focusing on those points that concern you. This can particularly occur if you are too task- or agenda-orientated, leaving you blinkered to hints of other potentially more important issues to tackle, or even closing down such discussion.*
- **Judging** *Where a person's views are disregarded due to our view of the person, for example, as being unqualified to comment.*
- **Dreaming** *Where we are attending to our daydreams rather than what the person is saying.*
- **Identifying** *Where we relate a person's experience to our own and interject our experience rather than listening to theirs.*
- **Advising** *Rather than listening to their whole account it is very easy to cut to offering solutions.*
- **Sparring** *Being quick to disagree rather than listening; or this can take the form of discounting, i.e. refusing to hear what someone has to say.*
- **Being right** *Unable to hear criticism or contrary views.*
- **Derailing** *Changing the topic and in doing so dismissing the other person's view.*
- **Placating** *Being so concerned with comforting or mollifying the person that we fail to listen to them.*

Comment

Miller (2012) would probably add to that list a preoccupation with the targets and bureaucratic demands of the organisation. I would also suggest that heavy caseloads can mean that at the end of a session a practitioner can become pre-occupied with the next person they are seeing. This is particularly problematic as it is often at the end of a session that a person will say what is concerning them most.

The tendency to offer solutions before all the issues have been explored is a problem which I have noticed seems to occur particularly within groups. I would also argue that daydreaming tends to occur after we have already become distracted. Your own comfort can be a considerable source of distraction. This may seem too trivial to consider but if you are tired, hungry or need the toilet, all of these factors will distract you from attending to what is being said. Seating and whether you are too hot or too cold can all play their part in blocking your attention. It should be noted that all of these points apply equally to people who are listening to us.

Active listening is not simply hearing, which is passive; it requires that we are focused on the here and now and on what is being said to us. It is not just a vital part of engaging with people but an essential aspect of anti-oppressive practice; to empower the other person to be heard and to be valued. This is a tiring activity but practice enables us to concentrate for longer.

When meeting carers or service users for the first time it is important to give them time to tell their story. When I was working on a hospital ward with people who had suffered traumatic, life-changing and life-threatening events, I was struck by how few of these people had been given an opportunity to really talk about what had happened to them. Professionals can become preoccupied with their expert intervention, rather than the individual's experience. Hearing their story can be validating to them and in turn build their trust in you as a professional. It is at this point that we are starting to build empathy with the person, developing an insight into their world. It is important to draw a distinction between sympathy, which is feeling *for* another person, and empathy, which is feeling *with* another person (Shulman, 1999). It can be a distressing and upsetting experience when, for example, a person talks of how they are losing their loved one to Alzheimer's disease. However, it is important to maintain perspective and purpose. Their loss is not your loss; you are merely a witness to their distress. Social workers are like participant-observers in anthropological fieldwork. If you hold yourself too distant from the person's experiences then you are likely to be perceived as uninterested, cold or uncaring, but if you become too immersed, then you may lose your professional and emotional boundaries, risking emotional burn-out.

ACTIVITY **6.4**

Displaying emotions

Are there any circumstances in which it would be okay to cry in front of a carer or service user?

Does it make a difference if the social worker is male or female?

Comment

Some social workers are unequivocal in their view that there are no circumstances in which this would be appropriate. From this perspective crying can be seen as a breach of boundaries, a loss of control and consequently of the ability to perform their role. However, others would argue that this view privileges instrumental care (caring for) over emotional care (caring about). Fox (1999) advocated that professionals should tend towards emotional care, in order to counter power differentials and avoid becoming too detached from their work. A critical element here seems to be the implied loss of control associated with crying. Crying by men, while growing in social acceptability, still holds a particularly strong risk of alienating people. As a general rule I would argue that it is better to contain your emotions, so that you are fully available to help the service user and do not risk closing them down, as they attempt to protect you. For example, a child who discloses to you that they have been abused may not only stop if they see your distress but also become less likely to disclose to another person. You may, however, need to debrief after hearing a particularly harrowing account or one that touches on your own experiences (see Chapter 1). In some cases you might require counselling support.

At times you may need to encourage a person to continue their account. Such prompts can be seen to exist on a continuum from the unobtrusive nod or tilting of your head to one side, to a simple *yes?* or *go on*, to repeating what they have said, to the much more directive *can you tell me about...?* Silence can be particularly powerful; it can make us feel uncomfortable and inclined to fill the space, but it can also encourage a person to expand further (see Chapter 7). In part this will depend on the culture that we come from, as the silence can hold negative or positive connotations.

Clarification, negotiation and planning

Having gathered information, it is important to clarify that you have understood correctly. This also provides validation of the other person's perspective. Using phrases they have used can help to build connections between you, but it is important that you check that you have a shared understanding of those terms.

The information they have provided is likely to have illuminated what they see as the issues and what their expectations are of you. It is important to clarify these points and to identify how they would like their situation to be after the intervention. Negotiation may be required to help the person to recognise the implications of issues they may have ignored or been unaware of and to gain agreement to act on these points. Negotiation can be particularly difficult where several people are involved who may have conflicting agendas (see Chapter 10). It is important that you are clear about your role. At times this will require considerable effort to remain neutral and at other times it will necessitate explicit clarification that you are advocating for a particular person's perspective (Mantell, 2013).

A key issue to address at this point is expectations. Any relationship you have established will be destroyed if you promise a Rolls-Royce and deliver a Mini. However, it is important not to destroy hope. A 24-year-old man who had suffered an acquired brain injury told me that it was the positive approaches of his social worker and physiotherapist that had motivated him to keep going. Nevertheless, we need to be clear and realistic and try to ensure that we are both working towards achievable goals.

Maintaining relationships

While engagement primarily occurs in the early stages of a relationship, it can take considerable work to sustain an individual's engagement over time. This can be the case particularly where the crisis that precipitated the intervention has passed and the drive for change has reduced. Here is where the quality of your relationship and of your empathy with the person can provide motivation and encouragement to remain engaged. Empowering approaches, as well as being desirable, have a real practical advantage as they are based around goals that the carer or service user wants to achieve (see Chapter 5).

It is at this stage of the relationship that the carer or service user can start to assess your performance – have you proved to be reliable? Maluccio's observation from 1979 (Lishman, 1994, p9) that initially warmth and sympathy are necessary, but later competence and knowledge are required, is still relevant today. If you have not delivered on what you have agreed (never promise), then their trust in and engagement with you will understandably deteriorate, regardless of whether or not you have a legitimate excuse.

It is also important to monitor the relationship to ensure that dissonance does not develop between you and the carer and/or service user. Even when we think we are working towards agreed goals it is easy for differences to emerge and the level of engagement to dissipate. For example, I once worked with a 22-year-old man who had cerebral palsy, and wished to enter a care home for younger people. We visited several homes and yet each time there was something different wrong with the home: one was too big, one was too small, one too isolated, another 'too busy'. He also seemed reluctant and slightly resentful at visiting. Speaking with him, it became clear that visiting the first home had made him realise what living in a care home would be like and he had changed his mind and now wished to live in his own accommodation. He had been waiting for the right time to tell me, as he knew I had gone to considerable effort. Reflection in action, i.e. your thinking at the time, as opposed to reflection on action, i.e. your thinking afterwards (Johnsson and Svensson, 2004, after Schön, 1983), can enable you to salvage a situation which would otherwise deteriorate (see Chapter 1). I had been too focused on the plan to fully appreciate the signals he was giving me.

Disengaging

Endings are often neglected, yet without them the benefits of a relationship both in itself and as a means to achieving a desired outcome can be eroded. At best the service user and the social worker can be left with a sense of unfinished business; at worst the service user may feel betrayed and abandoned. Their self-esteem, confidence and motivation may plummet and successful work on achieving empowerment and bias for action eroded. One of the main causes of this neglect may be the fact of social workers being task- rather than process-orientated. This may hide a social worker's own emotional difficulties in managing goodbyes.

Goodbyes provide an opportunity to evaluate your intervention and review what the carer or service user has achieved. Closure in this way can facilitate the service user in feeling confident to face the future without social work support, but can also confirm a positive experience of social work, if they do require further help. Closure actually begins at the start of our engagement: when we are agreeing what will be the nature of the relationship, we should be starting to cultivate an expectation of our involvement becoming unnecessary (see Chapter 10).

CHAPTER SUMMARY

This chapter has aimed to explore the skills necessary to engage with young people and adults. It has argued that engaging is the difference between developing an adequate relationship and a good relationship. The quality of your relationship enhances your ability to develop a more thorough assessment and increases the likelihood of achieving successful outcomes, even when managing difficult issues.

The Government's review of care and support services (DoH 2008) has at its heart the nature of the relationship between the state, the citizen, the family and the community.

The inevitable and welcome introduction of individualised budgets across England provides challenges for old systems of delivering services, but may release many workers from procedural practices more concerned with gatekeeping than supporting people. In the past, the relationships we created were considered a central aspect of social work and essential to good practice (Trevithick, 2005, p7). In the transformation from case managers to care navigators, advisors, guides and brokers it remains critical that we engage with carers and service users, if social workers' services are to be not just necessary but welcome.

FURTHER READING

Egan, G (2007) *The skilled helper.* 8th edition. Belmont, CA: Thomson.

A neglected gem, which should be essential reading.

Miller, E (2012) *Individual outcomes: Getting back to what matters.* Edinburgh: Dunedin.

An accessible presentation of the Talking Points: Personal Outcome Approach. Although focused on community care, it is equally applicable to work with young people.

Trevithick, P (2005) *Social work skills: A practice handbook.* 2nd edition. Maidenhead: Open University Press.

A comprehensive and critical exploration of the skills required within social work.

REFERENCES

Barker, R (2003) *The social work dictionary.* 5th edition. Washington, DC: NASW Press.

Boisvert, C and Faust, D (2003) Leading researchers' consensus on psychotherapy research findings: Implications for the teaching and conduct of psychotherapy. *Professional Psychology: Research and Practice*, 34, 508–13.

Braye, S and Preston-Shoot, M (1995) *Empowering practice in social work.* Buckingham: Open University Press.

Bronfenbrenner, U (1979) The ecology of human development. Harvard, Mass.: Harvard University Press.

Clarkson, P (1990) A multiplicity of psychotherapeutic relationships. *British Journal of Psychotherapy*, 7 (2), 148–63.

Cook, A and Miller, E (2012) *Talking points: Personal outcome approach, Practical Guide.* Available from: http://www.jitscotland.org.uk/action-areas/talking-points-user-and-carer-involvement/ (accessed 1 August 2012).

Cree, V and Myers, S (2008) *Social work: Making a difference.* Bristol: Policy Press.

Department of Health (2000) *Assessing children in need and their families: Practice guidance.* London: The Stationery Office.

Department of Health (2006) *Our health, our care, our say: A new direction for community services.* London: Department of Health.

Department of Health (2007) *Putting people first: A shared vision and commitment to the transformation of adult social care.* London: Department of Health.

Department of Health (2008) *The case for change: Why England needs a new care and support system.* London: Department of Health.

Department of Health (2010) *Prioritising need in the context of putting people first: A whole system approach to eligibility for social care – guidance for eligibility criteria for social care.* Available from: http://www.dh.gov.uk/en/Publicationsandstatistics/Publications/PublicationsPolicyAndGuidance/DH_113154 (accessed 2 September 2011).

Department of Health (2012) *Caring for our future: Reforming care and support.* London: The Stationery Office.

Duffy, S (2011) Personalisation in social care – what does it really mean? *Social Care and Neurodisability,* 2 (4), 186–94.

Egan, G (2007) *The skilled helper.* 8th edition. Belmont, CA: Thomson.

Forrester, D, McCambridge, J, Waissbein, C and Rollnick, S (2008) How do child and family social workers talk to parents about child welfare concerns? *Child Abuse Review,* 17, 23–35.

Fox, N (1999) *Beyond health: Postmodernism and embodiment.* London: Free Association.

Goleman, D (1996) *Emotional intelligence: Why it can matter more than IQ.* London: Bloomsbury.

Golightley, M (2011) *Social work and mental health.* Exeter: Learning Matters.

Greenson, R (1967) *The technique and practice of psychoanalysis.* New York: International University Press.

Howe, D (1994) Modernity, postmodernity and social work. *British Journal of Social Work,* 24 (5), 513–32.

Howe, D (2010) The safety of children and the parent–worker relationship in cases of child abuse and neglect. *Child Abuse Review,* 19, 330–41.

Hudson, B and Sheldon, B (2000) The cognitive behavioural approach. In M. Davies (ed.) *The encyclopaedia of social work.* Oxford: Oxford University Press.

Johnsson, E and Svensson, K (2004) Theory in social work – Some reflections on understanding and explaining interventions. *European Journal of Social Work,* 8 (4), 419–33.

Lefevre, M (2008) Assessment and decision-making in child protection: Relationship-based considerations. In Calder, M (ed.) *The carrot or the stick: Towards effective practice with involuntary clients.* Lyme Regis: Russell House.

Lefevre, M (2010) *Communicating with children and young people.* Bristol: Policy Press.

Leveridge, M (2002) Mac-social work: The routinisation of professional activity. *Maatskaplike Werk/Social Work,* 38 (4), 354–62.

Lishman, J (1994) *Communications in social work.* Basingstoke: Macmillan.

McKay, M, Davis, M and Fanning, P (1995) *Messages: The communication skills book.* 2nd edition. Oakland, CA: New Harbinger.

Maiter, S, Palmer, S and Manji, S (2006) Strengthening social worker–client relationships in child protection services: Addressing power imbalances and 'ruptured' relationships. *Qualitative Social Work,* 5, 167–86.

Mantell, A (2013) Chapter 5: The importance of the perspective of carers and people who use services. In T. Scragg (ed.) *Reflective Practice in Social Work.* Exeter: Learning Matters.

Miller, E (2010) Can the shift from needs-led to outcomes-focused assessment in health and social care deliver on policy priorities? *Research, Policy and Planning,* 28 (2), 115–27.

Miller, E. (2012) *Individual outcomes: Getting back to what matters.* Edinburgh: Dunedin.

Munro, E. (2011) *The Munro review of child protection: Final report, a child-centred system.* London: Department of Education. Available from: https://www.education.gov.uk/publications/eOrderingDownload/Munro-Review.pdf (accessed 24 August 2012).

Neville, M, Bayliss, L, Bolidson, SJ, Cox, A, Cox, L, Gilland, D, Laird, M, McIver, B and Williams C (1995) *Circles of Support.* Rugby: Circles Network, UK.

Rogers, K (1951) *Client-centred therapy.* Boston, MA: Houghton Mifflin.

Rogers, RW (1975) A protection motivation theory of fear appeals and attitude change. *Journal of Psychology,* 91, 93–114.

Saleebey, D (2012) *The strengths perspective in social work practice.* (6th edition). Harlow: Pearson.

Schön, D (1983) *The reflective practitioner: How professionals think in action.* London: Temple-Smith.

Shulman, L (1999) *The skills of helping: Individuals, families, groups and communities.* 4th edition. Itasca, IL: Peacock.

Smale, G, Tuson, G, Biehal, N and Marsh, P (1993) *Empowerment, assessment, care management and the skilled worker.* National Institute for Social Work Practice and Development Exchange, London: HMSO.

Stevenson, O (2008) A climate of fear, blame and mistrust. *The Guardian,* 20 November. Available from: http://www.guardian.co.uk/society/2008/nov/20/baby-p-child-protection (accessed 24 August 2012).

Thomas, V (2006) *Winnie the witch.* Oxford: OUP. CBeebies version available from: http://www.youtube.com/watch?v=0_f95a4MX7M (accessed 7 August 2012).

Thornton, A (2011) Blurred vision: Direct payments, funding cuts and the law. *Social Care and Neurodisability,* 2 (4), 218–25.

Weld, N (2008) The three houses tool: Building safety and positive change. In Calder, M (ed.) *Contemporary risk assessment in safeguarding children.* Lyme Regis: Russell House Publishing.

Chapter 7

Communication skills

Marie Price and Debbie Smallbones

Introduction

Communication is the medium for our everyday interactions and, consequently, is often unconscious and overlooked. Gesture, word, music, smell, touch and environment, for example, all communicate with us and us with them. As explained in Chapters 6 and 8, good communication skills are essential for establishing the quality of relationships that promote successful social work outcomes. These relationships are not only with carers and people who use services, but also colleagues and other professionals.

This chapter will explore communication in situations which can be demanding for us; for example, due to situations being distressing or intimidating, or to circumstances that challenge our own world view. It will also raise an awareness of the need to be sensitive to how we may unconsciously communicate our views and authority, potentially alienating or disempowering those we seek to enable. This in turn provides a link with the previous chapter, which looks at how workers can develop relationships which empower.

During the chapter we will explore identified communication skills, including areas such as keeping emotionally safe, self-awareness, barriers to open communication, hidden messages, spirituality, emotional engagement and keeping physically safe.

Communication skills

Many texts aimed at the caring professions, along with your social work training, provide insights into how to communicate well. Margaret Hough (2006, p57) summarised the generic communication skills for effective relationships required in counselling, which can be adapted to social work as follows.

- **Listening** Active attention to what is being said, rather than passive hearing.

- **Observation of non-verbal behaviour** Monitoring and analysing your own and other people's body language. It is through our heightened sensitivity and analysis of gestures, posture and facial expression that we become consciously aware of these often subtle messages.

- **Reflecting back** Repeating what the carer or person who uses services has said to you or seems to be feeling. This enables them to know that you have heard what they have said and provides them with the opportunity to question it.

- **Paraphrasing** Rewording what the person has said, confirming that you have a shared understanding of their situation.

- **Summarising** Précising what the person has said confirms that we have understood their concerns and can serve to clarify what can be complex and confusing information.

- **Asking appropriate questions** These questions need to be pertinent and sensitive to the situation. Sometimes this can be about choosing the right time to ask a question and at others it can be selecting the right wording.

- **Managing silence** We need to allow silences so that the person we're working with can gather their thoughts, reflect on what they've said and heard, and prepare a response. This skill isn't always easy to manage (see Activity 7.1).

- **Challenging** Used to help a service user to think about their behaviour and attitudes. Confronting these issues in a way that is helpful to the person involved.

- **Immediacy** Being present and not distracted in the moment of the session and using the information and the feelings that are available to us.

- **Self-disclosure** Sharing your own experiences can illuminate a situation or create a sense that you will understand the other person's experience due to your similar experience. However, this needs to be used with caution as it can be misleading; you have not shared the same experience, however closely aligned it might be. This can produce assumptions that the other person will feel what you felt and can manage the situation in the same ways that you have. Most of us like to speak about ourselves and our experiences and self-disclosure can easily become about us rather than the other person. Consequently this is a method to be used with extreme caution if used at all.

ACTIVITY **7.1**

List all the feelings you have when a conversation dries up and no one is speaking.

Do you feel differently if the other people are close friends, people you are working with or complete strangers?

Comment

You might have listed words like 'punishing' or 'awkward'. These feelings are often related to how silences felt for us as children, for instance when someone was punishing us by not speaking to us or at school when we needed to come up with an answer and weren't able to. Carers or people who use services may share or have very different responses to silence so we need to be alert and aware of what is happening to and for them as well as ourselves. Balancing our divergent needs can be difficult; our discomfort might make us less likely to want to stay silent, or if we are very comfortable with silence we might let it go on too long.

It is important to note that some people we work with will require us to take other factors into account to facilitate good communication; for example, if you are working with someone who has cognitive difficulties, such as an acquired brain injury. If this is the case you will need to ensure that the environment is quiet and without distractions and that you communicate in short, simple sentences, avoiding abstract meanings. A particular difficulty here is that while we tend to use open questions to facilitate gaining an understanding of the perspective of the person who uses services, this often does not work if they have cognitive difficulties. Instead our questions can seem vague and confusing. In these situations it can be more empowering to give the person a few clear options from which to choose.

RESEARCH SUMMARY

Research undertaken by Beresford et al. *(2007) highlighted the qualities in social workers that are appreciated by service users. Although the research for the book focused on palliative care, it recognises that these features are equally*

---

applicable to all areas of social work. The following areas are considered to be of paramount importance to service users.

- *Being able to determine their own agenda and work in partnership.*
- *Being listened to with a non-judgmental and respectful attitude.*
- *The social worker giving them time and being accessible and available.*
- *The social worker being reliable and delivering promised action.*
- *The social worker being available for both the service user and those close to them.*
- *The social worker having a good level of expertise and a willingness to learn.*
- *The social worker being available to talk about any issue of importance to the service user. This made people feel that their anxieties could be contained.*
- *The social worker offering a wide range of social work approaches that suited individual preferences.*

Keeping emotionally safe

As expressed earlier, interaction and communication is at the heart of all social work. However, these interactions can have unexpected and sometimes unwanted emotional consequences for us. We need to understand for ourselves in what circumstances this might happen and how we can recognise those feelings for what they are. Interlinked with this is the ability to know ourselves well, including our value base and belief system, in order to provide the best outcomes for carers and people who use services. As social workers with adults we need to provide a safe environment which enables carers and people who use services to fully express themselves while acknowledging that this may evoke difficult feelings in us. In these situations there is a need to maintain a balance between being open to listening and communicating while keeping ourselves emotionally safe in an appropriate manner.

ACTIVITY **7.2**

Think about situations that upset you.

In what ways do you protect yourself?

Comment

You may be aware of what triggers an emotional response in you. During your social work training you will have been/ be exposed to a range of situations which provoke this reaction. This isn't a sign of weakness but an acknowledgement that you are also human, with all the frailties that that involves. Consequently, it is important to become aware of what gets under your defences and makes you feel vulnerable.

While we may be aware of many of these triggers, others may catch us by surprise. This may be because we didn't know they were there or because someone else's story reawakens a situation that we thought we had dealt with. In such situations it is common to exhibit the fight-or-flight response. This can lead to our withdrawing physically and/ or emotionally from a situation or potentially becoming aggressive or intimidating. In these situations we need to be careful not to block someone else's communication while also ensuring that we don't become so upset that we are unable to function, or place undue responsibility on the service user. Our responses, of course, are not always triggered solely by our interactions with service users but can be evoked by colleagues and other professionals.

Self-awareness

Self-awareness – recognising what we feel, when we feel it and how we deal with it – is essential for effective communication. Patrick Casement (2002) advocates developing an *internal supervisor*. This enables the worker to develop an inner ear that attunes itself to pick up information, both from the person being worked with and from ourselves, and monitors how we are and what our responses are, enabling us to adjust appropriately to situations. Our internal supervisor shouldn't replace real supervision but should be developed as a way of monitoring our internal world and responses. This gives us the opportunity to enhance the way we are able to process and use the information available in order to make better relationships and decisions.

Should I or ought I?

We ignore how we feel emotionally and physically at our peril; the results can be detrimental to our practice, self-esteem and mental health.

Several years ago I suffered a bereavement of a close family member. It was a situation where, before the death, I needed to spend some time sorting various practical problems, sometimes at short notice. This occasionally resulted in my having to cancel meetings and commitments. After the death of this relative I didn't feel I could cancel any more appointments so proceeded to fulfil my obligations despite feeling that I wasn't fully present emotionally or able to communicate as effectively as I might otherwise have done. On one occasion the person I was working with could sense that something was wrong and neither she nor I were able to work in the way that we would normally work. This resulted in us both wasting time and energy and it was necessary on a subsequent occasion for us to work through the issues we needed to that day and also go back and address the difficulties from the previous time we had met. Whereas, if I had rearranged the time and come to the meeting emotionally available it would have avoided some of these problems. Similarly, despite feeling a migraine developing, a colleague decided that she couldn't cancel a teaching commitment or ask a colleague to take the session as she felt she *ought to get on with it*. The migraine affected her performance, causing her to take time from a subsequent session to unpick this interaction and explain again some of the concepts covered inadequately in the previous session.

Our growing self-awareness can enable us to manage anxieties about how we feel we ought to perform and to recognise what we should do when our ability to communicate at the high level necessary within social work has been impaired. It is important to realise that the pressure to act can come from our own expectations, those of others or our presumptions about the expectations of others. It is consequently essential to have an honest and open dialogue with yourself and other people involved in the interactions.

It is also important to understand that when carers and people who use services communicate with us they feel this same tension between what they need to say and do and what they feel they ought to say and do. Family members can feel obliged to provide care, guilty if they resent the demands of caring, and judged if they can no longer manage (Mantell, 2006). People who use services can feel that they have to be grateful for familial care and to act in a passive way. A social worker can be presented with a situation which superficially seems fine, but which is masking increasing conflict. It is in such situations that identifying dissonance between what is said and non-verbal communication often provides the key.

CASE STUDY

Mark, a newly qualified social worker, had been allocated to Sam, who was unable to speak due to an oral cancer that had required major surgery. Sam had not been involved with any services previously and lived in a caravan with limited facilities to cook or store food. Swallowing had become very difficult for Sam, requiring him to liquidise food. He also had to ensure that the nutritional content of his food was high as he was able to eat very little. No one had told Mark that Sam's ability to communicate had been significantly impaired. He was also unprepared for the emotional impact of seeing Sam's facial disfigurement and he found it hard not to stare.

Mark confirmed that Sam was prepared to write his answers after listening to Mark's questions. This was a slow, frustrating process for Mark, who was conscious that he had to visit another person that afternoon. He tried to speed up the process, asking each question as soon as Sam had answered the previous one, but soon realised that Sam was becoming fatigued and his answers were getting briefer.

Utilising his internal supervisor, Mark was able to reflect on the task and ask if Sam would like a break. He used this space to call his next client and say he would be late. He also managed to get hold of his feelings of disgust, pity and curiosity, recognising them for what they were, and to compartmentalise them, while making a mental note to discuss the way he felt with his supervisor.

Comment

As you can see from this example, myriad thoughts and feelings can go through our minds at any one point. It is not that we don't all have them; it's the way in which we respond to them that is important. If we are not self-aware we might let those feelings register on our faces, making it more difficult for the person we are working with to feel accepted, to trust us and be prepared to work with us.

Barriers to open communication

Why then might we be wary of entering or engaging with these situations? We have looked at some of the issues already but others may be around denial, a refusal to recognise the circumstances that we find ourselves in, and possibly a fear that we may get it wrong or get in too deep. The worker may also be working within too rigid a framework or theoretical base with little room for manoeuvre. There could be barriers between the worker and the service user. The barriers could be due to factors such as our gender, age, or a cultural issue, or something personal such as a fear that we will be weighed down by the problem or that we will feel inadequate in dealing with it. In these circumstances it is better to check out your concerns with the service user. Don't be too afraid of getting it wrong – take a risk, but do it sensitively. By taking risks we are able to offer the person we are working with an opportunity to voice their problem. I know that I have always appreciated the people who have been prepared to go that one step further to find a solution or to listen, even when they have been worried or overwhelmed by the information I might be sharing with them.

Hidden messages

One of the other very necessary messages to convey concerns the art of being non-judgmental. This could be seen as an anomaly, as social work is often about making judgments. However, the issue is to filter out personal views from more objective facts. Personally I feel that we are all judgmental to one degree or another. We all have areas that we are quick to form opinions about; these may have been influenced by our upbringing or the media or situations we have been involved with. We need to constantly monitor how our personal judgments might influence our thinking and our relationships with carers, people who use services and other professionals. For example, your own experiences of doctors, as well as their portrayal in the media, may have left you in awe of them; or you may have had negative experiences of doctors and be highly suspicious of the medical model. Both perspectives could lead to incorrect assumptions.

Judgments come in all sorts of guises – we may, for example, make them about someone's appearance, the way they speak or their accent. These sorts of judgments are usually made without us thinking about them, part of how we respond on a day-to-day basis. There are other sorts of judgments when we consider someone's skin colour, their religion, their gender or their age. It is worth stopping for a moment here to think about what other sorts of things about a person we can make judgments about; often these are linked to stereotypes and bear little resemblance to reality. We need to consider all aspects of the individual and how we respond to them as being different to us.

ACTIVITY **7.3**

Write down messages you were given from childhood about age, skin colour, sexual orientation, gender, culture, race, physical disability, mental health, learning disability, religion.

Which ones do you still believe and why? Which have you rejected and why?

Comment

Some of these ideas were probably handed down to you from parents, caregivers, teachers and peers. You may well find that, as you have matured and developed, and had your thinking challenged on a social work course, you have changed your ideas. Even if they haven't changed, you will have explored those ideas and will know why you believe what you do.

Spirituality

One area which can form a particular barrier to communication and trigger our personal judgments is spirituality. It is important to make the distinction between religion and spirituality. Religion can be described as *the corporate, organized and outward expression of belief systems and an attempt to describe and express faith, ordinarily in community* (Lunn, 1993 quoted in Sheldon, 1997, p23). Spirituality is the essence of what it means to be human; our ultimate existential concerns, questions about meaning and values and our deepest relationships, whether with others, with God or gods, or with ourselves.

So how do we address spirituality with the service users we are working with? First we have to have an understanding of ourselves as spiritual beings.

ACTIVITY **7.4**

How do you understand this question in relation to yourself? Do you have a religious belief? Do you have a feeling that there is something bigger than you? How do you answer questions about why we are here or what it's all about? How would you describe the very essence of yourself to someone else? What is important to you?

Comment

Some people describe their spiritual selves as their soul or consciousness, something that is distinct from their body and survives after their body. It is a natural part of being and can be described as humankind's ultimate nature or purpose. Existentialism is part of these ideas and is a philosophy which suggests that individuals create their own meaning as opposed to it being created for them.

CASE STUDY

Mary had been diagnosed with a rapidly progressing form of a neurological disorder and only had a couple of months to live. She had two small children both under the age of three. In my discussions with her the things that were uppermost in her mind were the practicalities of her situation: how to cope with mobility problems, feeding herself, keeping clean and all the everyday tasks that she was becoming less able to do. However, underpinning all of this was the pressing issue of what would happen to her children when she died. She had no partner but did have a very supportive family who had arranged to look after the children when the time came. As time went on and Mary was no longer able to care for herself, the conversations took a different turn and she became aware that the children would have no conscious memory of her voice or indeed what she stood for. We talked about the possibilities and decided that she would record some messages for the children to enable them to have a sense of who she was, her outlook on life, and what they, her children, meant to her. Mary was no longer able to hold anything, she had a very weak voice and spent most of her days in bed. On a prearranged day and time I made arrangements for a recording device to be placed on her pillow and agreed to check her every few minutes to ensure that the device was still in place and she was still happy to speak into it. She tired very easily so the monitoring was essential to enable her to achieve her goals.

Following the session Mary was able to feel that she had given her children part of herself that she wouldn't otherwise have been able to had she not had this opportunity. The essence of her had been passed on to her children via a recording that will be a lasting reflection of who she was.

Comment

This was a situation where I had to put my own emotions to one side. At the time my own children weren't very much older than Mary's and the thought of someone having to do such a thing for me was very difficult. It took a considerable amount of thinking through and planning in order for me to be sure that I was doing what was in Mary's best interests. I also had to be sure that it was something that I could manage and be supported to undertake through good supervision.

This was also an example of where we sometimes need to take risks with our service users and go that extra mile in order for them to meet their own goals. It would have been easy to say that this was too difficult for me emotionally or to have not heard what she had said or misinterpreted what she wanted to do. This was an exceptional set of circumstances that required careful handling; however, there are many situations where we need to create an environment where people can tell us what they would like and how they would like to live their lives. This may include things they may want to say and express that may be difficult for us to hear. Again this is where self-awareness is important, enabling us to better understand what we can tolerate and what we find difficult. This isn't a weakness; it is a real strength and promotes our own personal development.

It is important to note that if we offer something to a service user and they reject the idea it doesn't always mean that we got it wrong; it sometimes means that they are not ready to hear it yet. We can store it up and present it later, maybe in a different form. However, sometimes we have got it wrong as we are not experts in their lives, only witnesses to their situation as it is now. We need to be kind to ourselves also and tell ourselves that at least we were prepared to try.

Working with the children of service users

You may consider yourself to be working with either children and young people or adults, but in reality you are usually working with families at various points in their life course. So you will be communicating with people of all ages. According to Lefevre (2010, p1), *the importance of effective mutual communication between social workers and children and young people can no longer be ignored. It is now clear that, if they are to make a real difference to their lives, practitioners must be able to relate to children and young people, listen to them, support them, and fully involve them in matters that concern them.*

In communicating with children and young people, the worker should have a clear understanding of both the child's needs and the aim or objective of the intervention. Progress ideally will happen at the child's pace, taking into account their age, and stage of development. When communicating with children and young people, you will need to ensure that you are comfortable with a range of methods such as play, drawing, games and making things, in order to engage your subjects.

Herbert and Harper-Dorton (2005, p23) say that *interviewing children demands skill, patience, and respect for children* and they go on to state that *they cannot always tell their parents, let alone a comparative stranger, how they feel, but they have a language that adults can learn to translate – the language of behaviour and fantasy. What they do in everyday life and what they say indirectly through play or story telling can be most revealing.*

The following case study demonstrates how we might engage with the younger members of a family.

Ms Pink was partially sighted and had been working with social workers for most of her adult life. She was a single parent of three children who ranged in age from eight to 13. It was felt that Zoe, the eldest child, showed little respect for her family and regularly stayed out late at night as she had very few boundaries placed around her. She would often communicate by shouting and only attended school when she had lessons that she liked, most of which revolved around drama and art. The social worker established that the goal with this family was to re-establish some harmony into the family unit, in order to protect Zoe and to prevent her family from further breakdown. Although Zoe was seen as the 'problem', it soon became clear that she was feeling isolated and this was affecting her emotional well-being, as well as the family dynamics. Following a range of interventions it was decided that, as all the family enjoyed art, work that drew on their creative side was the best way to try and reconnect them to each other. Sessions were planned, and goals set, in order to achieve the aims identified by both the family and the social worker. Concentrating on painting enabled the whole family to talk to each other about a range of topics including drawing up a set of boundaries for behaviour, and 'rules' for communication. This was felt to be a less threatening situation than if they had to sit facing each other with nothing else to do and try and talk to each other. In this way parenting skills, boundaries and communication all had space to be discussed and agreed on.

Comment

This was a satisfactory ending for the family. In building trusting relationships, the social worker enabled a sense of value and respect for each family member to be re-established. On reflection the outcomes of the intervention could be divided into those that were positive and those that were less positive.

Positive outcomes

- Being able to explore ways of working that ensured all the family members were able to have their needs met.

- Working creatively with the family to enable them all to feel valued and respected.

- Ensuring that meetings and goals were planned in advance and aims were largely achieved.

Less positive outcomes

- Having to cease the work when it was felt the goals had been achieved.

- The difficulty of setting tasks due to the family's inability to communicate effectively.

- Having to remain consistent when some of the plans didn't work; for instance, if Zoe failed to turn up for an appointment, ensuring that she knew how important it was to attend and stressing the benefits. Equally, recognising the need to emphasise how important it was for Ms Pink to put boundaries in place and then make sure they were kept.

Emotional engagement

Both Pam Trevithick (2005) and Janet Seden (2005) accept that as human beings we are always communicating something, even if we do not always understand what we are giving or receiving. They cite the ability to build relationships as an essential part of the social work role and, in order to achieve this effectively, communication skills are paramount. Understanding and practising communication are necessary in order to provide the foundation for good relationships (see Chapter 6) and, consequently, meeting the needs of those we work with. Coupled with this is the ability to work with people creatively, as shown in the Case Study above, using methods other than dialogue in order to achieve positive outcomes for service users. Both Trevithick and Seden argue that social work is a highly skilled activity and the skills and interventions that we choose should focus on the individual, whether they are service users, colleagues or other professionals. Emotional engagement is the ability to connect with another person on a level that encourages understanding and a willingness to work with whatever the carer or person who uses services needs. Sometimes this can be the situation the person may be facing; sometimes it can be a dilemma of one kind or another. Other subjects that are sometimes difficult to tackle may include raw emotions; for example, in Mary's case above, sadness was one of the emotions that was prominent. As human beings we usually shy away from feelings that are going to hurt us or that we fear will damage us in some way. Sometimes we might feel overwhelmed by these emotions. Again we need to recognise what other people's feelings and experiences stir up in us and what we do to keep ourselves safe. Go back to Activity 7.1, earlier in the chapter, and think again about what upsets you and how you protect yourself.

Anger is another emotion that can be experienced as fearful or uncontrolled. Anger is often expressed when people are feeling unheard or backed into a corner with little power or control over the situation they are experiencing. While steps need to be taken to ensure our safety, we also need to be aware of what is happening for the service user and what steps we can take to alleviate the tension. Zoe would often shout in anger to get her voice heard but it's useful to note here that her feelings of anger and her need to express it diminished as her boundaries became clearer and she felt more supported. It may not be our situation to sort out but we can have some understanding of what is happening and attempt to empathise and give back some control to whoever we are working with.

Keeping physically safe

It is important to distinguish between anger, which can be a healthy expression of pent-up emotion, and aggression, which is where that anger becomes focused on a person or object. Working with a person's anger can be an uncomfortable experience but can be extremely valuable in helping a person to move on emotionally. However, if a person becomes aggressive, either verbally or physically, the most important thing is to keep you both safe. A zero tolerance (Department of Health, 1999) approach is recommended, in which you provide the person with clear, calm feedback that you will not accept that behaviour.

It is important though to note that most people follow a cycle of escalation in their aggressive behaviour, breaking down their social inhibitors; for example, starting by swearing, moving to kicking objects, before becoming violent towards you. If you give a person a clear, calm message that you will not tolerate their actions, they will sometimes escalate their behaviour to the next level, before de-escalating. So, if you consider they are close to assaulting you, withdraw immediately. For some people, however, there are limited inhibitors to violence – or none at all. This can occur particularly where someone has damage to the frontal lobe of the brain, which controls behaviour. Another example of where people may find it difficult to control their anger is when they feel they have no choices or voice in the decisions being made.

CASE STUDY

Ken Tenant

Mr Tenant was a 22-year-old boxer who had suffered an acquired brain injury following a fight outside a pub. He could stand with the help of two people and required a wheelchair for mobility. He had right-sided weakness and was unable to speak. He was receiving rehabilitation on a hospital ward. If he became annoyed or upset he would clench his right fist and then punch anyone within range. He was particularly aggressive when staff gave him a shower in the morning. The staff team worked to introduce a routine and cues, such as music, smells and verbal prompts, which would help Mr Tenant to understand what was happening to him, but to no avail. His partner explained that he always had his shower in the evening at home. The ward staff changed his shower time to the evening and his aggression around this issue stopped.

Comment

It is easy for people who have been aggressive to become labelled as an aggressive person. Young people with learning difficulties can be particularly vulnerable to this – you may have seen services referred as for 'challenging behaviour'; invariably they tend to be for people with learning disabilities. Such labels can become a lens through which all their behaviours are interpreted. This can lead to a failure to consider alternative explanations for behaviour, as the labels become squarely located in the individual. When told a person has challenging behaviour, it is always important to ask: *to whom?* and *why?*

A colleague of mine, having worked for several years on a unit for people with challenging behaviour, felt that one of the most important lessons learned from that experience was that aggressive behaviour communicates something in its own right. That does not make it acceptable, but understanding what a person is trying to communicate is central to preventing the behaviour occurring. The next step is to work with the person to develop more acceptable ways of communicating and getting their needs met.

Often people become isolated and this can increase their sense of vulnerability or hostility. It takes time and patience to work with people in this situation and build their trust. Usually this requires developing clear boundaries with the person, but also showing them positive regard and helping to build their self-esteem.

CHAPTER SUMMARY

In this chapter we have gone some way towards considering what we need to do to meet the needs of the service users we work with and to communicate in a way that is effective and as free from our own clutter as possible. While this is vital in the work we do, we also need to be aware of what is required to keep ourselves safe, both emotionally and physically, and again this chapter has considered how we might evaluate these areas. However, we need to recognise that our fear of new or potentially difficult situations must not stop us from trying to meet the needs of the service users with whom we work. It serves as a reminder that we must be aware of our internal supervisor. We should be able and prepared to take risks and provide opportunities for the people we work with in order to help them lead more fulfilling lives and provide ourselves with the satisfaction of having done a good job.

FURTHER READING

Lefevre, M (2010) *Communicating with children and young people: Making a difference.* Bristol: The Policy Press.

A comprehensive exploration of communicating with children.

Lishman, J (2009) *Communications in social work.* (2nd edition). Basingstoke: Macmillan.

This book introduces and examines all forms of communication in a variety of social work settings.

Trevithick, P (2005) *Social work skills: A practice handbook.* (2nd edition). Maidenhead: Open University Press.

This text provides a toolbox of skills from which to draw and enables us to begin to establish good relationships.

Beresford, P, Adshead, L and Croft, S (2007) *Palliative care, social work and service users.* London: Jessica Kingsley.

Casement, P (2002) *Learning from our mistakes.* London: Guildford Press.

Department of Health (1999) *We don't have to take this – NHS zero tolerance zone resource pack.* London: Department of Health.

Herbert, M and Harper-Dorton, KV (2005) *Working with children, adolescents and their families.* Oxford: BPS Blackwell.

Hough, M (2006) *Counselling skills and theory.* London: Hodder and Arnold.

Koprowska, J (2006) *Communication and interpersonal skills in social work.* Exeter: Learning Matters.

Lefevre, M (2010) *Communicating with children and young people: Making a difference.* Bristol: The Policy Press.

Lishman, J (1994) *Communication in social work.* Basingstoke: Macmillan.

Lishman, J (2007) *Handbook for practice learning in social work and social care.* London: Jessica Kingsley.

Mantell, A (2006) Huntington's disease: The carer's story. Unpublished DPhil, University of Sussex.

Riggal, S (2012) *Using counselling skills in social work.* London: Sage/Learning Matters.

Seden, J (2005) *Counselling skills in social work practice.* (2nd edition). Maidenhead: Open University Press.

Sheldon, F (1997) *Psychosocial palliative care.* Cheltenham: Stanley Thornes.

Thompson, N (2009) *People skills.* (3rd edition). Basingstoke: Palgrave Macmillan.

Trevithick, P (2005) *Social work skills: A practice handbook.* (2nd edition). Maidenhead: Open University Press.

Part 3
Working with others

Chapter 8

Skills for collaborative working

Janet McCray

Introduction

The International Federation of Social Workers (2013) describe social work interventions as ranging from primarily person-focused psychosocial processes to involvement in social policy, planning and development. These include counselling, clinical social work, group work, social pedagogical work, and family treatment and therapy as well as efforts to help people obtain services and resources in the community (IFSW, 2013). This cannot be achieved in isolation and, as the QAA notes:

> *Social work takes place in an inter-agency context, and social workers work collaboratively with others towards interdisciplinary and cross-professional objectives.*

> (QAA, 2008, p5)

At the centre of all practice is the person who requires support.

Bringing together values, goals, differing agendas and needs to create change through collaboration is an exciting and challenging prospect. Yet it can also seem daunting and complicated. In this chapter strategies for making collaboration effective will be presented. The landscape of service delivery is changing rapidly and the context of social work practice begins this chapter. A review of definitions and their meanings will follow. Collaboration as a practice will be explored while other language and terms often used interchangeably will be clarified. Components of good collaborative practice and strategies for its development are outlined. General protocols and practice will be charted. Examples of good practice with children and families and adults underpin the chapter content as some barriers to collaboration are considered. During the chapter attention is paid to frameworks to aid fair and appropriate social work practice.

The new landscape of practice

Changes in public health provision in England from 2013 (Healthwatch England, DOH, 2013) mean that there will be closer working between health and local authorities as they take responsibility for public health budgets to support communities. In order to give good value for money, effective collaboration will be vital. Partnerships between the public and third sector will drive service delivery and encourage the involvement of local communities. For adults in receipt of long-term care and their carers the quality of collaboration will be a key factor of success. In the new White Paper, *Caring for our future: Reforming care and support* (Department of Health, 2012), new roles for social workers may include community development roles. Adult social workers should, the White Paper states, help to connect people to community networks, get them involved in local activities and create community groups where there are currently gaps. New models of service delivery will be in place and some former public-sector roles may be outsourced and provided by social workers employed in social enterprises or in the private sector.

In children's services safeguarding and promoting the well-being of children centred on partnerships remains the responsibility of local authorities under the Children Act of 1989 (Department of Education, 1989) but, as in adult services, new frameworks and initiatives are being set in place. In particular, there is new guidance for collaboration in acute-care NHS settings.

What is collaborative working?

A simple definition of collaborative working is:

> *a respect for other professionals and service users and their skills and from this starting point, an agreed sharing of authority, responsibility and resources aimed at specific outcomes or actions, and gained through cooperation and consensus.*

(McCray, 2011, p393)

Often collaborative working forms an element of multi-professional and multi-agency teamwork (Taylor *et al.*, 2006, p19), while other terms such as multi-professional and multi-disciplinary are also used to mean the same thing.

These definitions provide information on what the intention and goals of collaborative working are, but the process of collaboration can take a number of forms.

RESEARCH SUMMARY

Findings on forms of collaborative working

In working with children and families collaborative working can be an effective and positive vehicle. Examples of success include reducing educational achievement gaps (Epstein and Van Voorhis, 2010) for supporting families to cope in adversity or to keep children safe. Collins and McCray (2012, p35) observe that such partnerships or collaborations may be dominated by the requirement to protect the child and, as a consequence, the building of relationships with other professionals can be constrained.

Often children's services teams may be working to targets and this focus creates a culture of competitiveness rather than collaboration.

Davey et al. (2004, p134) draw attention to the formal and informal models of collaborative working in social work with older people. They suggest that informal arrangements based on practitioner-driven activity are as influential for people using services as formal arrangements, such as those in integrated care teams, where health and social care agencies work within a formal strategically agreed framework to deliver a particular service. The writers continue their research to look at collaboration with general practitioners (GPs) in older people's services (Davey et al., 2005, p399). One finding was that informal collaborative practice which moved away from organisational or formal frameworks was needed to work through some of the very real differences between professionals and the challenges of tight resources (Davey et al., 2004, p134). So it was the informal relationships built with other professionals that were important, perhaps through networking activity, educational events or other contact.

Comment

Research shows that no single form of collaboration can work on its own. While successive governments have created legislation and formal frameworks for collaboration, often it is grass-roots workers who can make things happen based on their informal networks and connections to others, created through a shared commitment to service users. As Andy Mantell sets out in Chapter 6, often it is the building of relationships which serves to make or break good practice arrangements with other professionals and users of service. However, other factors also play their part and will become of more significance if the social work role and intervention are complex.

Components of good practice in collaboration

Many of the elements of good practice in collaboration, such as communication, teamworking and knowledge of the roles of other professionals and workers, have been described as 'common sense' by some professional undergraduate students (Gordon and Marshall, 2007, p47). Valuing other professional roles and contributions may also seem obvious. Of course, no one would dispute the importance of this knowledge and these skills in developing collaborative practice. What also need to be considered are their components. Increasingly, people in receipt of services are partners in their assessment and support processes, while other agency partners may also be involved. As we talk about communication, what do we mean? What form might it take and how important is the context in which the communication takes place? For example, positive communication may be easy in routine information-sharing activity by email or at an informal meeting with another professional. As you will know, some situations in practice are much more challenging for everyone involved. Begley and Monaghan (2004, p22) discuss the ethical dilemmas faced by professionals when disclosing a dementia diagnosis to individuals. They note the importance of collaboration with the service user and the critical role of inter-professional communication. What is important is clear, consistent information and responses from all involved, yet the different values held by professionals may mean communication is difficult. For example, not all professionals involved might want to give full information to the person in receipt of the diagnosis. It may not be appropriate as they might not be qualified to give a full answer. Mixed messages can be given to an individual which ultimately impact on future communication, support to the person and collaborative working. Talking about values may also seem a 'given' in collaboration. McCray (2011, p394) observes that personal values are something that individuals hold at the centre of their being. Values are developed over time and from experience, and personal values may reflect an individual's culture, moral stance or lifestyle.

When it comes to professional values another layer of strongly held and learned beliefs is added. All may be fine until there is a clash of professional values; for example, when ethics are at issue, as in the above case, and a decision on action needs to be taken. One group of professionals might see themselves as the rightful lead and final decision-holder in a case, based on the perceived value of their profession and its status. Hugman (1991) has written about inter-professional competition (Borthwick *et al.*, 2008) and the struggle to hold virtuoso or high-status roles by some groups of professionals. In collaborative practice a desire to hold higher status might get in the way of listening to the person needing support and their views and expectations about what they need.

Exploring the research on components of good practice shows that at times the givens of good collaboration might not be as easy to address as appears at first glance. Working with people who have complicated lives and lifestyles can impact on the degree and quality of communication in collaboration that takes place. As professionals are faced with ethical challenges and conflict around values, it is important that you are prepared to face up to, or prevent, any potential problems at an early stage. An important point here is not to make assumptions about the seemingly straightforward aspects of good collaboration.

CASE STUDY

Doreen and her Alzheimer's disease diagnosis

You are working with Doreen and a team of professionals from health and social care. Doreen has recently been diagnosed with Alzheimer's disease. She lives with her partner Jack in a small city centre flat. Their only son Anthony was killed in a car accident three years ago. At a meeting with the consultant and other health care professionals it was suggested that it might be better not to give Doreen the full extent of her diagnosis as it was felt this might compound the feelings of depression and helplessness she had described since her son's death. As the social worker you do not agree with this view and feel that the collaboration across professional groups is likely to be less successful and impact on communication with Doreen and Jack. You seek to understand why other professionals feel this was the correct intervention.

ACTIVITY *8.1*

Consider your thoughts and feelings about Doreen's situation.

Write down what you think has created a difference of opinion with other professionals about giving information to Doreen.

What are the positive and negative consequences of going along with the consultant's view from a collaborative perspective?

What action would you need to take to ensure that all professionals supported your position?

Comment

You will know from your earlier reading that often professionals' viewpoints on ethical decision-making are related to their initial professional education. Your professional position is founded on a belief in empowering social work relationships so that clients can influence person-centred decision-making (Gates, 2006). Doctors and other professionals also have their own professional values. Knowing about these and their basis is helpful in understanding and not judging other professionals. It is also important to avoid stereotyping other professionals and service users by making assumptions about their commonly held qualities.

To get past barriers to collaboration and gain good communication and consistent, honest messages for Doreen and Jack you will need to work on your own self-awareness and any stereotypical views you may hold. Plan, direct and review your collaborative activity and intervention from a user-centred position at all times. Use straightforward language and avoid jargon. Work to influence professionals to start from this shared common purpose which strengthens rather than diminishes relationships and communication.

Collaboration for positive outcomes

You have learned of the importance for collaboration of understanding components of other professional roles and their foundation. The context that is the social, economic and historical landscape in which professionals practice is also significant (McCray, 2011, p392). Services have undergone vast change in the last decades as the move from institutional to individualised care has occurred. Understandably this has impacted on how some professionals are viewed, valued and organised. For newly qualified professionals such change should not result in role conflict but, for more established professionals, policy directives may create dissonance. This is a type of stress caused by their being expected to act in a way that is contradictory to the role they prepared for. It might manifest itself as hostility or negativity, a seeming lack of commitment, and conflict in collaborative working. Understanding the context and its possible impact on the collaborative activity in process can help you decide on a strategy to ensure positive outcomes for the person in receipt of services.

The availability of resources and who should or can authorise their use or scope will also be a key issue in collaborative working. Only through agreement on the use of resources can collaboration work with trust and openness. Lingard *et al.* (2004) refer to 'trade' between professionals in collaborative working and its potential impact on present and future working relationships. Lingard *et al.* (2004) refer to this as trade in concrete commodities such as physical equipment and funding as well as social commodities such as goodwill and knowledge. In their study the writers noted the challenges of identifying the often intricate rules around trade in resources and the tension this created. For positive collaborative working, transparency was vital. The authors also viewed understanding the tensions and conflict around resources as paramount to maintaining balance in a teamwork setting.

Social workers in all services need to have a good knowledge and understanding of the context in which the collaborative activity is taking place. Changes occurring in service delivery may impact on professional interaction and the capacity and stamina of professional partners for collaboration. Clarity around funding can lessen tension and reduce conflict for collaborative partners. As a social work professional you should:

- keep up to date on social and health care policy for adults and children;

- regularly contact and meet colleagues from other professional groups and exchange information on change and its impact;

- take up opportunities for shared multi-professional education whenever possible;

- when resources are an issue, recognise the need for openness and provide updates on funding or knowledge as promised.

All of these actions can help you understand and work with other professionals effectively and enable you to be clear about boundaries for different professional intervention. Credibility and trust are gained through feedback and/or delivery of resources by an agreed time.

CASE STUDY

Enabling Eileen to live a more fulfilling life

Eileen is 90 years of age and lives alone. A recent fall resulted in a fractured pelvis and five weeks in hospital. Eileen is now housebound due to her reduced mobility and lack of confidence, and she is lonely and isolated. She has agreed to a referral to the community partnership team (CPT). Within 48 hours a worker from the team has visited Eileen and together they have decided on the goals that will enable her to live a more fulfilling life.

Eileen's goals are to:

- *conquer her fear of falling and eventually get out again;*
- *access practical assistance;*
- *access benefits advice;*
- *reduce the effects of loneliness.*

ACTIVITY 8.2

Write down what actions you think would need to be agreed to achieve those goals.

Comment

In the actions you identified you may have included the following.

- Appropriate walking aids arranged via the occupational therapist.

- Referral to a falls clinic with ongoing health trainer support.

- Practical services arranged via a package of care. This could, for example, be in the form of direct payments or a personal budget to enable Eileen to arrange her own care. Organisations such as Help the Aged might be utilised as brokers to help her.

- Referral to the Department for Work and Pensions regarding Attendance Allowance.

- Transport arranged, such as the WRVS Cars and Companions service.

This intervention had positive outcomes for Eileen. She now feels safer and significantly less at risk of falls; the additional services have led to improved self-esteem and ability to live independently; her income has increased as she now receives Attendance Allowance; and she is feeling less isolated (Potter, 2008, personal communication).

For a team such as the CPT to be effective there has to be a cohesiveness that goes beyond having a multi-agency, multi-disciplinary 'one-stop shop' approach. Integral to cohesion is sharing: sharing values, knowledge, skills, records and information.

It is the failure to share information that has been criticised in child protection inquiries since the death of Maria Colwell in 1973. In 1994 Timmins (writing for *The Independent* online) noted that:

> *About 40 child abuse inquiries have established that in almost every case the family was known to the social and health services and, among the many differing factors involved, in almost every case a breakdown in communication preceded the child's death.*

Despite subsequent high-profile cases such as that of Victoria Climbié and subsequent inquiries such as the Laming Report, which led to the policy initiative *Every Child Matters* (Department of Education, 2003) and The Children Act 2004, requiring agencies to work together, poor communication and collaboration have persisted in more recent cases such as that of baby Peter Connelly in 2009. The failings of multi-agency working can be summarised as follows.

- Professionals working in the isolation of their own agency 'silos' rather than with other professionals.

- Failure to pass on information due to the professional not seeing it as their role or due to concerns about confidentiality.

- Failure to send the information in the correct way (following procedures) or in a clear manner.

- Failure to notice the information or interpret it correctly.

- Lack of central co-ordination of information to allow all the pieces to be seen as a whole.

- Lack of clarity about roles and responsibilities.

- Poor interpersonal dynamic impairing the open and effective exchange of information, concerns and professional opinions.

- Stereotypical perspectives on other professionals undermining confidence in their opinions and actions. For example, a social worker confided to me that he told a doctor he wasn't sure he understood their view on what action should be taken in a particular situation that the multi-disciplinary team were concerned about. The doctor responded: 'Of course you don't – you are a social worker.' The doctor then walked off (after Ferguson, 2011, p183).

As previously discussed in this chapter, team members need to develop trust in each other and accept that all roles are of equal value and importance; sharing values, knowledge and skills helps to build this level of team spirit. However, sharing records and information can create an ethical dilemma. There is a legal responsibility under the Data Protection Act 1998 to keep personal information secure and confidential. It should usually only be shared with other organisations and individuals with the consent of the person concerned (see Chapter 3). In children's services, Collins (2011) observes that Sinclair and Bullock (2002) attributed poor inter-professional communication to practitioner uncertainty around issues of consent and confidentiality. The Victoria Climbié Inquiry Report (DoH, 2003) acknowledged obstructions to the exchange of information within and between agencies and recommended that they be addressed at national level by the government: *the free exchange of information about children and families about whom there are concerns is inhibited by the legislation on data protection and human rights* (DoH, 2003, p9, 1.46).

ACTIVITY 8.3

By definition a multi-agency team is made up of several organisations. Does this mean that information cannot be shared with other team members? Write down what you think are the boundaries to sharing information. What checks and balances are in place to ensure that personal information is respected?

Comment

Some staff may feel relatively at ease sharing information between statutory organisations but be more reticent about being open with workers from other sectors or with volunteers. There is no rationale for this; a team cannot collaborate effectively if important information is kept secret or only partially shared. Goble (2008, p132) tells us that a collaborative culture requires a commitment to ensure that the correct information is shared at the right time and in the right format among the people who need to know in order that the best outcomes can be achieved for the service user.

You need to ask permission to share personal information and explain what you will share with whom and the purpose of sharing it. It is good practice to ask a person to give you written, signed permission to share their information and to state on this with whom they agree or do not agree to share the information. If someone lacks the capacity to consent to the sharing of their information, section 5 of the Mental Capacity Act 2005 (DoH, 2005) allows this to take place as long as it is in the best interests of the person. On occasions you may find yourself with a legal obligation to share information without the person's consent (for example, if a vulnerable person is at risk of harm) but in these circumstances you would generally inform the person that you were going to take this action.

Fletcher gives us six questions to consider each time we are intending to share information or break confidentiality.

- What benefit will flow from this development?

- What invasion of personal liberty does it entail?

- Is it possible to achieve the benefit without the invasion?

- How do we inform and involve service users?

- Is confidential information compromised?

- Are the consequences of not sharing information greater than those of doing so?

(Fletcher, 2006, p54)

Shared recording can create similar ethical dilemmas within a multi-agency team; agreement to share information is a prerequisite of shared record-keeping as anything recorded will be accessed by other workers in the team. Joint files can also raise personal issues for some staff. It is one thing for your manager to access your case files but quite another for your peers to be looking over your shoulder. Some workers may feel uncomfortable or threatened by this level of openness and accountability within a team, particularly if they feel that other team members are more experienced or qualified than they are. In Chapter 3 Gill Constable explores record-keeping in more detail to increase your understanding.

CHAPTER SUMMARY

This chapter has explored the exciting possibilities and challenges of collaboration. You have read of the need to work informally as well as formally with other professionals to get good results. It is important to recognise different professional perspectives on giving information to service users. Values may be different across professional groups and they can impact on communication and positions about ethics and confidentiality. Tight resources may play a part in a reluctance to collaborate from some professionals, while different views on confidentiality and sharing of information could hinder effective collaborative practice. In your reading of this chapter you will have found that for the social worker prepared and equipped to move beyond the perceived givens and assumptions about multi-agency working, and other professional roles, there are many learning opportunities. Positive collaborative working offers the chance to look critically at your own practice within a team setting and offers the tools to create new strategies for co-operation in challenging ethical situations. At all times there is potential to learn from and value the positions and contributions of other professionals and service users and their families, who through the vehicle of collaborative working are enabled to retain control.

FURTHER READING

Barton, C (2007) Allies and enemies: The service user as care coordinator. In Weinstein, J, Whittington, C and Leiba, T (eds) *Collaboration in social work practice*. London: Jessica Kingsley.

This chapter tells it how it is: real people, real situations. It concludes with good practice guidelines to enable effective collaboration.

Davis, J and Sims, D (2007) Shared values in interprofessional collaboration. In Weinstein, J, Whittington, C and Leiba, T (eds) *Collaboration in social work practice*. London: Jessica Kingsley.

This chapter considers where and how social work values overlap with those of the health professions.

Quinney, A (2006) *Collaborative practice in social work*. Exeter: Learning Matters. Quinney's book explores collaborative working in depth.

REFERENCES

Begley, A and Monaghan, C (2004) Dementia diagnosis and disclosure: A dilemma in practice. *Journal of Clinical Nursing*, 13 (3a), March, 22–9.

Beresford, P, Branfield, F, Maslen, B, Sartori, A, Jenny, Maggie and Manny (2007) Partnership working: Service users and social workers learning and working together. In Lymbery, M and Postle, K (eds) *Social work: A companion to learning*. London: Sage.

Borthwick, A, Carr, E, Hammick, M and Miers, M (2008) Evolving theory in interprofessional education: Perspectives from sociology. Paper presented to the ESRC Interprofessional Education seminar series, June 2008.

Collins, F (2011) Interprofessional working: Cultures, identities and conceptualisations of practice. PhD thesis. Chichester University, UK.

Collins, F and McCray, J (2012) Partnership working in the context of UK services for children: Relationships, learning and teamwork. *The Journal of Integrated Care*, February 2012.

Davey, B, Iliffe, S, Kharicha, K and Levin, E (2004) Social work, general practice and evidence-based policy in the collaborative care of older people: Current problems and future possibilities. *Health and Social Care in the Community*, 12 (2), March, 134–41.

Davey, B, Iliffe, S, Kharicha, K and Levin, E (2005) Tearing down the Berlin wall: Social workers' perspectives on joint working with general practice. *Family Practice*, 22 (4), August, 399–405.

Department of Education (1989) *The Children Act 1989*. London: Department of Education.

Department of Education (2003) *Every Child Matters*. London: The Stationery Office.

Department of Health (2003) *The Victoria Climbié Inquiry: report of an inquiry by Lord Laming*. London: Department of Health.

Department of Health (2005) *Mental Capacity Act.* London: The Stationery Office. Available at: www.opsi.gov.uk/ACTS/acts2005/ (accessed 13 February 2013).

Department of Health (2012) *Caring for our future: Reforming care and support.* London: Department of Health.

Department of Health (2013) Healthwatch England. Available at: www.healthwatch.co.uk (accessed 13 February 2013).

Epstein, JL and Van Voorhis, FL (2010) School counsellors' role in developing partnerships in families and communities for student success. *Professional School Counselling*, 14, 1–4.

Ferguson, H. (2011) *Child protection practice.* London: Palgrave Macmillan.

Fletcher, K (2006) *Partnerships in social care: A handbook for developing effective services.* London: Jessica Kingsley.

Gates, B (2006) *Care planning and delivery in intellectual disability nursing.* Oxford: Wiley-Blackwell.

Goble, C (2008) Developing user-focused communication skills. In Mantell, A and Scragg, T (eds) *Safeguarding adults in social work.* Exeter: Learning Matters.

Gordon, F and Marshall, M (2007) Interprofessional learning in practice in South Yorkshire. In Barr, H. (ed.) *Piloting interprofessional education.* London: Higher Education Teaching Academy.

Hugman, R (1991) *Power and the caring professions.* London: Macmillan.

International Federation of Social Workers (2013) Definition of social work. Available at: www.IFSW.org (accessed February 2013).

Lingard, L, Espin, S, Evans, C and Hawryluck, A (2004) The rules of the game: Interprofessional collaboration on the intensive care unit team. *Critical Care*, 8 (6), 403–8, available at: www.pubmedcentral.nih.gov/articlerender.fcgi?artid=1065058 (accessed 26 June 2013)

McCray, J (2003) Towards a conceptual framework for interprofessional practice in the field of learning disability. PhD thesis. Department of Social Work Studies, University of Southampton.

McCray, J (2011) Nursing practice in an interprofessional context. In Hogston, R and Marjoram, B (eds) *Foundations of nursing practice: Themes, concepts and frameworks.* Basingstoke: Palgrave Macmillan.

Quality Assurance Agency for Higher Education (2008) *Subject benchmarks for social work.* Mansfield: QAA.

Quinney, A and Hafford-Letchfield, T (2012) *Interprofessional social work: Effective collaborative approaches.* Exeter: Learning Matters.

Sinclair, R and Bullock, R (2002) *Learning from past experience: A review of serious case reviews.* London: Department of Health.

Taylor, I, Sharland, E, Sebba, J, Leviche, P, Keep, E and Orr, D (2006) *The learning, teaching and assessment of partnership work in social work education.* Bristol: Policy Press.

Timmins, N (1994) Maria Colwell death led to legislation over two decades. *The Independent*, available at: www.independent.co.uk/news/uk/maria-colwell-death-led-to-legislation-over-two-decades-1431158.html (accessed 13 February 2013).

Chapter 9

Skills for group work

Marie Price and Bob Price

Introduction

All human interaction involves individuals at different levels coming together in order to be involved in or form groups of various kinds, be they formal or informal.

If you are a social worker or want to become one, then you cannot avoid becoming involved in all aspects of groups and group work on a daily basis as part of your role. As a social worker you will come across groups in various guises: as perhaps a member of a social work team or a learning set, at a team meeting, a child in need review, a hospital discharge meeting or perhaps at an adult or child protection conference. Therefore, whether you are a student social worker, a newly qualified social worker or a practitioner with many years' experience, you need to become familiar and at ease with the workings of groups; understanding both how they work and the roles you will play within them, as participant, facilitator or leader.

According to Trevithick, cited in Lindsay and Orton (2011, pxi):

> *In four out of the five areas of social work practice – work with families, groups, communities and organisations – an understanding of group work theory is clearly relevant. However, in the remaining area – work with individuals – it is equally relevant, since we cannot hope to understand individuals unless we also understand the groups to which they belong.*

A history of group work

It is difficult to pinpoint the exact origins of group work in terms of the concept we know today. However, it is believed that group work developed out of the 'settlement house' movement of mid-nineteenth-century England, pioneered by people like Augustus Samuel Barnett, who ran Toynbee House in the East End of London. The idea was to create a place where university students could work during their holidays among the poor, in order to improve their lives. The 'settlement house' movement subsequently spread to all parts of Europe and America and developed techniques for working with people in group settings.

It appears that much of the excitement that surrounded the initial group work explosion of the 1970s and 1980s, including intermediate treatment groups for young offenders, no longer exists. At the time there was a huge amount of text produced supporting and developing the processes of group work. This literature has been adopted by other professions such as counselling but is to a degree now alien to many social work practitioners. The demise of group work as a tool can be attributed to a range of factors including the emergence of the law as a central concern and, according to Adams *et al.* (2009, p117), the impact of *new managerialism with its focus on concrete and measurable outcomes*. Despite this, group work and its underlying principles are still relevant today, as a great deal of social work is still undertaken within and through groups. As a social worker, whenever you find yourself in a group setting the relevance of understanding group processes and the need to use group work skills once again come to the fore.

ACTIVITY **9.1**

Understanding groups

What do you think constitutes a group?

Write down the characteristics you associate with the following group-related terms (for example, 'support group: people with a similar difficulty or shared experience who offer and gain support from each other'):

- *class;*
- *gang;*

- *committee;*
- *militia;*
- *club;*
- *learning set;*
- *party.*

Comment

You may have recognised some common threads in the examples you came up with in terms of the fact that all groups will have implicit or explicit shared aims or goals, formal or informal structures and rules that govern behaviour and conduct.

What is group work?

In order for us to understand what we mean by the term 'group work', we first need to know what a group is. According to the *Oxford Dictionary* (2013) a *group* is a *number of people or things that are located, gathered, or classed together*. However, when you think more deeply about the issue it is not quite so easy to be so definitive about what constitutes a group. For instance, do you consider two people together in a place to be a group? Are a number of people gathered in a shopping centre a group? Do numbers in a group ever become so large that they become a mass or a crowd? So you can see that defining a group may not be as easy as we first thought. For the purposes of this chapter we are going to consider a group to be a set of people brought together for a common aim and consisting of the generally recognised optimum number for group work of between eight and 12.

While the above goes some way towards helping us to understand what may define a group, we now need to consider the notion of group work itself. There are various definitions from authors such as Konopka (1963, p29), who describes group work as a *method of social work that is utilised in order to help individuals to enhance their social functioning through purposeful group experiences, and to cope more effectively with their personal, group or community problems*, and Brown (1994, p8) who talks about group work in terms of providing:

A context in which individuals help each other; it is a method of helping groups as well as helping individuals; and it can enable individuals and groups to influence and change personal, group, organisational and community problems.

In this chapter we focus on group work as a means of social work intervention in either formally constructed groups (for the purpose of group work) or those pre-existing groups that you, as a social worker, will be involved with.

139

Why set up a group?

In order to answer this question it is probably right to acknowledge that group work is not the only method or intervention open to social workers, but it can nevertheless provide a valuable technique for working with groups of individuals. Group work will not be appropriate for everyone or every situation; however, it may for example be considered when dealing with issues involving:

- parenting;
- dementia reminiscence;
- bereavement support;
- young people's anti-social behaviour;
- community-based support;
- young carers;
- substance misuse;
- teenage parents.

It should be noted that the primary aims of some of the above groups will be focused on providing support (for example, setting up a group for bereaved children) and are more likely to be open-ended in nature; that is, members may join and leave the group, so that its composition can be quite fluid. There will also be other groups which will be task-orientated and closed groups, run for a fixed number of sessions, with new members unable to join.

The stages of establishing a group

There are a number of stages to consider when setting up a group, but perhaps the most important of these is the planning. Lindsay and Orton (2011, p19) suggest *you should invest at least as much time and effort in the planning of the group as actually working with it*. However, alongside the planning, we also need to consider the progress of the group and the process of review and evaluation, which are touched on later in this chapter.

Planning the group

In setting up a formal group it is vital that the following areas are carefully considered.

- **Purpose** It is important to be clear about the identified aim or need the group is trying to address. One example is an adult dementia reminiscence group, which is attempting to trigger the memories of often older people with the use of photographs, recordings and other artefacts. Another example can be found in the current government initiative around 'troubled families', which could be seen as an area that would lend itself well to a group work approach; perhaps for adolescents in relation to antisocial behaviour, or their parents in relation to parenting.

- **Co-ordination** You will need to consider and make decisions concerning the following issues at this stage.

  o Authority – do you require consent/agreement from your organisation or employer to set up the group?

  o Leadership/facilitator – who will be leading or facilitating the group and does it require someone who is elected or are you hoping a leader will gradually emerge from the membership?

  o Planning group – will you have a number of people involved in the planning and delivery of the group?

  o Membership – will it be an open or closed group (with an open group membership can change through the life of the group; with a closed group membership is fixed)?

  o Referral process – will attendance be compulsory or optional?

  o Contract – what are the stated expectations of both the group members and the leader/facilitator?

  o Venue – where will the meetings be held?

  o What day and at what time will the group meet? How long will the sessions last?

  o Will the group be fixed-term or open-ended, i.e. will it run for as long as anyone wants it or for a defined period of time?

  o Cost/funding/resources – how will the group be funded?

  o Administration – how will the group be run?

  o Supervision of facilitator – how will this be carried out?

  o What will be the balance of the group/gender mix?

- **Methodology** When planning your group you will need to decide what methods you might employ. These might include discussion, role-play or activity-based sessions. Although there are no rights and wrongs when it comes to content, you need to be clear which method or combination of methods would best suit your purpose. You may also decide that you will start with some activities in order to stimulate the group into a discussion and then let the group decide topics for themselves.

- **Leadership and facilitation** It is important to decide whether you require a leader or a facilitator and which approach will best meet the group's set aims. A leader, put simply, will be the person who takes responsibility for both the group content and process; this will be regardless of whether or not the leader encourages a high level of member participation in shaping the group and its direction. On the other hand, a facilitator adopts a more neutral position within the group by working as a conduit on behalf of the membership to achieve their stated goals or aims. The boundaries between leadership and facilitation are not absolute and so as a leader you will some-times find yourself facilitating group sessions rather than leading them and vice versa.

When undertaking the planning process you could, depending upon the size of the group and the type of activities being undertaken, consider having more than one facilitator. In order to positively take forward co-facilitation you would need to ensure that both workers were available for the duration of the group and had a largely similar attitude and approach to the process. The advantages of co-facilitation are that it can take the pressure off a single leader/facilitator and allow for more rounded reflection upon group processes. Clearly the disadvantages can occur when there are differences of opinion and can potentially lead to splitting in the group. Splitting is the process whereby group members may side with one or other of the facilitators and this can lead to schisms both inside and outside the group, with each leader holding something of the feelings of the group, i.e. good and bad, happy or sad.

There isn't space within this chapter to cover extensively the theme of leadership/facilitation styles but you will find recommendations for further reading at the end of the chapter.

Group processes

Whether you are a social worker who is at the point of setting up a new group or are reading this because you want to learn more about working with groups or understanding the workings of them, knowledge of group processes will be crucial.

If you are starting a new group you may have been involved in meeting poten-tial group members or inviting them to the first session; giving them informa-tion about the date, time and venue of the group, transportation arrangements, and what they should expect from the group. This is your opportunity to make a good first impression with potential members and it can showcase your skill at managing the initial group processes. You are now ready to move on to the 'contract stage', which is when you have gathered everyone together for your first session, completed your introductions and are about to commence the group processes outlined below.

The 'contract stage' is a way of being clear with group members about issues such as:

*   group aims/objectives;

*   confidentiality;

*   session – venue/date/time;

*   content;

*   ground rules (sanctions may need to be considered for any breaches).

ACTIVITY 9.2

What ground rules do you think a group should include?

Comment

If you think back to when you started on your social work course you may remember a list of ground rules covering, for example, confidentiality; respect; mobile phone use; challenging the behaviour and not the person; swearing; punctuality; absence procedures. If you were involved in establishing those boundaries then you will be more likely to *own* them and consequently respect them, more so than if they were just imposed upon you. Note that while some rules tend to be universal – for example, respecting other members – others may be specific to a particular group.

The life cycle of a group

While there are a number of writers who have attempted to quantify the processes that groups go through within their life cycle, according to Lindsay and Orton (2011, pp75–8) it is hard to move away from Tuckman's work, which described a developmental sequence for the life of a group: forming, storming, norming, performing; and finally the fifth stage, usually called adjourning or mourning. While Tuckman's linear model is perhaps the best known, it should not be considered the only way of describing and understanding group processes; there are other relevant models including those of a cyclical type where it is recognised that groups will go through certain stages and return to them regularly until the task is complete, through to Manor's (2000, pp211–2) own description of 'the evolving stance'.

ACTIVITY 9.3

Understanding roles within groups

You have just moved to a new property in an area that you are unfamiliar with. After a few days of settling in you awake one morning to find a note from your next-door neighbours inviting you to a dinner party the following Saturday evening. When you arrive at the neighbours' house all the guests are sitting around a large dinner table talking among themselves. There are eight other people in addition to yourself and you do not know any of them.

Consider the following questions.

- *What do you feel when you walk into the room?*
- *How do you negotiate your way into the group?*
- *What is your preferred role?*

    o *I remain on the outside.*
    o *I gradually integrate into the group (by invitation or opportunity).*
    o *I am the life and soul of the party.*

Comment

This gives you an idea of some of the ways in which you may approach becoming part of a group, your preferred role and the feelings associated with this process. The reason this is important is because it helps you to recognise the ways in which others function in a group setting and also understand how members may be feeling as they negotiate their way into a new group. If you are able to distinguish between the positions people adopt within groups and be aware of their feelings, then you have an opportunity to address them.

As highlighted by Llewelyn and Fielding (Dwivedi, 1993, p316), Tuckman's model of developmental sequences is as follows.

- Forming is *the initial coming together of a group, any group, where the criteria for membership and the purpose of the group are known.* There will be a range of spoken or unspoken anxieties within the group about the need for acceptance, fitting in, being liked, through to rejection and feeling unwanted, plus loss of power and control. An example of the sort of behaviour you may see at this point in your group could be nervousness from individuals, who may either compensate by being loud and boisterous or withdraw into themselves; people may stay close to anyone they already know or consider to be similar to them. The conversation may largely consist of 'safe' topics that keep the individuals protected.

- Storming is *when the group begins to sort out behavioural roles and individuals within the group begin to find out where their place in the pecking order is.* It can be identified by power struggles, arguments and testing out within the group, but could equally be punctuated with a process that is co-operative and far less traumatic. An example of the sort of behaviour you may see at this point in your group is the individual who wants to dominate group discussions, arguments between group members, or individual/collective challenges to your leadership or authority.

- Norming is *a time when the group has formed an idea of who is who and is accepting of the reality of the situation. Functional roles are decided upon and rituals and procedures agreed.* An example of the sort of behaviour you may see at this point in your group is when the group begins to function less as a group of individuals and more as a collective body, where members consciously or unconsciously accept their roles and the function of the group.

- Performing is *the time when the group begins to achieve the set task.* The group appears to be at its height in terms of problem-solving by utilising the resources within the group. An example of the sort of behaviour you may see at this point in your group is where members are working well together in pursuit of the aims of the group and the level of conflict has diminished. However, it is hoped that the members of the group will still be comfortable providing challenges to each other and the process.

- Adjourning/mourning is the point *when the group's original reason for being a group has ended and the life of the group is officially finished.* The group members may turn to finding other ways of meeting in the future or may accept the inevitable and begin the process of final goodbyes and mourning. The authors believe that group endings are one of the most important parts of the whole group work experience and therefore it is essential that this is well planned and that sufficient time is set aside for it. An example of the sort of behaviour you may see at this point in your group is where members start to act up again, withdraw, or become sad, with the realisation that the end of the group is near. You will need to be aware of the importance of endings and that for some members this will be extremely difficult, and could result in their not turning up for the final session or being disruptive. It is hoped that group members may evaluate the group experience and consider how they have previously dealt with endings. This learning will enable them to experience endings in a different and, hopefully, more productive way in the future.

Comment

It should be noted that groups can get stuck at particular stages and move back and forth between them from one session to the next; the linear process described by Tuckman is not as clear a template for the life cycle of groups as it may at first appear. The authors have facilitated groups which have not moved beyond the storming phase, determined to keep themselves in a state of unhelpful conflict. Alternatively some groups have moved quickly through the first few stages and have worked effectively until the very last session.

CASE STUDY

Marie had been facilitating a group for two years and it was due to come to an end in the following couple of months. Over the last eight weeks the group worked towards the ending, with Marie flagging up its approach and encouraging the participants to consider what they were thinking and feeling. Responses to the coming end were mixed, with individuals reflecting on how they dealt with endings generally. Most were able to contemplate the ending, with some wanting to deal with it differently from the way they had dealt with previous endings; to consider how they felt and their need to resist the end. Others were able to embrace the ending, while recognising their sadness and sometimes their ambivalence towards the approaching end. Generally the members wanted to share the ending with the group and recognise the importance of the process both for themselves and the rest of their group. However, there was a small sub-group who resisted the process out of a fear that they wouldn't be able to cope with their feelings. These participants were not able to manage the ending and didn't show up for the last session, citing illness, work commitments and other engagements in order to avoid the perceived difficulties.

Comment

It is important to introduce the concept of endings at an early stage in the group process to encourage the members to think about and prepare themselves for this stage. Sometimes, despite our best efforts in preparing a group for the ending, this does not always happen in the way we envisage, due to the fact that individual members have their own agendas on both a conscious and an unconscious level. Although from their absence it appeared that some members were not able to manage the group ending, and thus denied other members the opportunity to conclude the experience together, it is hoped that the importance of acknowledging and dealing well with endings is nevertheless embedded in their thinking.

Group dynamics

What then are group dynamics and why is it so important that we understand the impact they have on group processes and their product? Burnes (2009, p335) highlights that, according to Cartwright (1951, cited in Burnes, 2009), group dynamics *refers to the forces operating in groups* and the study of them. He goes on to point out that Kurt Lewin was the first psychologist to write about 'group dynamics' and the importance of the group in shaping the behaviour of its members. It is worth noting that this applies as much to existing groups that you as a social worker will operate within as it does to any new group-work setting. In the following paragraphs we highlight what we consider are some of the key concepts that may manifest themselves in terms of group dynamics but recognise that this is not an exhaustive list.

- **Power and anti-oppressive practice** In order to understand the influence of power and anti-oppressive practice in group work, the leader or facilitator requires a level of self-awareness and sensitivity. First the leader or facilitator needs to be aware of the authority invested in their role by the group and the inherent power differential between them and group members. This power or authority could be something that is real, i.e. in an assessed group of students, or perceived by group members as a result perhaps of previous experiences, but nonetheless is an important dynamic. Leadership styles could feed into this dynamic, as an autocratic leader or facilitator may be less willing to recognise or address any power differentials and therefore minimise anti-oppressive behaviour. The leader or facilitator needs to be conscious of their group members' diversity and culture in order to ensure that both an anti-discriminatory and anti-oppressive approach is taken in leading the group. Here it should also be recognised that group members can take power away from the leader or facilitator in certain situations. An example of this could be where the members feel very strongly about something and choose to work against the original intended aims of the group.

Comment

Issues of power and anti-oppressive practice should be addressed in both the planning and contracting stages of the preparation for the group, including strategies that you might employ when they arise (also see Chapter 5 on empowerment).

- **Roles in groups** Although we may not consciously be aware of the role we or others may play in a group it is well documented that there are certain aspects of behaviour that can be located in either an individual or sub-group that constitute a recognisable function for the group as a whole.

  For the purposes of this chapter we have concentrated on Doel and Sawdon's work, *The essential groupworker* (1999, pp179–93) in which they identify 'Individual Behaviours in the Group'. Here it is important to remember that the roles and behaviours are usually a product and example of the group process rather than an opportunity to provide a label for an individual member and therefore need to be considered as such.

  Doel and Sawdon identified eight distinct roles and indeed devised a set of cards that encouraged the reader to consider what these roles may involve. The set of cards also included a ninth card with a question mark for individuals to consider any other behaviour they may have witnessed as part of a group.

> **ACTIVITY 9.4**
>
> **Group roles**
>
> *Consider the following list of group roles identified by Doel and Sawdon and write down what behaviours, thoughts or feelings you would associate with each one.*
>
> - *Monopolising*
> - *Leading from within*
> - *Challenging*
> - *Keeping silent*
> - *Gatekeeping*
> - *Joking*
> - *Being different*
> - *Scapegoating*

Comment

As we have stated a number of times, understanding group dynamics and the roles people play in groups is a vital skill for every social worker to master, whether you are a participant, facilitator or leader, because unless you can identify these behaviours you will not have the opportunity to address them. We have selected the following two Doel and Sawdon group roles to discuss in more detail.

- **Challenging** What is evident is that when you as a leader or facilitator of a group are challenged by a member this can feel uncomfortable for both you and sometimes other group members. However, challenge should be seen as healthy practice as groups without challenge are often those that have a high degree of consensus leading to a lack of creativity. As a leader or facilitator you may be seen as the person setting the rules and thus a legitimate target for attack or challenge; and you may find that other members either join in or come to your rescue. What is key is that the group members will be watching how you respond to this challenge and will take their lead from you in terms of the way you manage the situation. There are a range of ways you can respond, which may include simply reiterating the rules of the group on that issue, being clear what is up for negotiation and what is not, seeking a compromise, opening up discussion for others views or agreeing to take the issue away and make a decision by the next session.

Sabotaging can be seen as a form of conscious or unconscious challenge and can manifest itself in a variety of ways, including members turning up for sessions late or intermittently, refusing to undertake tasks or deliberately deflecting meaningful group discussions.

- **Scapegoating** The term scapegoat is one that is well known and used widely in day-to-day conversation. However, in the group work setting, a scapegoat is a member who is singled out on a regular basis by other members and on whom the group take out their frustrations when things go wrong; the scapegoat may be a reluctant recipient of this unwanted attention or may be happy in this role, as it fulfils some need in him or her. In order to address scapegoating in any group, first you need to recognise when it is happening, then decide at what level, and finally what action is warranted.

CASE STUDY

Scapegoating

Y was a member of a group that was set up as part of a professional course. Participation was compulsory and the members generally had no say in who would be part of their group. It was clear from the outset that Y wasn't comfortable with conversations that were perceived as becoming too deep. Y would use the state of her health to deflect any attention away, asserting the constant need for time off, repeated surgery and pain as reasons for not becoming involved in the group.

It certainly had that effect but also ensured that it stopped the progress of the other participants who had initially felt sympathetic towards their peer. However, as the group progressed, the other members would not include Y in their discussions or would actively choose topics which they knew would distress Y; thus making Y a scapegoat for their frustration and anger at the lack of progress of the group.

Comment

While we acknowledge that scapegoating behaviour is often directed towards one individual, it should be recognised that the behaviour in itself may have a benefit for others in a group, namely that it deflects attention away from individuals (and the group) in having to deal with difficult issues. In order to manage and address any scapegoating that may be occurring in the group, you will first need to identify the fact that it is happening. It is important to note that there is a range of feelings and potential consequences associated with scapegoating, for both the person being scapegoated and those scapegoating.

Monitoring and evaluation

When planning a group it is important to consider the benefits of setting up a process of monitoring and evaluation. Monitoring of the group work process is useful in recording your reflections on each session and the events and processes that occurred during them (see Chapter 1). It helps to show progress within the group as well as highlight any setbacks that occur, and ultimately will contribute to the overall evaluation. In terms of evaluation you need to think about whether you seek written or verbal feedback from group members about their experience of the group. Evaluation can hopefully lead to improved learning in some of the following areas and to the positive development of future groups.

- What specific exercises and/or sessions worked well; and which didn't?
- Were the initial group aims/goals achieved?
- Did group work members feel the process was beneficial?
- How could the process have been improved?

While most of this chapter concentrates on groups for adults we should not forget that they can be a very effective way of working with children too. However, it should be noted that when you are setting up a group for working with children, as opposed to adults, you need to take account of some subtle but very important differences.

According to Dwivedi (1993, pp 7–8), *in groupwork with children and adolescents there is a tendency towards action, also the pace and style of communication is very different from that in adult groups. Themes of conversation may change very rapidly, jumping from topic to topic often unconnected and in parallel.* In addition we need to consider the developmental age of the group we are targeting. If, for example, we are concentrating on a group for teenagers there would be little point in providing toys as the target group may well feel belittled or not taken seriously, whereas if we are planning a group for primary school children then toys or games may well be an advantage in engaging them. Although creating boundaries is important in any group, it is particularly the case when you are working with children in order to ensure that group members feel safe.

Comment

The creation of boundaries is about constructing a safe and trusting environment for group members to work within. This can best be achieved through ensuring that children and young people understand why they are attending the group and that the 'contract stage' referred to above is built into the process.

When working with any group you will be incorporating a range of different activities and exercises, depending on the type of group, including art, role-play/drama, activities, games and talk. However, there will be differences depending on your audience and Koprowska suggests that *groups for children will always involve activities, while some for young people and adults consist solely in talk* (2010, p119). There is a range of activities, exercises and resource materials that can be helpfully employed with children to assist you, from the initial 'ice-breaking' group stage, when members get to know each other, right through to the issue of dealing with endings.

This chapter has highlighted how important it is to plan thoroughly for any group you may be attempting to set up for whatever reason. Coupled with this, thought should be given to the stage before the first session, as this is your first contact with the potential members of your group.

We have gone some way towards helping you to understand group processes, dynamics and roles, and the importance of endings, not least as a way of helping group members rework earlier poor endings.

While the focus has been largely on the setting up of a group it must be remembered that the behaviours and responses of group members apply to all manner of groups that we may be involved with.

Finally, we have begun to think about the importance of supervision in managing the complexity of groups (see Chapter 4).

FURTHER READING

Doel, M and Sawdon, C (1999) *The essential groupworker.* London: Jessica Kingsley.

A helpful look at the dynamics necessary for successful groups.

Dwivedi, KN (ed.) (1993) *Groupwork with children and adolescents.* London: Jessica Kingsley.

A comprehensive resource on group work with children and adolescents.

Lindsay, T and Orton, S (2011) *Groupwork practice in social work.* 2nd edition. Exeter: Learning Matters.

A good introductory text to group work.

REFERENCES

Adams, R, Dominelli, L and Payne, M (eds) (2009) *Critical practice in social work.* Basingstoke: Palgrave Macmillan.

Aveline, M and Dryden, W (1988) *Group therapy in Britain.* Milton Keynes: Open University Press.

Brown, A (1994) *Groupwork.* 3rd edition. Great Yarmouth: Ashgate.

Burnes, B (2009*) Managing change.* 5th edition. Harlow: Pearson Education Limited.

Doel, M and Sawdon, C (1999) *The essential groupworker.* London: Jessica Kingsley.

Douglas, T (1991) *Groupwork practice.* London: Routledge.

Dwivedi, KN (ed.) (1993) *Groupwork with children and adolescents.* London: Jessica Kingsley.

Konopka, G (1963) *Social groupwork: A helping process.* Englewood Cliffs, NJ: Prentice Hall.

Koprowska, J (2010*) Communication and interpersonal skills in social work.* 3rd edition. Exeter: Learning Matters.

Lindsay, T and Orton, S (2011) *Groupwork practice in social work.* 2nd edition. Exeter: Learning Matters.

Manor, O (2000) *Choosing a groupwork approach.* London: Jessica Kingsley.

Oxford Dictionary (2013) www.oxforddictionaries.com

Chapter 10

Negotiation skills

Chris Smethurst and Rebecca Long

Introduction

Trevithick (2005, p222) provides the following simple definition of negotiation: *achieving some form of agreement or understanding*. Although this definition does not suggest the potential complexity of the negotiating process, it does indicate the extent to which negotiation is part and parcel of our everyday lives. Certainly, negotiation appears to be integral to social work practice. However, it could be argued that, because negotiation is so embedded within the activity of social work, it is taken for granted. There are some texts which specifically focus on negotiation in health and social care, for example Fletcher (1998); yet, in many social work skills textbooks, it is noticeable that discussion of negotiation skills is frequently incorporated, or subsumed, within chapters on assessment or care planning. This is in sharp contrast to texts relating to business, where negotiation is given a far greater profile.

An instruction manual approach to negotiation, which breaks down the skills of human interaction into simple, sequential steps, may not be appropriate for social work: arguably, the subtlety and fluidity of the processes of communication are not so easily simplified. Similarly, an increasing amount of attention has been given to the fact that social work is frequently practised in an environment that is highly pressurised, adversarial and emotionally charged (Ferguson 2011, Munro, 2011, Kinman and Grant 2011). Consequently, although this chapter will explore some models of negotiation, we will attempt to avoid the reader having to memorise sequential techniques that they may struggle to recall in real-life practice situations. Instead, this chapter will refer to models of negotiation that draw upon those skills and qualities with which social workers are already familiar. The chapter will also address negotiation in situations of conflict, ethical issues and dilemmas.

Negotiation skills: the practice context

Social work practitioners employ negotiation skills in interactions with:

- people who use services, carers and others who provide assistance and support;
- managers, colleagues and other staff within the practitioner's organisation;
- service providers;
- other professionals/organisations.

Students on qualifying and post-qualifying courses most typically refer to negotiation in the context of their direct work with service users and when attempting to secure resources. Of course, the two are frequently inextricably linked. Interestingly, research suggests that service users value practitioners who can act as 'go-betweens'; negotiating and mediating between the service user and the local authority (Manthorpe *et al.*, 2008). However, practitioners often report feeling ethically compromised and inadequate when negotiating to meet the needs of service users within the constraints of limited resources. Therefore, it is important to stress that better negotiating skills, on their own, cannot enable practitioners to bridge the gap between the legitimate demands of service users and the inadequate resources that are available to meet them. Nevertheless, practitioners who develop their negotiating skills are likely to improve their effectiveness when working on behalf of service users. Similarly, social workers who enhance their skills may well feel more confident and capable.

Standardised eligibility criteria and procedural approaches to decision-making could undermine the practitioner's influence upon the allocation of resources. However, there is evidence to suggest that practitioners can and do exercise discretion and professional autonomy in their interactions with service users (Evans and Harris, 2004) and that the skills and knowledge of the worker do make a difference in securing resources (Newton and Browne, 2008). Of course, this raises the ethical and political issues of service users effectively being placed in competition with each other for resources, with access to these resources being determined less by individual need than by the negotiating ability of the practitioner. Clearly, this situation places those most marginalised and excluded in our society and who lack advocates at a considerable disadvantage. While arguing that part of the social worker's role is to challenge unfair systems, we acknowledge that social workers also practise in the world as it is, not as it should be. Consequently, social workers, as advocates (see Chapter 5), need to try to maximise the support that they can secure for service users. Practitioners will therefore probably wish to enhance their negotiating effectiveness on behalf of service users, and for reasons of professional competence.

ACTIVITY **10.1**

On a scale of 1–5 (with 5 being the highest score), how would you assess your negotiation skills?

Does the effectiveness of your skills vary in different contexts?

Now consider what factors need to be present for your skills to be particularly effective?

Comment

It is likely that you will have concluded that how well you negotiate varies according to a number of factors. Some people may feel quite comfortable negotiating on behalf of someone else, but less capable when they feel they are asking for something for themselves; for example, you may find yourself to be an assertive advocate for service users but feel far less capable of negotiating a pay rise for yourself (of course, the converse could be true). Similarly, as a social work practitioner, you may find yourself negotiating on behalf of your agency for a course of action that perhaps is uncomfortable. This discomfort may affect your ability to empathise with the individual with whom you are negotiating; you may find yourself in an entrenched position and saying things that, upon reflection, you may not agree with. This is a relatively common occurrence in potentially conflictual situations. Diplomats, police officers and probably most parents would recognise the social worker's experience of situations that start out as a reasonable and promising discussion, then quickly and bewilderingly escalate into heated argument.

Conflictual situations often elicit strong emotion. Therefore, it is wise to acknowledge the emotional element of negotiation, since emotion is an integral feature of human interaction. Anxiety, frustration and anger are likely to have an impact upon any negotiation, as will emotions like sympathy and a sense of guilt. Similarly, it is likely that if you feel anxious, unsure of your facts and are fearful of 'losing', your negotiating ability may be severely inhibited.

CASE STUDY

Sarah is employed by a local authority adult services team working with disabled people. She is very passionate about her job and is committed to what she calls 'getting the best for the people I work with'. However, she is

---

frequently frustrated by the negotiations she undertakes on behalf of disabled people, concerning the amount of personal assistance her local authority is willing to fund. Even before she enters into discussions with her managers, Sarah feels stressed and anxious about 'losing'. Although she tries to find a compromise solution, she frequently finds herself feeling defensive as she is asked questions which she struggles to answer. She feels that these negotiations often end up as interrogations, where her competence, values and professional judgment are called into question. Sarah finds herself embarrassed in these discussions; especially when she is accused of not being 'realistic', or is criticised for not having followed some aspect of agency procedure. She gets anxious reporting back to the individuals for whom she is advocating. She tries to put an encouraging slant on disappointing decisions, but gets upset when the individuals she is working with appear to perceive her as an unthinking functionary of the social services department. Sarah frequently feels that she is trying to reconcile the impossible, with her role reduced to that of a mouthpiece for decisions she does not always believe in.

ACTIVITY **10.2**

What steps do you think Sarah could take to address some of the difficulties highlighted in the case study?

Comment

It is relatively easy to empathise with Sarah's experience. Her situation is reminiscent of the ambivalent and contradictory position occupied by many social work practitioners: attempting to advocate for service users, while simultaneously being the representative of an organisation that is restricting access to resources. Of course, these professional anxieties and dilemmas are real for front-line practitioners in a variety of public service agencies (Lipsky, 1980). Can social workers really claim to have a strong commitment to anti-oppressive practice if they are focused on gatekeeping resources for their organisations? Consequently, the reflective practitioner has to grapple with the potential inconsistency between these principles and the realities of practice.

Numerous studies identify the extent to which the priorities of social care agencies have been driven by resource constraint (Postle, 2002; Gorman and Postle, 2003; Ferguson, 2008). These resource concerns add legitimacy to the restructuring and remodelling of social work practice as an administrative activity. This construction of practice seems to place limited value on interpersonal skills, can seem at odds with the concerns and priorities of service users and frequently conflicts with the professional values of practitioners (Dustin, 2007; Dominelli 2008; Munro, 2011). This has important implications for practitioners: ambivalence, contradiction and confusion in professional roles can be a major source of stress (Handy, 2005; Kim and Stoner 2008). Similarly, Ferguson and Lavalette (2004) argue that the increasing bureaucratisation of social work has resulted in social workers experiencing their work as a series of *alien* practices, over which they have little control. This theme was placed in a contemporary context by Munro (2011) who concluded that the demands of bureaucracy have limited the capacity of social workers to work directly with service users. In addition Munro notes a trend towards standardised and prescriptive services that are insufficiently flexible to meet the variety of need encountered by social workers.

The managerial and bureaucratic remodelling of social work practice is indicative of the lack of trust afforded to social workers by government (Jones, 2001). Coincidentally, but for different reasons, many in the disabled people's movement are apparently hostile towards the social work profession. Here, this hostility is born of the interference, insensitivity and abuses of power; perpetrated by both individual workers and social work agencies (Beresford, 2008; Leece and Leece, 2011). In these circumstances, it is not surprising that Sarah may feel so unhappy. Yet, research with service users reveals that the following social work skills and qualities are valued:

- commitment to social rather than medical models;

- ability and willingness to listen and be non-judgmental;

- willingness to advocate on behalf of service users;

- relationship with the worker based on genuineness and honesty;

- human qualities of warmth, empathy and respect.

(DHSS, 1985; McKeown, 2000; Beresford *et al.*, 2005; Branfield *et al.*, 2006)

These qualities are valuable, if sometimes undervalued, in both adults' and children's services. In fact, they form the key components of relationship-based social work, which is seen as integral to effective child protection practice (Munro, 2011). Miller (2012) has argued that adopting a personal outcome approach can shift the focus back to service users' and carers' concerns and encourages the practice of these skills and qualities (see Chapter 6).

In the next section on negotiating styles, you may wish to consider whether the case study gave any clues about the negotiating styles which may have been adopted by Sarah and her managers.

Negotiating styles

Shell (2006) identifies five negotiation styles. He suggests that individuals may have a strong preference for a particular approach or approaches. However, he argues that individuals may adopt differing approaches according to the situation. Similarly, awareness of one's own preferred styles, their strengths and weaknesses, can enable the individual to be more adept in negotiating scenarios.

Shell (2006) identifies that some individuals enjoy the competition of negotiation; they literally 'play to win'. In employing a *competing* style, negotiators may well secure an initial perception of victory. However, this may be to the detriment of the relationship with the other party. In a profession which places a high premium on the establishment and maintenance of positive relationships, the risks of an over-reliance on a competing style are clear.

A competitive approach may be favoured by individuals who wish to establish and maintain control. These individuals can seem strong and intimidating, particularly if occupying a supervisory position. Yet, the impression of control and confidence can be illusory. Insecurity and anxiety may be revealed by a lack of willingness to depart from a narrowly defined agenda. Similarly, a refusal to acknowledge perspectives other than one's own can be masked by a claim to rationality; a dismissal of others' arguments as being irrelevant; a belief that the other party is over-emotional and insufficiently objective. Gabriel (1998) suggests that the fear of losing control of situations leads many managers to disguise their uncertainty behind an illusion of objectivity and emotional detachment. Munro's review of child protection notes that, once they have reached a decision, social workers may prove to be reluctant to evaluate objectively evidence that contradicts their opinion (Munro, 2011).

Perhaps diametrically opposed to the competing style is the *avoiding* style; many practitioners may have witnessed this in action. Avoiders are not confident and dislike negotiation; they are more likely to skirt around potentially contentious or conflictual issues. Unlike those who enjoy a competitive style of negotiation, avoiders may appear to place a high value on positive relationships. Unfortunately, this can be to the detriment of the relationship if a degree of dishonesty is present. When social work practice has gone wrong, the subsequent inquiries have often highlighted the extent to which anxiety about damaging the relationship with service users has led to practitioners not addressing areas of concern. In fact, important work by Dale *et al.* (1986) suggests that a practitioner's need to be liked may result in their being insufficiently assertive, leading to dangerous practice. Of course, this is interesting when examined in the context of research which suggests that, even where conflictual relationships existed between service users and social work agencies, service users respected practitioners who were 'honest' and 'genuine' (DHSS,1985). It is sobering to acknowledge that both these pieces of work are over 20 years old, yet the lessons have still not fully permeated social work practice.

Shell (2006) identifies *accommodators* as individuals who value relationships and enjoy problem-solving. The inherent risk of this approach is that the individual can be too accommodating and may feel taken advantage of; this feeling may be particularly acute following an encounter with another individual who adopts a more competitive style. Similarly, *compromisers* may too readily give concessions that may be regretted later. However, where there is fundamental disagreement between parties, willingness to compromise, at least to a certain degree, is probably essential to avoid deadlock.

A *collaborative* approach appears to be attractive within social work practice: a high value is placed upon empathising with the perspectives of others and working out complex issues together. However, there is a risk that negotiation can get bogged down in the complexity of detail if an attempt is made to reach a consensus on a myriad of issues where there may be fundamental disagreement. Occasionally, parties may have to 'agree to disagree' and accept that not all issues can be resolved by consensus.

ACTIVITY **10.3**

Consider a recent practice situation or experience and reflect upon the negotiating style that you adopted.

What negotiation style do you think the other individual employed?

How successful was the negotiation?

Did the other individual's, or your own, style of negotiation enhance or inhibit the process?

What could you have done differently which might have improved the outcome?

Comment

In dynamic and fluid practice situations it is frequently difficult to adhere to fixed models and methods (Payne, 2007). A positive feature of the Shell (2006) framework is that it provides sufficiently overarching concepts that can be witnessed in practice. Hopefully, you will have been able to identify your own and others' preferred styles of negotiation and the practice implications of these. In the next section we will explore a sequential model, where Shell (2006) provides a structure for understanding the negotiating process itself.

The stages of negotiation

The introduction to this chapter cautioned against the rigid application of step-by-step instruction manual approaches to the complexities of real-life practice situations. Nevertheless, Shell (2006) provides some illuminating insights into the processes that occur during negotiation. It is worth exploring these and considering the extent to which they can be applied in social work practice. Shell (2006) suggests that the negotiation process can be broken down into four interdependent stages.

Preparation

In the case study above, Sarah felt defensive and struggled to answer questions that were asked of her. Possibly, a lack of prior preparation, allied with uncertainty about her facts, led to low confidence and poor performance when negotiating. Adequate preparation is a precondition of successful negotiation. According to Shell (2006), this preparation does not extend only to the possession of factual information. Knowledge of an individual's negotiating style, alongside strengths and weaknesses, would appear also to be a prerequisite. Interestingly, Shell (2006) emphasises the necessity of acknowledging one's own value base and the values of the other party. Recognition of these seeks to avoid the emergence of intransigent negotiating positions, perhaps the result of emotional responses to the negotiating process.

The activity of preparation, when engaging in negotiation, has some parallels with the process of 'tuning in', as described by Woodcock Ross (2011). She suggests that this can be likened to tuning in to a radio station by blocking out background noise. She also refers to it as 'preparatory empathy'. Woodcock Ross (2011) draws on Shulman (2009) to suggest that in preparing to communicate with service users, practitioners may consider the following questions.

- How might the service user see you? How might they react?

- What may be the issues or difficulties being experienced by the service user at present?

- How might the service user have experienced similar situations? How might they have been treated? How might this affect how they behave now?

Although Woodcock Ross has focused on preparation to work with service users, the principles can be seen to have resonance in a range of professional interactions.

Exchanging information

Shell (2006) argues that successful negotiators ask more questions than poor negotiators. The purpose of these questions is to understand the other party's views, values and anxieties. A successful negotiator aims for an empathic understanding of the other individual's perspective. Of course, this does not just involve asking questions; active listening, and other skills used in daily practice, form the foundation of successful negotiation.

Interestingly, this aspect of Shell's model is very similar to the Exchange Model of Assessment (Smale *et al.*, 1993, 2000). In this model, the exchange of information between practitioner and service user, or others in the immediate support network, is important in ensuring a shared understanding of issues and differing perspectives. There are obvious parallels with the *collaborative* style of negotiation identified by Shell (2006). He argues that a collaborative style may run the risk of contributing to negotiations getting 'bogged down' in detail and minor disagreement. Interestingly, Smale *et al.* (1993) suggest that practitioners employing the exchange model may use their skills to act in various ways: as an 'honest broker'; to challenge and confront others with their responsibilities; to avoid becoming enmeshed in the problematic relationships that may characterise the client's social situation.

Bargaining

Negotiation is often associated with bargaining and, especially when under pressure of time, there is a tendency to 'get down to business', or 'cut to the chase'. However, Shell (2006) identifies bargaining as only one of a number of stages in the negotiating process; the success of this stage is conditional upon the success of those preceding it. It is argued that too little attention is paid to the exchanging of information. In fact, the model proposes delaying the bargaining stage for as long as possible, to ensure that there has been a comprehensive and effective discussion beforehand. The rationale is that effective information exchange allows the parties to understand each other, identify common ground and values and perhaps allow possible, previously unidentified, options or solutions to emerge.

Arguably, the concept of bargaining suggests the act of reaching compromise, giving something up to secure something else or, to use a less delicate phrase, 'horse trading'. Although this may be acceptable, practitioners need to be aware of the dangers of a form of moral relativism; where everything is open to negotiation. This may not be the case when negotiation compromises service users' rights or where the issue being discussed involves legal duties and responsibilities, for the agency or for the service user.

Closing and commitment

Once an agreement has been reached, mechanisms should be in place to ensure that the parties involved in a negotiation fully understand precisely what has been agreed, and that the record of the agreement and any actions arising from it are unambiguous. However, it is possible for both parties to come away from a negotiation with subtly, and occasionally radically, different interpretations of what was said and agreed. Pressure of time, and possibly the relief at reaching agreement, may result in insufficient attention being paid to accurate phrasing and recording of the nature of the agreement.

ACTIVITY 10.4

Preparation for negotiation is vital. Using another practice experience, reflect upon the people you were negotiating with.

What difference would it have made to know more about who they were and what they wanted?

Comment

We have already noted that the pace of much contemporary social work practice does not appear to lend itself to the development of long-term professional relationships. Consequently it can be difficult to establish the trust that can be the cornerstone of successful negotiation. However, it is probably fair to say that crisis-driven work carries its own momentum, which can make it difficult for the practitioner to slow down, think, prepare and reflect (Gilligan, 2004; Munro, 2011). Nevertheless, it is probably worth remembering that social workers, generally, are skilled at 'putting themselves in others' shoes': empathising with and understanding other people's perspectives. No matter how stressed, or pushed for time, practitioners should arguably allow at least a little time to 'tune in' to the other individual's possible wishes, needs, anxieties and hopes (Woodcock Ross, 2011). Simple preparation such as this is likely to improve the negotiating process and enhance the practitioner's confidence and sense of focus.

Ethical issues and questions for practitioners

When engaged in negotiation activities, practitioners may face a number of ethical questions and dilemmas: they may find themselves caught between the interests of service users and the demands of the organisation; their professional values may be subject to challenge and contradiction, leading to discomfort; they may be left feeling that social work practice is inherently concerned with compromise, ambivalence and doubt.

Bateman (2000) explores the links between negotiation and advocacy and asserts that not all situations are appropriate for negotiation. For example, social workers should not engage in negotiations that diminish service users' rights and legal entitlements. The Health and Care Professions Council's Standards of Performance and Ethics require practitioners to *act in the best interests of service users* (HCPC, 2012, p3). Practitioners could be seen to be in breach of their terms of registration if, for example, they contravened legislation when negotiating reduced levels of support for a service user.

Social work and social care legislation is complex and ambiguous in the way it is often interpreted (Clements and Thompson, 2007). Consequently, there is considerable scope for confusion and misinterpretation on the part of practitioners, local authorities and service users. Practitioners may seek to resort to agency procedure to resolve the questions that legal complexities generate. However, there is no guarantee that these procedures, or at least the interpretation of them at a local level, conform to the requirements of law. Therefore, a practitioner's knowledge of the legal framework in which they operate is essential to ensure that their practice conforms to HCPC requirements. Specifically, it enables practitioners to recognise when the role of acting as a 'go-between' between service users and agencies should not be one of negotiation, but that of advocate. In these circumstances it may be appropriate for the practitioner to cease their own negotiating role and arrange for independent advocacy (Bateman, 2000).

Nevertheless, negotiation on principles of law should not be rejected out of hand when the legal framework allows agencies to exercise discretion in the interpretation of their duties. Practitioners and agencies may interpret their own policies and procedures as absolutes, with little room for discretion (Dustin, 2007; Munro, 2011).

However, these policies are frequently local interpretations of legislation or national policy.

It must be recognised that it can be very difficult and uncomfortable for practitioners to occupy the position of advocate or negotiator on behalf of service users. If the practitioner is in an oppositional role to the demands of their organisation, they can find themselves marginalised and their opinions discounted. Hawkins and Shohet (2007) discuss some of the forms this may take in those organisations which are characterised by an authoritarian or defensive culture. Similarly, they argue that organisations, if primarily concerned with administrative efficiency, often focus on tasks to the exclusion of personal relations. These conclusions correlate with what we know about the implementation of bureaucratic, and specifically computerised, systems within social work (Broadhurst *et al.*, 2010; Munro, 2011). This focus does not just extend to the relationship between the employee and the organisation, but to the way in which work with service users is defined and carried out. Beresford (2008) discusses the way in which social care has become increasingly defined in terms of measurable tasks and outcomes, to the exclusion of process. Yet service users' own definitions of quality in public services highlight the importance of 'how' the work is done, not just 'what' is done. Miller (2012) noted that services frequently confuse output with outcome, meeting the needs of the organisation rather than those with whom they work.

These issues are integral to the ethical basis of negotiation in social care: if the practitioner conceives of themselves primarily as a gatekeeper for scarce resources then they may embark on the negotiating process with a particular, procedural mindset. Specifically, they may pre-empt the outcome of the exchanging of information stage of negotiation by filtering anything that is said by the other party through their internalised and restrictive definition of the agency's eligibility criteria. This procedural approach may be oppressive and severely restrict the opportunity for free discussion and the identification of creative solutions to problems (Thompson, 2000).

CASE STUDY

Danny is a busy hospital-based social worker. He enjoys the work, but finds it difficult to manage his workload. This primarily consists of arranging the discharge of older people. The work is highly pressurised and potentially conflictual: Danny frequently feels that he has to negotiate and mediate between the desires of the ward staff and the needs of older people and their families. He feels under pressure to arrange a quick discharge; yet, he is aware that it can take time to make potentially life-changing decisions. The nature of the work results in Danny not necessarily having time to develop a relationship with the individuals with whom he is working, before he is engaged in negotiating their discharge from hospital. When Danny tries to support service users to take time to reach a decision, he feels that he is criticised by the hospital for working too slowly and for contributing to the 'bed-blocking' crisis.

Comment

The case study illustrates some of the tensions previously discussed. The following research summary highlights some of the wider problems that can arise from the local day-to-day conflicts between the principles of anti-oppressive practice and the organisational pressures of resource constraint.

RESEARCH SUMMARY

Research by CSCI (2004, 2005) explored the process of hospital discharge. The research concluded that the process was largely driven by the need to release beds to allow further admissions. There was some evidence to suggest that patients were pushed into making complex and profoundly important decisions when they were unwell. Similarly, discussions and negotiations often took place in a hospital ward environment where it was difficult to make these decisions; the absence of privacy being not the least of the concerns. Consequently, individuals may have agreed to courses of action which they later regretted; possibly leading to inappropriate admissions to long-term care.

Later research by McLeod et al. (2008) revealed that social care workers had a key role in supporting and negotiating re-engagement with social networks following hospital discharge. These contributed to improvements in physical health and psychological well-being. Effective skills included advocacy, the ability to challenge the restrictive time frames of intermediate care and the provision of sensitive interpersonal interaction.

The Care Quality Commission has recently reviewed the experience of hospital discharge in England (CQC, 2012). The CQC notes that there are increased numbers of people moving from hospital to social care services more quickly, and that these individuals have increasingly complex needs. Although the CQC report does not provide the same level of detail about the patient experience as the CSCI studies, it does reveal that poor discharge arrangements are closely correlated with an increased risk of emergency readmission. In a disturbing parallel with the earlier CSCI studies the Care Quality Commission indicates that poor communication with patients and carers was among the most common concerns along with insufficient planning and incomplete discharge plans (CQC, 2012).

Negotiation in situations of conflict

Negotiating where there is conflict can be particularly stressful and challenging. The work of Ury (1991) provides some useful ideas for those social work practitioners who may be approaching a negotiation with some trepidation. Central to this model is recognition of one's own and others' emotions. Specifically, Ury (1991) suggests that, when confronted by difficult situations, individuals may get angry and strike back, break off the discussion and withdraw, or give in to the other's demands. None of these alternatives is likely to lead to an effective resolution.

163

Ury (1991) cautions against negotiating when angry; his first suggestion is: *Don't react: Go to the balcony.* This requires the negotiator to be aware of themselves, and how they may be perceived; be aware of what makes them angry and attempt to control their own emotional reactions; try and dispassionately observe the other party's tactics and the other party's motivation. Fletcher (1998) identifies that it is easy to mirror aggression with aggression but, as Ury points out, this merely sustains the confrontation. It may also be exactly what the other party wishes; it enables them to deflect attention from the central issue of concern. Consequently, Ury recommends taking time *to go to the balcony*; to pause, take a break, review the discussion and not be pressurised or bullied into making a concession that may be later regretted. These concepts have particular resonance for social work: Ferguson (2005; 2011) illustrates how social workers are often subjected to overt, and sometimes covert, processes of manipulation and intimidation by service users. Without proper space for reflection, these processes may go undetected by the worker, who may agree to courses of action, or inaction, which are placatory but ultimately unsafe .

Ury (1991) is clear that arguments are unproductive, not least because the heightened emotional content of the confrontation is likely to polarise the negotiation into a battle of winning and losing. Individuals are less likely to reach a negotiated agreement if they perceive offering concessions as losing. Consequently, instead of taking an oppositional stance, Ury recommends *stepping to the side.* In essence, Ury recommends those skills that are familiar to social workers: the skills of active listening, to demonstrate your awareness of the other party's point of view, their difficulties and their feelings. Effective negotiators should never be afraid to apologise if appropriate and, as Shell (1999) recommends, ask questions.

Questions are also key to the third element of Ury's model, which focuses on reframing problems or sources of disagreement. Asking 'why' questions helps clarify the other party's interests, and it may be possible to reframe firm positions as aspirations. 'What if' questions help identify possible solutions in a hypothetical way which may not be perceived as a direct challenge to the other party's entrenched position. Underlying this use of questions is Ury's suggestion that solutions to problems can frequently be found by focusing on the shared interests of the parties, rather than on what divides them.

The fourth and fifth elements of the model focus on not backing the other party into a corner. Ury (1991) argues that the negotiator should allow the other party to retreat, make concessions, or reach agreement without losing face. Drawing on the words of an ancient Chinese general, Sun Tzu, Ury suggests that negotiators should not push, but should build their opponent a golden bridge to retreat across. The fifth stage of negotiation comes into play if the other party refuses to reach agreement. Again, Ury cautions against escalation and displays of power: it may be possible to force an agreement, but it is likely to lack the commitment of both parties and may not last.

Ury recommends using questions to ensure that the other party considers what could happen if an agreement is not reached: what will the consequences be?

What will they do? What do they think you will do? Even if it is possible to secure a 'victory', achieving a lasting agreement through negotiation is recommended; this may require assistance from a third party.

CHAPTER SUMMARY

Negotiation is an integral but often underexplored feature of social work practice.

Management and business literature provides a wealth of negotiating models and techniques. However, their application in social work practice may be limited.

Nevertheless, the exploration of models of negotiation does highlight many similarities with accepted good practice in social work; for example, the principles of effective information sharing in negotiation bear many similarities to the key aspects of the Exchange Model of Assessment.

Professional and organisational cultures have a major impact on the autonomy of the practitioner, and the nature of the negotiating relationship with service users and other professionals.

FURTHER READING

Fletcher, K (1998) *Negotiation for health and social service professionals.* London: Jessica Kingsley.
A useful introduction to negotiation in the context of social care.

Hawkins, P and Shohet, R (2006) *Supervision in the helping professions.* 3rd edition. Maidenhead: Open University Press.

This book provides a valuable exploration of negotiation in the area of supervision, with frameworks for considering the issues and improving practice.

Shell, R (2006) *Bargaining for advantage: Negotiating strategies for reasonable people.* New York: Penguin Books.

A good introduction to individual roles and styles in negotiation.

REFERENCES

Bateman, N (2000) *Advocacy skills for health and social care professionals.* 2nd edition. London: Jessica Kingsley.

Beresford, P (2008) Viewpoint: What future for care? *JRF Viewpoint* (September 2008, Ref: 2290).

Beresford, P, Shamash, O, Forrest, V, Turner, M and Branfield, F (2005) *Developing social care: Service users' vision for adult support* (Report of a consultation on the future of adult social care). Adult Services Report 07. London: Social Care Institute for Excellence in association with Shaping Our Lives.

Branfield, F, Beresford, P with Andrews, EJ, Chambers, P, Staddon, P, Wise, G and Williams-Findlay, B (2006) *Making user involvement work: Supporting service user networking and knowledge.* York: Joseph Rowntree Foundation.

Clements, L and Thompson, P (2007) *Community care and the law.* 4th edition. London: Legal Action Group.

Commission for Social Care Inspection (2004) *Leaving hospital – The price of delays.* London: CSCI.

Commission for Social Care Inspection (2005) *Leaving hospital – Revisited.* London: CSCI.

Dale, P, Davies, M, Morrison, T and Waters, J (1986) *Dangerous families: Assessment and treatment of child abuse.* London: Tavistock.

Dustin, D (2007) *The McDonaldization of social work.* Guildford: Ashgate.

Evans, T and Harris, J (2004) Street-level bureaucracy, social work and the (exaggerated) death of discretion. *British Journal of Social Work*, 34, 871–95.

Ferguson, I and Lavalette, M (2004) Beyond power discourse: Alienation and social work. *British Journal of Social Work*, 34 (3), 297–312.

Gabriel, Y (1998) Psychoanalytic contributions to the study of the emotional life of corporations. *Administration and Society*, (30) 3, 291–314.

Gilligan, R (2004) Promoting resilience in child and family social work: Issues for social work practice, education and policy. *Social Work Education*, 23 (1), 93–104.

Gorman, H and Postle, K (2003) *Community care: A distorted vision?* Birmingham: Venture Press.

Jones, C (2001) Voices from the front line: State social workers and New Labour. *British Journal of Social Work*, 31 (4), 547–62.

Kim, H and Stoner, M (2008) Burnout and turnover intention among social workers: Effects of role stress, job autonomy and social support. *Administration in Social Work*, 32 (3), 5–25.

Leece, J and Leece, D (2011) Personalisation: Perceptions of the role of social work in a world of brokers and budgets. *British Journal of Social Work*, 41 (2), 204–23.

Lipsky, M (1980) *Street level bureaucracy: The dilemmas of individuals in public service.* New York: Russell Sage Foundation.

McLeod, E, Bywaters, P, Tanner, D and Hirsch, M (2008) For the sake of their health: Older service users' requirements for social care to facilitate access to social networks following hospital discharge. *British Journal of Social Work*, 38, 73–90.

Manthorpe, J, Moriarty, J, Rapaport, J, Clough, R, Cornes, M, Bright, L, Iliffe, S and OPSRI (2008) There are wonderful social workers, but it's a lottery: Older people's views about social workers. *British Journal of Social Work*, 38, 1132–50.

Miller, E (2012) *Individual outcomes: Getting back to what matters.* Edinburgh: Dunedin.

Newton, J and Browne, L (2008) How fair is fair access to care? *Practice*, 20 (4), 236–49.

Payne, M (2007) Performing as a 'wise person' in social work practice. *Practice*, 19 (2), 85–96.

Postle, K (2002) Between the idea and the reality: Ambiguities and tensions in care managers' work. *British Journal of Social Work*, 32, 335–51.

Smale, G, Tuson, G, Biehal, N and Marsh, P (1993) *Empowerment, Assessment, Care Management and the Skilled Worker.* London: HMSO.

Smale, G, Tuson, G and Statham, D (2000) *Social work and social problems: Working towards social inclusion and social change.* Basingstoke: Macmillan.

Thompson, N (2000) *Understanding social work: Preparing for practice.* Basingstoke: Palgrave.

Trevithick, P (2005) *Social work skills: A practice handbook.* 2nd edition. Maidenhead: Open University Press.

Ury, W (1991) *Getting past no: Negotiating with difficult people.* New York: Bantam Books.

Part 4

Making sense of a complex world

Chapter 11

Applying legislation and policy

Sue Bull

Introduction

The Professional Capabilities Framework highlights the fact that applying law in social work is far more complex than simply knowing the relevant legislation. It is vital that as a social worker you understand how the values and ethics of the profession, the function of your employing organisation, and your role within it, combine to inform and empower you to act in the best interests of your service users and the wider public.

This understanding relies on your ability, on the one hand, to know the principles of the legislative context in which you are working and, on the other, to use your knowledge of the law effectively and ethically on behalf of service users. This includes recognising how and when to seek legal advice; being confident in your professional expertise in your field; and making decisions, with management support, based on this advice. You also need to know how, in turn, to instruct lawyers and inform legal processes. This role may, at times, pose ethical dilemmas or conflicts of interest that test your ability to prioritise the values of the profession.

In this chapter we will explore the key concepts and the skills necessary for judicious application of the legislation. It will focus primarily on the development of the understanding, confidence and attitudes that will stand you in good stead in working within legal processes, both inside and out of the court system.

Definition and explanation of legal skills in social work

It is essential in any social work task to first define your terms. This is crucially important when it comes to the legislation, because how a term is defined can make the difference between a person receiving a service or not. For example, under the current legislation, to be deemed to be a carer, a person must provide 'regular and substantial' care, but what counts as 'regular' or indeed 'substantial' has been the subject of considerable legal debate. In their recent review of adult social care law the Law Commission recommended that:

> The new duty to assess a carer would remove the existing requirement for the carer to be providing a substantial amount of care on a regular basis. In our view, this test is overly complex, subject to a range of different interpretations by local authorities, and creates inefficiency by requiring local authorities to undertake pre-assessments.

> (Spencer-Lane, 2011, p229)

ACTIVITY **11.1**

What do you think are the legal skills required by social workers? List as many as you can.

Comment

In order to be critically competent in applying the law, social workers require the ability to:

articulate legal knowledge, debate the relationship between law and professional practice, share ethical dilemmas and options for their resolution, and explain their decision-making. It includes a commitment to tackling discrimination and oppression alongside individual need, responding to the impact of the law on people's lives, and taking action when the law disadvantages particular social groups.

(Braye and Preston Shoot, 2010, p2)

In other words, legal skills require knowledge and the skilled application of that knowledge. For example, you may know the two-stage test for assessing mental capacity, but applying it, while others are trying to assert their views, can be difficult. It is essential that you are competent in the following areas.

- Understand and apply the values and ethics that social workers must adhere to as registered members of the Health and Care Professionals Council (HCPC).

- Have a basic knowledge of general legislation that may relate particularly to social care work: for example, the Human Rights Act 1998, the Data Protection Act 1998, health and safety legislation, criminal law.

- Have a basic knowledge of legislation that is directly relevant to areas of social work in which you do not practise, for example a social worker in a children and family team should still have an understanding of community care legislation. This includes understanding the key principles underlying legislation; for example, an adult services practitioner should know that the welfare of the child is paramount under the Children Act 1989.

- Have a more detailed knowledge of general legislation that may be particularly associated with your specific service, such as domestic violence.

- Have a detailed knowledge of the legislation pertaining to your role; for example, an approved mental health professional (AMHP) must know how to apply the Mental Health Act 1983 as amended by the Mental Health Act 2007. If they use the legislation incorrectly they may find that they have inadvertently illegally deprived a person of their liberty and could face civil proceedings from the person (AMHPs are personally liable for their actions).

- Understand the relationship between national policy, legislation, local policy and procedures and how these interact and continuously develop.

The related legal skills include the following.

- Knowing how, when and where to acquire further information or advice, particularly within your specific role and agency function.

- Understanding and actively developing your approach to how, why and when the legal system and your agency powers and duties can be helpful to service users.

- Adhering to agency recording policies and being mindful of data protection and information sharing in report writing and other forms of communication.

- Developing skills in your written presentation (see Chapter 3); writing witness statements and reports for legal forums, including private and public family proceedings, mental health tribunals and appeals.

- Developing skills in your public presentation (see Chapter 2) and awareness and clarity regarding your status within the legal and court system: is your role that of advocate, or witness, officer of the court or party to the proceedings, for example, and what are the implications of this? This understanding will help you become confident in your role, knowledge and expertise as a practitioner.

- Becoming confident and effective in your dealings with lawyers. Developing an understanding of how your role differs from that of a lawyer, learning to use their services for advice while retaining your position as the agency representative, and to give instructions. This includes understanding the different roles lawyers themselves may have, particularly within the court setting.

- Developing courtroom skills. Learning how to be effective as not only a witness generally but as a party to the proceedings if acting for your employer, or independent professional (for example, approved mental health professional, children's guardian) and also as an expert witness.

- Keeping up to date with current legal developments and case law in your field, through newsletters, journals and training.

These skills take time and experience to develop. An introduction to and basic understanding of legal systems and legislation will start in your university, but the confidence to apply that knowledge and understand the nuances of its application comes with experience over time. Classroom teaching and practice, even role-play, cannot substitute for learning from standing in the witness box and being cross-examined. Similarly, fully comprehending how the exact interpretation of a particular section of a piece of legislation has been translated into agency procedures requires experience of applying these procedures, and supervision on doing so. Reflection (see Chapter 1), however, enables you to prepare yourself in advance and consider how you have applied the legislation.

Attitudes to legal interventions

Our attitudes and previous experience of the law can significantly enhance or inhibit our approach to how we use it professionally. It is important not only to be aware of what these influences are, but also to realise their impact and the possible need to moderate them.

ACTIVITY **11.2**

Consider the following situation: you are a child and family referral and assessment social worker. As a result of a referral from his school, you have conducted an initial assessment concerning a four-year-old boy, Gary, who has

---

significant learning difficulties and whose 20-year-old single mother lives with him in one room, rented from a friend. Given all the information you have collected, your view is that this is unsuitable accommodation and that, although the child is being well supported through education services, his mother is isolated and struggling to understand or meet his basic needs. You would like to continue working with the family, as you consider Gary to be a child in need (Children Act 1989, Section 17), while you provide a care package to support the family and continue a core assessment. Your manager disagrees and tells you the family does not meet the criteria for social care involvement and suggests you close your involvement.

What are your immediate thoughts on this situation? How might you feel? What would you do?

Comment

You are likely to encounter this sort of situation in any area of practice at one time or another. While every situation needs to be considered individually, how you approach this may depend on your underlying attitude to your legal mandate. The teaching you have received may influence this. Preston-Shoot and McKimm (2012) identify three broad approaches to the teaching of law in social work: a rights-based approach, a technical/rational approach and an ethical approach. Similarly, different orientations that social workers may take to applying the law are described in the Social Care Institute of Excellence (SCIE) e-learning resources, *Law and social work* (2009) as:

- a **technical/rational orientation**: where you base your judgments and intervention on a close attention to the detail, and an up-to-date knowledge, of the law;

- a **needs/procedural orientation**: where you base your actions on understanding and assessing needs, and matching those needs with available resources;

- a **rights orientation**: understanding how the law limits or promotes service users' rights and seeking to justify your interventions on that basis.

Clearly, these different approaches are not mutually exclusive, but are a balance between the potentially conflicting principles of your professional code of conduct, the spirit of the legislation under which you operate, the priorities and policies of your employer and your personal views. The end result will probably be a pragmatic compromise and may not necessarily meet what you, personally or professionally, would choose.

You may need to work to achieve an approach that balances all three orientations. As your experience develops, and the culture of the environment in which you are working exerts an influence, you may find your approach changing. Reflection on what informs and influences your practice is consequently essential for retaining professional autonomy (see Chapter 1).

A further example of how conflicting factors can result in professionally and legally questionable practice is described below.

CASE STUDY

Part 1: (McDonald) v. Royal Borough of Kensington and Chelsea (adapted from Clements, 2011)

The applicant was 67 and a former principal ballerina with the Scottish Ballet. In 1999 (aged 56) she suffered a stroke and subsequently a broken hip which left her with reduced mobility. She was assessed by the council as needing assistance at night to access her commode. Once a community care need of this nature has been assessed as eligible, then domestic law obliges the local authority to meet that need: it is what is known as a 'non-resource-dependent' duty. Assessed community care needs of this kind must be met, regardless of the cost of meeting them.

Although the council provided this support, it decided in 2008 (a decision that coincided with the economic recession) that it could save money by putting the applicant in incontinence pads and on 'special sheeting' at night and sorting her out the next day: effectively withdrawing existing support and requiring her (as Baroness Campbell of Surbiton expressed it) to lie in [her] own urine and faeces. There was, however, a domestic law problem with the council's approach. Elaine McDonald's need was not for incontinence pads (because she was not incontinent): her need was quite different; namely, to access her commode. To address this problem (albeit that nothing had changed) the council undertook a desktop reassessment and redefined her need as a need to be kept safe from falling and injuring herself. Consequently night-time care was not provided.

(adapted from Clements, 2011, p3)

ACTIVITY **11.3**

What are your thoughts about this case? What sort of approach to using the law do you think it reflects (needs-led, rights-led, technical)? How does this decision reflect social work values? Could it be challenged; and under what legislation?

CASE STUDY

Part 2

Elaine McDonald appealed to the Supreme Court. However, the argument that there might be a human rights issue was dismissed. The court cited three European Court of Human Rights disability-related judgments, particularly Sentges v. The Netherlands. Lord Brown observed that one only has to consider the basic facts of those three cases to recognise the hopelessness of the article 8 argument in the present case. *In Sentges the court observed that the national authorities are in a better position to carry out this assessment than an international court. In other words, the Strasbourg Court defers to national courts, which then use that deference as justification for rejecting similar claims.*

(adapted from Clements, 2011, p3)

Comment

As Clements explains, this example vividly illustrates how the law can be used to prioritise agency over individual needs. The argument can legitimately be made that individual needs have to be subsumed by the greater needs of the general public and budget constraints. However, in this case, the local authority appears to have used detailed knowledge of the legislation to undermine the spirit of community care law by using the loophole of reassessment, and to be completely at odds with the personalisation agenda's espoused aims of choice, control and dignity (Mantell and Simonson 2011). The power of the human rights legislation to challenge such decisions is clearly more restricted than it might appear.

Clements goes on to make a case that the rights of people with disabilities are in this sense less than those of prisoners, based on the Napier v. Scottish Minister judgment, where the practice of 'slopping out' in Barlinnie Prison was deemed *to expose the prisoner to conditions of detention which, taken together, were such as to diminish his human dignity and to arouse in him feelings of anxiety, anguish, inferiority and humiliation* (Clements, 2011, p5).

Such ethical conflicts underline the need to reflect deeply on your beliefs and values in your practice.

Understanding and applying the principles of legislation

Whatever your role, it will be guided by some legal mandate or policy that emanates from legislation. Understanding what this is, where it has come from, how it relates to your task and therefore guides your practice, is essential to effective social work. Understanding the key principles of the Children Act 1989, for example, should underpin the work of every practitioner in children and family work.

> ## CASE STUDY
>
> *Jane is 30 and six months pregnant. She and her partner Tom, 35, are both known to have misused a mixture of drugs and alcohol over many years. They have had two children (now aged five and three) removed and adopted due to their drug abuse and resulting lifestyle.*
>
> *A pre-birth child protection conference has agreed that Jane's unborn baby will be made subject to a child protection plan and that a pre-birth assessment should take place. You are allocated the case. The parents say they 'will do anything to keep the baby'. They claim to be drug free. However, you have had difficulty in seeing them so far as they continue to have an erratic lifestyle and live in a squat. You are also aware from health professionals that it is suspected that the couple continue to misuse both alcohol and other substances. There is concern from her GP that Jane's mental health is fragile and that she may not be caring for herself properly. There have also been police reports of domestic abuse over the past year, but no charges have been pursued.*

> ## ACTIVITY 11.4
>
> *Consider how the following principles of the Children Act 1989 could apply to this situation.*
>
> - *Working in partnership (local authorities have a duty to do this, with families and other agencies).*
> - *Providing services for children in need.*
> - *The welfare of the child is paramount.*

Comment

To work in partnership you would need to include the parents and other significant relatives, such as grandparents and other extended family members. Other agencies would include the GP, midwifery, substance misuse services, housing and benefits agencies. You might want to involve family support services, such as children centres, outreach workers and so on. Applying the partnership principle is not just a matter of contacting people, but involves making every effort to do so as creatively and openly as possible in ensuring good practice. Information sharing, for example, can present challenges, and the priorities of differing agencies may require you to be very clear about the risks and need for this to occur, and the legislative mandate behind it.

In respect of providing services, you will need to consider immediate and longer-term support. Financial considerations may challenge your plans and require you to advocate effectively, using the spirit of the legislation to support you. Ethical dilemmas may emerge, particularly where adult and child needs may conflict and you will want to consider how, for example, you interpret the welfare of the child being paramount in real-life situations. While removing the child may ensure their short-term welfare and safety, the distress caused to the parents may have such a deleterious effect on their mental health, potentially increase the risk of substance misuse, and generally have such a harmful impact on them that some agencies might feel this outweighs the short-term benefits, or is indirectly also harmful to the child.

Each situation will differ, but you need to be as inclusive and open to the possibilities as possible. To help you to think in this way, it is useful to ask yourself, and others who know this case, the following questions.

- Who has been involved, accepted and helpful before; how and why?

- Who could support the parents?

- What is known about them already?

- How have they engaged previously?

- What can previous social workers tell you, or previous lawyers?

- What is the way in to working with the family?

Being informed, knowledgeable and authoritative

Student placements are key to learning practice skills and this is as relevant to the understanding and application of law as to any other subject. This can be a neglected area of focus (Preston-Shoot and McKimm, 2012), especially if the service where you are placed is not a front-line child protection or mental health service. It is important that you make the most of any opportunity afforded, and actively seek out others. If you have not already done so, consider trying the following.

ACTIVITY 11.5

Consider what you think to be the key legislation and regulations your placement operate and then ask your supervisor, practice educator and colleagues for their views.

Comment

Being informed and authoritative depends on you taking responsibility for your own development and being proactive in seeking out knowledge and experience. You may feel daunted or uncertain about this, particularly as the language and processes of law can seem remote at first. If so, discuss this with your practice educator, tutor and peers, and ensure that the subject is discussed at any placement meetings. Listed below are some other tasks you can undertake to develop your understanding of the law and how it is applied in your service.

- Find and study any policy and procedure documents relating to your placement and look for the legislation on which they are based. Ask colleagues how this impacts on what they do.

- Discuss in supervision the legislation that relates to every individual case or area of work you are involved in, including any that may have been relevant previously (e.g. a service user who was previously subject to a section under the Mental Health Act but is now a voluntary patient).

- If appropriate, and with guidance, discuss with service users their experiences of the law.

- If you are not working in situations involving legal intervention, ask to read files and shadow workers who are, particularly if they are going out on emergencies or going to present to court.

- Read any literature about the law concerning your client group and bring this to supervision.

- Consult your team and look for recent case law that could be relevant to your service user group. Bring it to team meetings for discussion.

- Bring examples from your placement into university for discussion (bearing in mind issues of confidentiality).

Keeping informed

Think about how, as a matter of everyday practice, you keep informed of current legal and policy developments. To an extent, it is inevitable that we will seek specific information only when we need it. Depending on the organisation you work for, and where it is, you will have differing resources available. Local authorities, and some other organisations, will have legal services that can be used for specific advice. Policies and procedures may be abundant. Day to day you may find yourself relying more on voluntary organisations that specialise in giving advice, such as the Citizens Advice Bureau, Shelter, the Family Rights Group, for up-to-date legal information. You also need to know your local area and who the advisory organisations are that have a presence and can help service users directly.

Internet resources can be particularly convenient and useful for keeping abreast of social-care-related policy and legislation. Whether you are looking up a specific issue, acquainting yourself with a new resource or gaining regular legal updates by electronic newsletters, they are invaluable tools.

The major newspapers and the BBC (Radio 4 especially) all provide accessible and up-to-date sources of news and views concerning social care legislation and policy. They also have website areas devoted to these issues. Some specialist lawyers and law firms maintain websites with extremely useful updates and articles on recent case law as well as more general news. The Joseph Rowntree Foundation is a particularly useful source of social policy research and news.

Working within legal processes and the courts

Depending on your role, you will be likely at some stage, and possibly regularly, to be involved in court-related activity. Even if this is a small or infrequent part of your work, it is one that requires a very professional approach in order to be most effective on behalf of your service users.

ACTIVITY **11.6**

Court work skills

Think about a recent time when you have attended court, in any capacity. If you have never done so, arrange to sit in on a case through placement or as a member of the public. What were your first impressions of being in court? How would you feel being a witness in this situation?

Comment

It is quite likely that you will feel intimidated, out of place and generally uncomfortable when you first attend court. You may not understand what is going on, who all the officials are, or what is happening. You may find yourself sympathising with the defendant, or feeling angry with a pugnacious advocate. As a social worker representing your employer in court, it can be very difficult to assert yourself if you are not sure what is happening. Imagine how much more frightening this can be for service users who, on occasions, have to listen to the intimate matters of their lives being described and discussed in forensic detail. There are a number of pointers for helpful practices that can assist in managing and enhancing court work.

- **Ensure you provide high-quality information** This includes accurate, well-designed, evidence-based reports or statements that follow any agency-specific guidance. Have them proofread and/or peer- or manager-audited against quality standards. If such protocols do not exist in your team, suggest them. Pay attention to detail: spelling, names, dates, etc. Any slight mistake may be leaped upon as evidence of your unreliability.

- **Be well informed** Know your evidence and arguments. Knowledge of your case will not only improve your self-confidence, it will also enhance the impression of expertise you give the court and give more authority to your arguments. If you have any doubts, discuss these in advance with your manager and lawyer. Understand the opposing position. Read all the other evidence and formulate counter-arguments.

- **Ensure professional and mutually respectful relations with your legal representatives** Set up regular and clear channels of communication with any legal representatives (you may be more skilled at this). Be confident about your expertise: do not agree to anything just because your lawyer or the court suggests it. If you have justifiable reason to believe you know better, make sure the court knows. Seek advice, but also be confident in giving instruction to lawyers – use management to support this if necessary. It is likely that you will know and understand more about the situation than they do. Get the best from your lawyer – follow up and check that they understand and are doing what you need.

- **Follow court protocols and practice** At court, be aware that conversations with lawyers or other parties outside the courtroom may be overheard and used. Be on time, dressed appropriately, but comfortably. Remember that the other parties (particularly service users) may be even more nervous than you. Acknowledge them; do not ignore them or see them as adversaries (even though this may be how the court treats you). Understand that the court is a deliberately very formal situation and one in which you may feel disadvantaged by lack of familiarity. The lawyers and other court officers may seem far more relaxed in this environment, but this does not need to detract from your authority.

- **Develop your witnessing skills** Watch and learn how more experienced witnesses deal with court. If possible, once in the witness box, keep eye contact with the judge or magistrates as much as possible. Avoid getting sucked into arguments or battles with the opposing lawyer. Stand with your body facing the bench. Do not rush to answer or be badgered to give a yes or no response. Try to think carefully before answering any question that requires you to give an opinion. Showing the court you are considering carefully what you say is not a weakness.

In summary, if you are the social worker making the application, take charge of the case. You will feel more in control of the situation and confident of yourself if you do so.

Confidence in your arguments and in the evidence supporting them will be enhanced by knowledge of up-to-date research that informs your decisions.

Research in social work law

The following is an example of how research is contributing to the development of legal processes in family law.

CASE STUDY

Ministry of Justice Research Summary 6/11, Outcomes of family justice children's proceedings – A review of the evidence

Key points

Evidence on our key questions was mainly based on studies with small and/or select samples. Taken together, however, they do provide an indication of some key outcomes for children involved in care proceedings and children involved in contact and residence cases.

Public law

The evidence suggests that maltreated and neglected children remaining in care or adopted fared better, at least in the short/medium term, than those returned home. In some cases those children that were returned home faced further maltreatment. Attempting to return children home, although important, has been found to be among the key reasons of delay in care proceedings.

Length of time in finalising care proceedings can limit the options for the child, in particular the chances of being adopted. Other adverse consequences include further parental maltreatment, placement moves, anxiety and distress.

Although many children are eventually placed in the type of placement envisaged in their plan, a substantial minority of care plans are either not achieved or subsequently fail. In particular, care plans to return children home have often proved unsuccessful. Some children go through a number of placement moves and care plans while in care.

Stability of placement is affected by age at entry into care with older children less likely to find stability.

Private law

Residence cases tend to resolve more quickly than contact cases and they tend to be guided by the status quo principle. When there is hostility between parents, contact cases can last longer. Direct contact is eventually granted in most cases.

Both contact and residence disputes tend to be fuelled by underlying issues around financial and housing matters and resentment.

There is a trend for contact to decrease over time. Geographical distance between non-residential parents and children, children's gender, new relationships and children growing up and making new independent arrangements with their parents were all found to affect contact over time.

(Giovannini, 2011, p1)

The above is a summary of a much more detailed report, based on various pieces of research. It is of course helpful to read the whole report to have a more in-depth understanding of the issues and of how the report's authors have interpreted them. You may want to consider particular cases you know of or are working with in the light of this research. This report led to the Family Justice Review (Family Justice Review Panel, 2011), which made various recommendations, and the consultations that followed. The Ministry of Justice is now making plans that would legislate for family proceedings to be dealt with more swiftly. At the point of writing it remains to be seen how far these will be implemented.

Applying legislation effectively is not just about understanding the legislation; you also need to keep abreast of research and know its relevance. This can be challenging in the busy workplace, but is essential to competent social work. It can also be stimulating and potentially time-saving in the longer term.

Managing ethical dilemmas

To end this chapter we will return to thinking about the ethical dilemmas that are part of everyday life in social work. The following extract from *The Independent* cites just one extreme example of the sort of situation you could be involved with.

ACTIVITY **11.7**

Imagine you are a social worker involved with this man.

It is impossible not to be moved by the details of Tony Nicklinson's life, as revealed in the High Court this week. Paralysed by a stroke in 2005, the former businessman is locked inside his malfunctioning body and able to communicate only by blinking. With no hope of release, he wants to take his own life – but is too disabled to do so.

Mr Nicklinson is asking two things of the court. He wants any doctor who enables him to die to be able to cite the common-law defence of 'necessity' if subsequently arrested. And he wants the law forbidding assisted suicide declared incompatible with his rights of autonomy and dignity under the European Convention of Human Rights.

Few lawyers expect him to succeed. But concern at the dangers of a new precedent must come second to the inhumanity of condemning a person to so intolerable an existence. Mr Nicklinson must be allowed to make his choice.

(The Independent, *Wednesday, 20 June 2012*)

Consider the following. Suicide is not illegal: should society discriminate against a person who is disabled by denying them this right? What do you think about The Independent's view? Do you have an instinctive feeling about this situation?

Comment

It is important to consider how you would feel if you were involved with service users, their families or carers in such highly charged and difficult situations. Under what, if any, circumstances might you consider promoting an individual's rights above the existing law?

Such issues raise strong personal emotions, as well as challenging professional, moral and potentially religious principles. Although in this situation it was medical professionals in the front line, social workers can just as easily be confronted with similar situations. Even the legal system can be unclear about how to proceed. Less newsworthy but equally difficult judgments may face you when working with children, young and vulnerable people: disputes concerning the age at which children can consent to medical treatment (controversially, abortion and contraception) but also, for example, blood transfusion, or surgical intervention against the wishes of parents. How would you judge at what age, or stage of development, a child is able to make other decisions, such as with whom they live or have contact? When is a child old enough to be left at home alone? Similar questions, such as those concerning confidentiality and information-sharing against the wishes of a vulnerable person, will regularly give you cause for deep thought, close attention to any agency policy and precedents and, inevitably, your personal views. Balancing the developmental needs of children with their parents' rights to a family life, or the needs of a carer with the wishes of the cared-for person, will test your ability to be impartial.

The SCIE e-learning site identifies the following tensions in how the law may be critically applied within social work. Consider and reflect on these in relation to the above situations.

- **Care versus control** Social workers intervene to provide care or to control behaviour. These are not always alternatives but can be two sides of the same coin: you may be attempting to provide care, but in the process may be constraining freedom.

- **Needs versus resources** Services may be needs- or resources-led. Budgets, policies and attitudes all have an impact on the tension between these approaches.

- **Legalism versus professionalism** The weight given to legal rules as against professional values and knowledge may vary from professional to professional, within teams or agencies.

- **Professional versus partnership** Where the power lies between professionals, service users and carers, and what affects this, is complex and not always transparent.

- **Individual versus collective interests** An individual's rights may be promoted first and foremost, or weighed against the collective interest.

- **Rights versus risks** The law can be used to promote rights or control risks.

- **Autonomy versus protection** An individual's rights may be overruled in order to protect him or her.

Understanding and navigating these tensions, and the questions they raise, has to be considered in relation to making every social care or social work decision, no matter how minor. In that sense, all social work practice is inextricably linked to a legal mandate and principles, even if you are working in a setting that appears to undertake no statutory tasks.

The Professional Capabilities Framework states that you must be able to work within the principles of human and civil rights and equalities legislation, differentiating and beginning to work with absolute, qualified and competing rights and different needs and perspectives. Perhaps what is missing here is an acknowledgement that while understanding and trying to apply these principles is a good start, in reality there is rarely a 'right' answer, or one that satisfies everyone. Practice wisdom may come with experience, but the dilemmas do not get easier: as a newly qualified worker you can only be expected to do your best. This chapter has aimed to provide you with a few suggestions that might help.

CHAPTER SUMMARY

This chapter has explored key concepts and skills in applying law in social work. It focused on the development of understanding, confidence and attitudes inside and out of the court system.

By the time you qualify you will be expected to be an autonomous professional who is able to understand and take responsibility for your own continuous development. Awareness of your approach to the law, and that of your agency, understanding of the principles behind the legislation, and of how your own values can impact on the way in which you exercise the powers and duties conveyed by it, are all required to practise effectively. Being up to date in your knowledge of the law and taking responsibility for this will add to your competence, enhance your confidence and facilitate you to manage the legal and ethical dilemmas that occur in daily social work practice.

FURTHER READING

For more provoking thought on this subject, and to test how you might approach the application of legislation, it's worth exploring the SCIE e-learning materials and particularly the following.

All in a day's work. Available at: www.scie.org.uk/assets/elearning/law/law10/resource/flash/index.htm

The SCIE e-learning law exercise on courtroom skills, available at: www.scie.org.uk/assets/elearning/law/law05/resource/flash/index.htm

REFERENCES

Braye, S and Preston-Shoot, M (2010) *Practising social work law.* 3rd edition. Basingstoke: Palgrave Macmillan.

Clements, L (2011) Disability, dignity and the cri de coeur. *European Human Rights Law Review*, 6, 675–85. Available at: www.Lukeclement.co.uk/resources-index/files/PDF%2001.pdf (accessed 30 June 2013).

Family Justice Review Panel (2011) Final Report. Available from: www.gov.uk/government/publications/family-justice-review-final-report (accessed 21 May 2013).

Giovannini, E (2011) *Outcomes of family justice children's proceedings – A review of the evidence.* London: Ministry of Justice. Available at: www.gov.uk/government/uploads/attachment_data/file/162327/outcomes-family-justice-childrens-proceedings.pdf (accessed 30 June 2013).

Joseph Rowntree Foundation Available at: www.jrf.org.uk (accessed 30 June 2013).

Mantell, A and Simonson, P (2011) Editorial. *Social Care and Neurodisability*, 2 (4), 184.

Preston-Shoot, M and McKimm, J (2012) Tutor and student experiences of teaching and learning law in UK social work education. *Social Work Education*, 31 (7), 896–913.

Social Care Institute of Excellence (2007, updated 2009) e-learning resources *Law and social work.* Available at: www.scie.org.uk/publications/elearning/law/index.asp (accessed 30 June 2013).

Spencer-Lane, T (2011) Legal: The Law Commission's final recommendations for a new adult social care statute. *Social Care and Neurodisability*, 2 (4), 226–33.

The Independent (2012) Editorial: Tony Nicklinson deserves the right to die. Wednesday, 20 June. Available at: www.independent.co.uk/voices/editorials/leading-article-tony-nicklinson-deserves-the-right-to-die-7869901.html (accessed 30 June 2013).

Chapter 12

Assessing need

David Gaylard

Introduction

This chapter critically examine assessment, with a focus on assessing needs (also see Chapter 13, which focuses on assessing risk), one of the core activities undertaken by social workers. It examines what is meant by social work assessment; and the important practice considerations, plus service users' perspectives, will also be highlighted alongside the current legal context of children and adult assessments as well as Law Commission Review of adult social care law for England and Wales.

Important themes as well as of what we ourselves bring to assessments, models of assessment, and the main purposes of adult assessments will be presented. Multi-disciplinary assessments, common assessment dilemmas and dominant theoretical influences upon assessment processes are evaluated alongside the basic principles of effective assessment involving children and young people in need. The chapter concludes with a discussion on how practitioners can demonstrate good assessment skills. Interspersed throughout this chapter are exercises aimed at promoting reflection, individual personal development and self-awareness.

Assessments do not occur within a vacuum and the ability to conduct assessments requires not only knowledge about the assessments process, but also the ability and professional confidence to draw upon a broader repertoire of social work skills and social science knowledge. This includes knowledge regarding the needs of particular user groups and social problems, skills pertaining to related research, critical thinking and interviewing, and cultural competence in terms of diversity and sensitivity.

Social workers must also adhere to the profession's fundamental principles and values, now underpinned by the Health and Care Professions Council (HCPC) Standards of Conduct, Performance and Ethics (HCPC, 2012) and the revised British Association of Social Workers (BASW) Code of Ethics (2012). You will also need to have a clear understanding of the concerns of and restraints upon the other professions with whom you work.

Crucially, assessments require you to gather and analyse information from differing and sometimes competing perspectives. This process is undertaken within the context of recognising your legislative duties, powers and limitations, while steering between competing pressures during a period of austerity that is significantly impacting across both statutory and voluntary social care sectors across the UK and on those who depend upon these services for their continuing independence and well-being.

Defining assessment

There are numerous, often diverse, definitions with regard to what a social work assessment consists of but not one common universal definition. The most helpful definition which captures the frequently contested and complex nature of social work assessment is the one provided by Walker and Beckett (2003, p21)

> Assessment is a purposeful activity. It is the art of managing competing demands and negotiating the best possible outcome. It means steering between the pressures of organisational demands, legislative injunction, limited resources and personal agendas. It includes having the personal integrity to hold to your core values and ethical base whilst being buffeted by strong feelings. An assessment should be part of a perceptual, analytical process that involves selecting, categorising and synthesising data.

As a tutor, team manager and practice educator I sometimes observe students developing a preoccupation with the assessment paperwork. While this is often a valid learning objective that provides a tangible contextual framework of understanding, it may produce an assumption that the assessment process is primarily a bureaucratic one. There may be potentially dangerous practice implications for becoming solely dependent upon the documentation for making a sound assessment. An over-focus on the forms may locate the expertise in a questioning or procedural model of assessment (see models of assessment later in this chapter). However, as the definition above implies, assessment also involves the skilled application of fundamental values of good listening, honesty, trust, sensitivity and empathy. A sense of proportionality and genuine non-judgmental or person-centred approaches are also vital elements of the decision-making process inherent within good assessments.

ACTIVITY **12.1**

Try to recall a situation in which you have been assessed. It can be any experience where your competency has been formally evaluated; for example, a driving or cycling proficiency test, an academic examination, a medical consultation with a doctor, a job interview, a musical audition or artistic presentation, or a practice-based observation. Reflecting upon the experience, ask yourself the following questions.

- *What did the process involve?*
- *How did you feel about this situation before, during and after being assessed?*
- *What key characteristics adopted by your assessor facilitated or perhaps hindered the process?*

Comment

You may have found you were unclear about what was expected of you and what the criteria for the assessments were. This can often leave you feeling anxious, apprehensive, powerless and frustrated even after the assessment and may include anticipation or fear, especially if one is waiting for a swift outcome. Conversely, experiences of disappointment or accomplishment are common once the outcome of an assessment is known. There may be some similarities in the above experiences, common factors or feelings with the experiences of service users when they are the subject of an assessment by a social worker.

It is worth acknowledging that few of us cherish being assessed, so it is sobering to think about what a social worker may represent to some service users e.g. interfering, intrusive, a sense of failure or inability to cope. Thus, clear and concise assessments enable practitioners and service users to share a sound understanding of the purpose, process, nature and extent of professional involvement.

RESEARCH SUMMARY

What do service users want from social workers?

Peter Beresford (a social work academic and former mental health service user) and colleagues (Beresford et al., 2006, 2011) provide a convenient summary of service users' views as to what essential qualities they require in social workers.

Relationships are crucial

Above all else the evidence highlights that service users value the relationship that they have with social workers. It is seen as the crucial starting point for getting help and support on equal terms; for working with rather than on people. Service users talk of relationships based on warmth, empathy, reliability and respect (see Chapter 6). This is the antithesis of form-filling approaches to assessment, which reduce the connection between service users and practitioners to formulaic and bureaucratic contact. It isn't surprising that service users sometimes talk of social work practitioners as 'friends'; not because they confuse the professional relationship they have with them with an informal one, but because they associate it with all the best qualities they hope for from a trusted friend. One of the most important of these qualities is being able to listen to and not judge them. If we do not listen to people we cannot hope to understand their needs.

Good social work is social

Positive social work practice, as its name makes explicit, comes from a social perspective. It is based on seeing people's lives in the round, not just their problems, not just what they can't do, but also what they can do. Service users talk about the strengths of social workers who see them in their community, among their families and friends, and who don't just interpret their problems as their fault – as a matter of individual deficiency or pathology to be blamed – but rather take account of the broader barriers and difficulties they may face.

Support should be practical as well as emotional

Service users particularly value the fact that social workers can offer both practical and emotional support. They bring the qualities of a counsellor alongside the practical skills of a hands-on worker. They know how to navigate the housing and benefits system, fill in forms and sort out practical problems from debt to infestation. But they also offer 'talking therapy' and a shoulder to cry on, and don't treat psychological and emotional difficulties in isolation from people's real worlds. However, the modern history of the helping professions has been to separate practical and emotional support, creating assistant roles to handle more mundane practical tasks. What service users highlight though is that through such mundane tasks they can build the trust and confidence to confide in social workers and be in a position to gain emotional strength from their support.

Rediscover a community-based approach

The rise of 'managerialism' and the adoption of care management have undoubtedly created barriers in the way of social workers in local authorities

(Continued)

189

(Continued)

being able to deliver these qualities with adults. But these aren't inherent problems for statutory social work. After all, local authorities have a strong tradition of encouraging community work, which has supported local neighbourhoods, citizens and service users, and fostered empowerment and anti-discrimination. This approach sometimes means taking social workers' sides against their employers and other state agencies. Despite the challenges this tension poses, this community-oriented tradition needs to be rediscovered and social workers supported to feel that their first loyalty as professionals must always be to the people they work with, not those they work for.

The legal context of adult assessments

All assessment activity is bound by a legal framework so practitioners need to be aware of this when undertaking their roles.

Before a local authority social services department decides whether someone is eligible for social care support, they need to identify an individual's needs, therefore an assessment is required. Assessments of adults are carried out under the legal framework provided by the NHS and Community Care Act 1990, Section 47. Where it appears to a local authority that any person for whom they may provide or arrange for the provision of community care service may be in need of any such services, the authority:

a) shall carry out an assessment of their needs for those services; and

b) having regard to the results of that assessment, shall then decide whether their needs call for the provision by them of any such services.

Local authorities in England and Wales continue to operate under a national eligibility framework, Fair Access to Care Services (FACS), devised by the Department of Health (2002) with updated guidance in 2010. This framework consists of four eligibility bandings (relating to the risks associated with remaining without support); for example, critical, substantial, moderate and low. FACS aims to provide a consistent approach across the UK by helping to address inequalities and discrepancies in funding across the country, sometimes referred to as the 'postcode lottery'. Local authorities are able to determine their own eligibility thresholds in terms of need, services and resources. However, nearly all now operate from a critical or substantial banding as a consequence of austerity cuts to social care budgets.

While the NHS and Community Care Act 1990 currently remains a significant piece of legislation setting out the duties of a local authority social services department to assess individuals who may be in need of services, duties under several other pieces of legislation are also in place.

- **NHS and Community Care Act 1990, Section 47 (2)** If the person is identified as being disabled, that person has additional rights that require a local authority to make a decision as to the services required under Section 4 of the Disabled Persons (Services, Consultation and Representation) Act 1986.

- **Disabled Persons (Services, Consultation and Representation) Act 1986, Section 4** This imposes a duty on a local authority to decide whether the needs of a disabled person call for the provision by the local authority of any services in accordance with Section 2 (1) of the Chronically Sick and Disabled Persons Act 1970.

- **Chronically Sick and Disabled Persons Act 1970, Section 2** This places a duty on local authorities to assess the individual needs of everyone who falls within Section 29 (provision of welfare services for those who are ordinarily resident in their area) of the National Assistance Act 1948.

- **National Assistance Act 1948, Section 29 (1)** To qualify for services under this section, persons must be: aged 18 or over who are blind, deaf or dumb, or who suffer from mental disorder of any description, and other persons aged 18 or over who are substantially and permanently handicapped by illness, injury, congenital deformity or such other disabilities as may be prescribed by the minister.

- **Carers and Disabled Children Act 2000, Section 6** This section provides that a person with parental responsibilities for a disabled child has the right to an assessment from the local authority of their ability to provide and continue to provide care for the child. The local authority must take that assessment into account when deciding what services (if any) to provide under Section 17 of the Children Act 1989.

- **Disabled Persons (Services, Consultation and Representation) Act 1986, Section 8.** Carers also have rights under this section, which requires local authorities to have regard to the ability of the carer to provide or continue to provide care when deciding which services to provide to the disabled person. In these circumstances the assessment of the cared-for person must take account of the carer's situation and record this part of the assessment of the cared-for person. This requirement exists even if the caring role is not of a regular or substantial nature.

Social work practitioners need to ensure that they know what legislation they are acting under before undertaking an assessment. Being clear about the remit of your role is an important aspect of professional, competent practice which ensures that the information you give to service users and carers regarding their rights to assessment is accurate and based within a sound legal framework.

The Law Commission Review of adult social care law for England and Wales

As you can see from the brief legislative framework summary above regarding assessment, adult community care legislation is often incomprehensible and outdated. So the overall aim of the review was to provide a clearer, modern and more cohesive framework for adult social care. To this day it remains a confusing patchwork of conflicting statutes enacted by piecemeal development over a period of 60 years. The scope of some legislation now encompasses outdated definition, language, concepts and expectations. There is no single, modern statute to which practitioners, providers and service users can look to understand whether (and, if so, what kind of) services can or must be provided.

A draft Care and Support Bill implements the Law Commission's recommendations following an extensive consultation. Following the announcement in the Queen's Speech on 9 May 2012, a draft bill on adult social care was made which implements the Law Commission's recommendations and it was issued on 11 July 2012 for pre-legislative scrutiny before the current coalition government introduces a full bill sometime during the 2013 parliamentary timetable. In summary, the draft bill aims to:

- **modernise** care and support law so that the system is built around people's needs and what they want to achieve in their lives;

- **clarify** entitlements to care and support to give people a better understanding of what is on offer, help them plan for the future and ensure they know where to go for help when they need it;

- **support** the broader needs of local communities as a whole, by giving them access to information and advice, and promoting prevention and earlier intervention to reduce dependency, rather than just meeting existing needs;

- **simplify** the care and support system and processes to provide the freedom and flexibility needed by local authorities and care professionals to innovate and achieve better results for people; and

- **consolidate** existing legislation, replacing law in a dozen Acts which date back to the 1940s with a single, clear statute, supported by new regulations and a single bank of statutory guidance.

What do you bring to an assessment?

Who we are has a big impact upon the professional relationships we have; for example, what you bring with you to an assessment and how you carry it out. So both our personal and evolving professional identities are based upon such features as our gender, ethnicity, class, moral or political belief systems. Some of these are more important than others, and may be dependent upon the context, but both personal and professional identity is something we need to be mindful of when undertaking assessment work. We cannot stop being ourselves, but we can adapt and monitor our weak spots by becoming more self-aware; by confronting our fears and prejudices, or the gaps in our skills or knowledge, and recognising how they affect us when we are embarking upon assessments. Therefore, utilising good supervision to aid reflective practice, professional understanding and personal development remains crucial.

Models of assessment

It is important to remember that gathering data essentially involves conversations so, fundamentally, assessments remain a human interaction. Invariably, people will say different things depending upon who is speaking to them, in what context and in what way. We do not reveal all of ourselves to everyone and what we choose to divulge depends very much upon our perceptions of the individual to whom we are talking.

Assessment involves a range of activities in which social workers, service users and carers attempt to describe, explain, predict, evaluate and sometimes prescribe. Smale and Tuson (1993) identified three different models of assessment which still remain closely linked to social work practice in terms of assessing risk, resources and needs.

- **Procedural model** In this model of assessment the social worker fulfils the agency's functions by gathering information to see whether the individual 'fits' defined eligibility criteria for service. Often little professional discretion or judgment is required as checklists may also be used, e.g. a traditional care management or task-centred approach.

- **Questioning model** The practitioner holds the expertise, follows a format of questions, listens to and processes the answers. This process primarily reflects the social worker agenda in which the gathered data is shaped to fit the practitioner's theories regarding the nature of people, e.g. a psychodynamic approach.

- **Exchange model** In this model all users are viewed as experts on their own problems, therefore greater emphasis is placed upon exchanging information. The social worker 'tracks' what other people are saying rather than placing interpretations on what they think is meant. The practitioner works in collaborative partnership to identify how the service user may mobilise either internal or external resources in order to achieve their desired outcomes defined in their own their terms, e.g. a strength-based or solution-focused approach.

ACTIVITY 12.2

Selecting your model of assessment

- *Can you reflect upon a placement scenario in which you combined elements of all three assessment models?*
- *Which model do you tend to use in your current practice context?*
- *Which model do you feel most comfortable working with? Why might this be?*

Comment

The procedural model is frequently adopted during times of austerity when public services are subject to rationing. If one adopts a purely procedural approach
it could be experienced as officious, cold or even alienating, especially if a 'tick-
box' style of assessment is adopted when asking probing personal questions.
Professional ethical tensions will always exist when demands for scarce resources
exceed supply, resulting in needs-led versus resource-led assessment dilemmas.

A questioning model tends to place the practitioner 'in charge' as they ask the
questions while the service user answers them. Therefore, a questioning model is
most likely to be used when risk factors provide the emphasis of the assessment
or when it includes a substantial *procedural* element, such as interviewing prospective foster carers or adoptive parents. The questioning and procedural models are often found in combination.

The exchange model is often cited as the most desirable model assessment of
choice. Routine service-led assessments are the antithesis of an empowering
approach to assessment and care management (Smale, 1994). The exchange
model comes nearest to meeting a needs-led assessment. However, inviting service users to be experts on their own lives and equal participants in the assessment process is often not entirely straightforward. There can be a tendency,
when acknowledging the expertise of service users, to overestimate their ability
to identify solutions to their problems. In addition, difficulties can arise when
practitioners deny or fail to acknowledge their own professional expertise. In
developing collaborative partnerships it is important that practitioners do not
underestimate their professional perspective and the expertise they bring to the
assessment process. Baldwin and Walker (2005, p43) acknowledge this dilemma.

> A partnership approach can recognise an individual's rights to autonomy, safety,
> inclusion and having their voice heard without denying power differentials,

Why assessment?

Undertaking something new or starting a task for the first time can often be
challenging and so can sometimes generate some level of anxiety or doubt.
Wilson *et al.* (2008, p268) provide a useful summary of key questions practitioners
should contemplate before embarking upon assessments.

- What am I trying to achieve and where do I begin?

- What information is pertinent, why, and according to whom?

- Whose views do I incorporate?

- How do I make sense of, interpret and most accurately record and represent
  the information gathered?

It is also vitally important before embarking upon an assessment that you are
clear about your precise role, the purpose and goal of the assessment and what

your approach may be. Sometimes a rushed, poorly planned assessment may make you unsure about why the assessment is being done, for whom, and for what purpose. If this situation arises it may become confusing for both service user and practitioner, resulting in an inaccurate assessment and poorly informed decision-making and outcomes. Table 12.1 captures the main purposes and related roles in relation to adult assessments.

Table 12.1 The main purposes of adult assessments (adapted from Whittington, 2007, p25)

Why are you there?	What is your role?
Individual and public protection	Risk assessor or evaluator role
Service user and carer needs	'Traditional' professional role
Service user and carer representation	Advocacy role
Agency function, policy and priorities	Agency representative function
Other professional or agency	Proxy (e.g. providing information about a service user to facilitate decisions made by others)

Assessment of children in need

Unlike assessing the needs of adults, the needs of children are primarily covered under s17, the Children Act 1989 (see also Chapter 11). All children and young people are different and have different needs. Similarly, a family's ability to respond to and meet all of their needs may also differ. In some circumstances, professional assessment may be required to identify strengths and needs, to ensure that all children, young people and their families receive appropriate support. Assessment can be defined as a systematic process of gathering a range of information relating to a child, to help identify their strengths and needs, in order to decide on appropriate further action (or to confirm that no additional help is required). Assessment can provide a baseline of information against which a child or young person's future development can be measured. The information may be gathered from a wide range of sources.

Basic principles of effective assessment

The purpose of effective assessment is:

- to gather information;
- to identify strengths;
- to identify needs;
- to inform action.

Assessment should follow the non-deficit model or strengths/needs model, where focus is placed on a child or young person's strengths and needs, rather than their weaknesses, which has been shown to lead to more positive outcomes. However, issues and problems also need to be considered. The assessment process should be a positive experience and practitioners should work with a child or young person, their parents/carers and other agencies, to gather information to establish the issues that need to be addressed and assess the most suitable response (Department for Children, Schools and Families, 2006).

Children who are defined as in need under Section 17 of the Children Act (1989) are those whose vulnerability is such that they are unlikely to reach or maintain a satisfactory level of health and development, or their health and development will be significantly impaired, without the provision of services, and/or the child is disabled.

The *Framework for assessment of children in need and their families* states that:

> the critical factors to be taken into account in deciding whether a child is in need under the Children Act 1989 are what will happen to a child's health and development without services. Determining who is in need, what those needs are, and how services will have an effect on outcomes for children requires professional judgement by social services staff together with colleagues from other professional disciplines.

(Department of Health, 2000, p 5)

The Children Act (1989) clearly sets out the responsibilities of the local authority with regard to children in need.

> It shall be the general duty of every Local Authority to safeguard and promote the welfare of children within their area who are in need; and so far as is consistent with that duty, to promote the upbringing of such children by their families, by providing a range and level of services appropriate to those children's needs.

The *Framework for the assessment of children in need and their families* (DoH, 2000) provides a pictorial representation to assist social workers in exploring the key areas of need for children and their families (see Figure 12.1).

This assessment tool has remained unchanged as the principle guiding tool when exploring the needs of children under s17. However, in addition to using this tool, social workers must also consider the following as underpinning key principles to ensure that the needs of children and their families are accurately assessed.

- All assessments are child-centred.

- They are rooted in child development.

- They are ecological in their approach.

- They ensure equality of opportunity.

- They involve working with children *and* families.

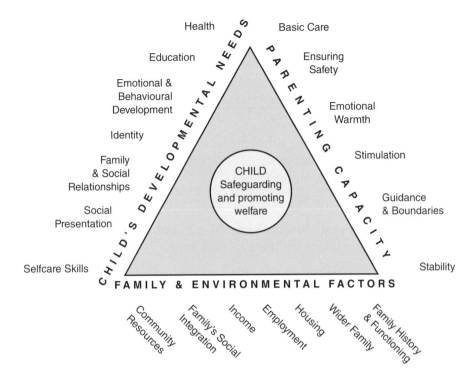

Figure 12.1 The framework for the assessment of children in need and their families (DoH, 2000)

- They build on strengths as well as identify difficulties.

- There is an inter-agency approach to assessment and provision of services.

- Assessment is a continuing process not a single event.

- Assessment is grounded in evidence-based knowledge.

Multi-disciplinary assessments

Due to the nature of collaborative social work practice – for example, safeguarding children and adults at risk, NHS continuing health care, mental capacity tests – social workers inevitably request, build upon or contribute to other professionals' assessments, such as occupational functioning or physiotherapy mobility assessments, district nurse or dietician evaluations, clinical psychologist or community psychiatric nurse assessments. It does sometimes feel as if people with different job titles find it difficult to trust each other's professional judgment (especially when this is associated with risk management), so can find it difficult to work together constructively in service users' best interests. So how can cultural or occupational barriers to collaborative assessments be resolved? Whittington (2007, p40) suggests some key good practice guidance (also see Chapter 8).

- Remember that assessment is a key skill in other professionals allied to social work, so never underestimate your colleagues.

- Confront your own prejudices (in terms of medical model expectations). How may some medical staff adopt a more holistic (as opposed to a narrow, purely medical) perspective? If you have grudges against certain individuals you must try to resolve these.

- Think about what prejudices other professionals involved might have – how much do they trust your assessment? How could you help them develop their trust in you and your professional role?

- Seek out other professionals' specific areas of expertise and utilise them.

- Have confidence in your own professional role and be clear about what your distinct contribution is to a multi-disciplinary team.

- Remember that you are all there for the same reasons; focus upon positive service user outcomes.

Common assessment dilemmas

Wilson *et al.* (2011) identify four key dilemmas frequently encountered when undertaking assessments.

Assessment: a one-off event or an ongoing process?

One of the limitations of some assessment models is the propensity to present assessments as a linear process with each stage neatly following a set sequence resulting in a definite outcome. However, in the real world of social work practice the assessment process may often be convoluted, relevant to a specific context, time and relationship in which it was procured. The linear assessment model still appears to have a dominant influence over official guidelines and prescriptive procedural formats, which tend to oversimplify the ambiguities, complexities and uncertainties of operational practice. Assessments need to be seen as integral components to social work intervention from beginning to end. It is often argued that assessments are a never-ending process, an integral part of planning, interviewing and reviewing involvement with service users. So assessments need to be understood as a dynamic process, as opposed to one-off events, to ensure they remain relevant for the service user concerned.

Objectivity versus subjectivity (understanding 'the self' and others)

This relates to whether there is a definitive assessment outcome, a 'truth', or whether assessments should be approached as a negotiated process which involves the practitioner and service user constructing 'a truth' relevant to that unique situation. Linked to the art–science debate is the question of whether it is possible to undertake objective assessments. The more scientifically orientated, checklist-informed approach suggests that it is. Increasingly, however, acknowledgement is being given to the unavoidable subjectivity built into assessment processes (Milner and O'Byrne, 2009). A clear implication of adopting a relationship-based perspective on assessments is the potential for an assessment to contain subjective bias or error. If this is recognised as an integral, unavoidable component of the assessment process it need not be a problem and can be used to engage more openly and honestly with the individuals concerned.

Commencing an assessment relationship requires practitioners to resist assuming that an individual will conform to a service user label or stereotype, such as an elderly man with limited mobility; or that an individual's needs can be predetermined by criteria that have been recorded on the referral form – for example, a single parent on benefit, a person leaving care, a person with schizophrenia. Each referral needs to be unique as each individual will experience their particular difficulties uniquely. This is important when referrals are received from service users with whom social work departments are familiar. Previous involvement with service users can, on occasions, unhelpfully influence how new assessments are undertaken. Accurate, non-judgmental recording is central to avoid such issues.

Risk-focused versus holistic assessments

A particular challenge arising from the wider political influences that shape the nature of the assessment process is the tension between narrowly defined assessments that focus exclusively on risk and those that attempt to retain a broader, person-centred brief and include risk as one aspect of the assessment process. A comprehensive assessment requires practitioners to weigh up the risks, needs and resource implications of a particular situation. Difficulties arise from the pervasive preoccupation with risk in contemporary society, which is responsible for two distinct characteristics of current practice. These are:

(a) an unrealistic search for absolute truths and definitive, right interventions;

(b) a blame culture which constrains creative or effective professional practice.

The fear of being accused of having misjudged or wrongly assessed a situation or of getting it wrong causes practitioners to operate defensive practices and so to err on the side of caution. Practice of this nature fails to consider fully the implications, risks and potential benefits of the decision reached and actions taken; for example, deciding to remove an adult at risk from an abusing situation is not a risk-free decision. The potential harm that could arise from an alternative (but inappropriate) placement has to be balanced against the risk of leaving the adult in the abusing situation. An integral feature of a constructed collaborative model of assessment is the need to define risk in conjunction with service user(s) alongside your professional assessment of need and risk, research evidence and resources. Reductionist definitions of risk often equate it with danger and seek its elimination. More helpful understandings, by adopting a more person-centred approach, relate it to individual uncertainty, risk management while balancing risk factors with supported decision-making, risk enablement processes, safety and protective factors (Sanderson and Lewis, 2012).

Collaborative partnership versus expert professional

When embarking upon a new assessment it is important that practitioners acknowledge that both they and service users probably hold preconceived ideas about what the assessment may entail and what the desirable outcome may be. Upon your first meeting it may be helpful for these preformed ideas to be discussed, enabling the assessment process to commence from both a shared understanding and baseline. It can be hard to agree on what is an acceptable starting point but it will at least ensure that a transparent approach is being implemented from the start and unreasonable expectations are acknowledged and addressed at the outset.

Theories behind assessments

Students frequently struggle with the concept of social work theory. The truth is that there is no such thing as one definitive social work theory, if what one means by theory is a body of knowledge which serves the same role for social work as, say, medical science does for the practice of medicine.

Current social work education promotes an eclectic approach to theoretical teaching, requiring practitioners to draw upon elements from different practice methods according to the context and individuals involved; combining whatever seems the best or most useful rather than following a single theoretical approach. Many competent practitioners invariably adopt an eclectic approach, often at an unconscious level.

By promoting a mixed bag of ideas or explanatory models, social work invariably draws from psychology (e.g. *attachment theory*), sometimes working models developed by therapists (e.g. humanistic , psychodynamic or cognitive behavioural therapies), or from within social work itself (e.g. *task-centred practice*). Some of these ideas are more akin to belief systems or value positions (e.g. *empowerment*); or generalisations about society derived from academic disciplines such as sociology; or political stances adopted by activists (e.g. *social model of disability, radical or feminist social work, anti-oppressive practice*). They are then lumped together as 'theory'. Eclecticism can also aid practitioners to challenge or complement theoretical approaches.

Despite social work education promoting the value of eclecticism, students often still struggle to attempt to shoehorn real-life practice placement experiences into one or other of these social work theories, sometimes wondering whether it is really necessary at all. But as Beckett (2010, p39) stresses, *the fact is, though, you simply cannot do a meaningful assessment without resource to some kind of theory.*

Theories behind assessment

Consider the following case example of Chantelle and Declan.

You are a second-year student social worker (in a voluntary sector placement) based within a busy inner city children and families centre. Chantelle is a 24-year-old single mother who refers herself because she feels unable to cope with the destructive, aggressive behaviour of Declan, her five-year-old son, and thinks he needs to 'come into care' for a while in order to calm him down and to teach him a lesson. You're the family centre duty worker this week.

Think of five key questions you may want to ask Chantelle, then take a piece of paper and draw a line down the centre. In the left-hand column, write down these questions. Having written your five key questions, now reflect upon why you asked these specific questions and write down your answers in the right-hand column.

Comment

Whatever you have written in the right-hand column constitutes some form of formal or informal 'theory'. You may not be able to give it a distinct name but it represents your immediate thinking behind your choice of question(s). As social workers we have no business asking any question at all if we are unable to give a reason for it. None of us would like to be asked a set of random questions by a professional who had no idea what the purpose of those questions was. This does not just apply to your choice of questions. In order to explain the decisions you make at every stage of the assessment – decisions in weighing the data, the way you analyse the data – you would have to come up with 'theory'.

As Beckett (2010, p41) highlights, *assessment is not simply about the facts – it is always an 'interpretation' of those facts.* So as a professional you should be able to be explicit as to what the theory is and spell out the reasons why you think your theory makes sense, based upon evidence or research. How you carry out an assessment is shaped by theoretical assumptions; this is true whether or not you are consciously using named theories of the kind found in books, or simply applying your own personal theoretical framework. Some examples of different approaches are explained below.

- If you adopt a more **psychodynamic** approach or a personal perspective influenced or akin to psychodynamic theory, you are more likely to ask a lot of questions about Chantelle's early history on the basis that early history is a major factor in the 'here and now'.

- Alternatively, you may take a **behavioural** approach (consciously or not), in which there will be less emphasis on the past but more emphasis on the detail of Chantelle's present circumstances because this theory suggests that any behaviour which persists must be being reinforced in some way in the present.

- If you adopted a **task-centred** approach you may want to identify key problems (identified by Chantelle) and then work with her on prioritising them and developing strategies to address them in order.

- If you took a **strengths-based** or **solution-focused** approach you might avoid too much emphasis on problems and want to explore with Chantelle her successes in dealing with problems.

- If you're interested in a **family systems** perspective you may want to look at patterns of interactions that take place within Chantelle's wider family, as much as at what each individual family member says or does.

- Finally, if you tend to have a more **political** perspective you may be inclined to look more at service users' external circumstances: neighbourhood, financial situation, the messages they are given by the rest of society. So you may be inclined to view Chantelle's difficulties as a consequence of her oppression, poverty, discrimination, or gender power imbalances rather than personal problems. You may perhaps adopt more feminist, anti-oppressive or radical social work approaches to your assessment focus and interventions with Chantelle.

(adapted from Beckett, 2010, pp40–41)

Good assessment management skills

Espinal-Roberts (2012, p16) summarises key fundamental considerations or 'good manners' in terms of how practitioners may actually demonstrate respect for services users and carers when undertaking assessments. It is not simply a matter of efficient form filling in of the questions asked but also how you manage the assessment.

Negotiate the timing of your visit Ideally timings should be negotiated rather than imposed. Unannounced visits are rare (unless required for legitimate safeguarding concerns). Occasionally, early-morning visits may be required if service users have known substance dependency or mental health patterns.

Consider the length of the assessment Do consider the usefulness of a lengthy, prolonged assessment visit in terms of both you and service users' concentration and how this might affect the quality of answers. Does it really have to be done in one sitting? Assessments must be proportionate; are the scale and depth proportionate to the needs? Take time checks as you go along; it's your role to set reasonable limits.

Consider the location of the assessment Assessments are frequently undertaken in all sorts of locations, such as an office setting, a hospital ward, a care home, a noisy and chaotic front room. So try to forward plan by considering factors like privacy, soundproofing, interruptions and personal safety.

Establish the purpose of your visit As indicated earlier in this chapter, although you may know you need to complete an assessment of need, does the service user or carer have the same understanding? Try to conceptualise your key questions and give reasons as to why certain (more probing) questions are being asked.

Generate a sense of trust and friendliness As identified by the service user research summary, these characteristics are of crucial importance to the social work relationship. We may work with individuals for months or years, or perhaps see them only once or twice. So we need to establish a proportionate sense of trust by, for example, being courteous, capable, friendly, sensitive, knowledge-able, and by acting with integrity. Punctuality, reliability and appearance are also important factors to consider when establishing or maintaining an ongoing pro-fessional working relationship.

Listen properly and show interest As practitioners undertaking assessments we really need to listen and be receptive to everything that is being said. Facilita-tive listening is what you should be aiming for (to understand fully and help the other person to be able to say what they want to say). Listen to the individual's narrative, for the kind of language used, including images and descriptions, may reveal personal strengths that you can pick up on, as opposed to focusing solely on problem-based talk.

Record what you are hearing Capturing what people say is no mean feat. Although it may often seem awkward, making a record of conversations does mean that you are getting as close as you can to what the person is actually say-ing. Some practitioners fill in assessments at the time; others take concise notes then write them up afterwards. But with the development of self-assessment the notion is moving towards needs being 'self-' rather than 'professionally defined', offering opportunities for greater lateral thinking and assessment creativity on behalf of service users and practitioners.

Outline what will happen next It is always important to summarise (or recap) key assessment areas explored: areas of agreement, uncertainty, disagreement, or needs that may require further or specialist assessment. Outlining what will happen next at the end of an assessment is important as this often reduces fear, anxiety and uncertainty, and prevents the emergence of individual priorities, mis-understandings or prejudices.

CHAPTER SUMMARY

This chapter has presented an overview of the topic of assessing need. Good assessment remains the cornerstone of good social work (McDonald, 2006). Therefore, this chapter supports the notion that effective social work assessments should be grounded in

(Continued)

203

(Continued)

knowledge, i.e. theory, research findings and practice experience in which confidence can be placed to assist in the gathering of information, its analysis and the choice of intervention in formulating a plan. To be effective and empowering (see Chapter 5) it is an activity which needs to be done with rather than to people.

As is the case when assessing risk (see Chapter 13), assessing needs is not simply a discrete skill, but requires the effective application and combination of the skills covered in the other chapters within this book. Self-presentation, good communication and skills in engaging are necessary to be able to establish a relationship. Reflection is necessary to reduce subjectivity and to keep focused on empowering practice. Collaborative and group working are crucial to gathering information and effectively acting on the assessment, and this in turn is formulated through negotiation and decision-making, informed by the legislative remit in which you are working. Accurately recorded assessments require good written skills; and achieving all of this within the time pressures that invariably apply requires good self-management.

FURTHER READING

Beckett, C (2010) *Assessment and intervention in social work – Preparing for practice.* London: Sage.

A well-crafted, highly recommended text for students and practice educators. Full of excellent reflective activities and case studies supported by insightful chapters covering assessment, intervention, judgment, need, risk, change and evaluation.

Espinal-Roberts, E (2012) *Assessment in social work with adults.* Maidenhead: Open University Press/McGraw Hill Education.

An excellent, concise pocket guide for both students and practitioners which will assist you in making more effective, person-centred assessments. Full of invaluable advice, tips and practice illustrations.

Koprowska, J (2010) *Communication and interpersonal skills in social work.* 3rd edition. Exeter: Learning Matters.

This third edition enables the reader to develop a flexible and responsive approach to communicating with a diverse range of people. The author critically explores in accessible detail all approaches to communication, paying particular attention to children, young people, adults and families.

Martin, R (2010) *Social work assessment.* Exeter: Learning Matters.

An engaging text covering definitions, key skills and values underpinning assessments plus applied chapters on risk, children and adult service community care assessments.

Milner, J and O' Byrne, P (2009) *Assessment in social work.* 3rd edition. Basingstoke: Palgrave.

An accessible generic text on social work assessment which focuses upon anti-oppressive practice.

USEFUL WEBSITES

www.scie.org.uk **The** Social Care Institute for Excellence currently provides an excellent online e-learning resource entitled *Gathering information*, aimed at assisting practitioners to assess and gather information from service users and carers of all ages.

REFERENCES

Baldwin, N and Walker, L (2005) Assessment. In Adams, R, Dominelli, L and Payne, M (eds) *Social work futures: Crossing boundaries, transforming practice.* Basingstoke; Palgrave Macmillan.

Beckett, C (2010) *Assessment and intervention in social work – Preparing for practice.* London: Sage.

Beresford, P, Lesley, A and Croft, S (2006) *Palliative care, social work and service users: Making life possible.* London: Jessica Kingsley.

Beresford, P, Fleming, J, Glynn, M, Bewley, C, Croft, S, Branfield, F and Postle, K (2011) *Supporting people: Towards a person-centred approach.* Bristol: Policy Press.

British Association of Social Workers (2012) *The code of ethics for social work, statement of principles.* Birmingham: BASW.

Department for Children, Schools and Families (2006) *An introduction to assessment, to support the CAF training: A handbook to support practitioners.* London: DCSF.

Department for Education and Skills (2004) *Every child matters.* London: The Stationery Office.

Department of Health (2000) *Framework for the assessment of children in need and their families.* London: The Stationery Office.

Department of Health (2002) *Fair access to care services: Guidance on eligibility criteria for adult social care.* LAC (2002) 13. London.

Espinal-Roberts, E (2012) *Assessment in social work with adults.* Maidenhead: Open University Press/McGraw Hill Education.

Health and Care Professions Council (2012) *Standards of conduct, performance and ethics.* London: HCPC.

McDonald, A (2006) *Understanding community care: A guide for social workers.* 2nd edition. Basingstoke: Palgrave Macmillan.

Milner, J and O' Byrne, P (2009) *Assessment in social work.* 3rd edition. Basingstoke: Palgrave Macmillan.

Saleebey, D (2012) *The strengths perspective in social work practice.* 6th edition. Harlow: Pearson.

Sanderson, H and Lewis, J (2012) *A practical guide to delivering personalisation: Person-centred practice in health and social care.* London: Jessica Kingsley.

Smale, G (1994) *Negotiating care in the community.* London: HMSO/NISW.

Smale, G and Tuson, G (1993) *Empowerment, assessment, care management and the skilled worker.* London: HMSO/NISW.

Walker, S and Beckett, C (2003) *Social work assessment and intervention.* Lyme Regis: Russell House Publishing.

Whittington, C (2007) *Assessment in social work: A guide for learning and teaching.* London: SCIE.

Wilson, K, Ruch, G, Lymbery, M, Cooper, A (2008) *Social work: An introduction to contemporary practice.* Harlow: Pearson Longman.

Wilson, K, Ruch, G, Lymbery, M and Cooper, A (2011) *Social work: An introduction to contemporary practice.* 2nd edition. Harlow: Pearson Longman.

Chapter 13

Skills in working with risk

Chris Smethurst, Jenny Robson and Viv Killner

ACHIEVING A SOCIAL WORK DEGREE

This chapter will help you to develop the following capabilities from the **Professional Capabilities Framework**.

- **Diversity.** Recognise diversity and apply anti-discriminatory and anti-oppressive principles in practice.
- **Knowledge.** Apply knowledge of social sciences, law and social work practice theory
- **Critical reflection and analysis.** Apply critical reflection and analysis to inform and provide a rationale for professional decision-making.
- **Intervention and skills.** Use judgment and authority to intervene with individuals, families and communities to promote independence, provide support and prevent harm, neglect and abuse.
- **Contexts and organisations.** Engage with, inform, and adapt to changing contexts that shape practice. Operate effectively within your own organisational frameworks and contribute to the development of services and organisations. Operate effectively within multi-agency and inter-professional settings.

It will also introduce you to the following standards as set out in the 2008 social work subject benchmark statement.

5.5.4 Intervention and evaluation
5.6 Communication

Introduction

Risk, risk assessment and risk management are arguably the primary preoccupation of social workers and certainly of their managers in most organisations. When assessing need (see Chapter 12) in these financially straitened times, it is invariably the degree of risk entailed that is the key determinant of resource allocation. This chapter will explore what is meant by risk, its impact on social work practice, and the skills social workers require to assess and work with risk.

It is a cliché that risk is an inevitable feature of everyday life. Probably, from an early age, readers will have been made familiar with the possibility that at any time they could *leave the house and be knocked down by a bus*. This overused phrase is revealing because, at a very basic level at least, human beings are made aware of the potential for random misfortune; the early origins of the word *accident* derive from the notion of an unforeseen event. It is interesting that, until recent times, *risk* was also typically understood in terms of chance and random fate (Kemshall, 2002).

It would perhaps be reasonable to assume that social work should be understood within a context of uncertainty; that the 'real world' of practice is characterised by events that are not always easy to predict (Webb, 2006). Predictability is made easier when events (or people) follow prescribed, linear pathways of cause and effect. Social work practitioners will know that this is rarely the case and that the complex inter-relationship of changing factors in an individual's life can indeed lead to unforeseen consequences.

Predictability is further enhanced when it is possible to discern patterns of cause and effect from the behaviour and characteristics of large numbers of people. The use of *probability* to calculate insurance risk relies on the ability to make generalisations from statistical evidence. Consequently insurance companies may, for example, conclude that young male drivers are statistically more likely to have a car accident than older, female ones. However, that does not mean that a specific young man is more likely to have an accident than a specific young woman. Consequently, the EU has recently banned this discrimination, with the consequence that the cost of women's insurance has now gone up (Bachelor, 2012).

ACTIVITY 13.1

What risk factors do you most associate with child abuse?

If some or all of those factors are present should a child be removed?

Comment

The Centre for Disease Control and Prevention (2012, online) in the United States lists individual risk factors for abuse which can be summarised as follows.

- The child being under four years old and/or having special needs, which increase the burden of care of the parent(s) or guardian.

- Parents' lack of understanding of children's needs, child development and parenting skills.

- Parent having experienced abuse in their childhood.

- Substance abuse and/or mental health issues.

- Parental characteristics such as young age, low education, single parenthood, large number of dependent children, and low income.

- Non-biological parents, transient partners in the home.

- Parental thoughts and emotions that tend to support or justify abusive behaviours.

The CDCP (2012, online) also identified familial risk factors such as social isolation, domestic violence, negative interactions, family disorganisation and stress. At a wider level they highlight the significance of factors like high unemployment, poverty, residential instability and violence in the community.

Putting aside the problems of applying statistics from one country to another, consider again the question: *If some or all of those factors are present should a child be removed?* If all children, where these factors were present, were removed it is clear that many children would be removed who had not been abused, nor would be abused. The statistics do not suggest an *inevitability* that in homes where the risk factors are present abuse *will* occur. This would assume that the risk factors in some way pre-programme the behaviour of parents or other care givers. This is simply not the case; therefore draconian, pre-emptive intervention would be highly questionable in terms of the principles of natural justice and, of course, ethical social work practice.

In addition, the CDCP (2012) statistics do not take into account the impact of protective factors, such as early childhood services, and safer neighbourhoods (Parton, 2006). Sinclair (1997, cited in Parton, 2006) likened childhood to a game of *snakes and ladders*, with the role of preventative services to be to remove or ameliorate the effects of the *snakes*.

The notion of probability, when applied in a social work context, is often problematic, with the often heard accusations that social workers are either *overzealous* or tardy in their responses to potential risks. These apparently diametrically opposite responses are perhaps less puzzling when viewed in the context of the difficulties of assessing probability.

Munro (2011) demonstrates that in social work practitioners are often attempting to predict events that have severe consequences, but are statistically very rare. Similarly, social workers are frequently making judgments in fast-changing situations, with confusing, contradictory, or at least partial, information. Titterton (2005) notes that inquiries following child deaths can often assume an inevitability of cause and effect. A similar phenomenon has been identified in relation to mental health practice: a belief that what is obvious with the benefit of hindsight should have been similarly evident at the time that risks were being assessed (Szmukler, 2000).

There are further elements to consider when discussing how social workers understand and respond to risk: the psychological and emotional aspects of working with risk; and the influence of societal attitudes to particular risks, and to social work itself.

Risk, social work and society

Social workers will be familiar with the idea of *positive risk taking*: an understanding that life necessarily involves risk and that risk taking is an inevitable and desirable feature of human growth and development (see Chapter 5).

ACTIVITY 13.2

Consider activities that you did as a child – did you have more or less freedom than your parents at a similar age?

Think of your own children if you have them, or the children of other people you know. Do they have more or less freedom than you did?

Comment

Ferguson (2011) noted that in 1971 eight in every ten children went to school on their own, but this figure had dropped to less than one in ten by 1990. At an instinctive level we are aware that it is impossible to insulate ourselves and others from all potential harm; indeed, the overprotective parent or restrictive health and safety regulations are familiar, and sometimes ridiculed, features of British popular culture. However, these stereotypes do not evolve in a vacuum and are perhaps windows to underlying societal attitudes and beliefs about risk; attitudes and beliefs that may permeate policy and practice, or at least unconsciously influence individual practitioners.

Alberg *et al*. (1996, p9) provide the following definition of risk: *The possibility of beneficial and harmful outcomes and the likelihood of their occurrence in a stated timescale.* This quote incorporates an acknowledgement that risk can lead to positive as well as negative outcomes. However, there is evidence that risk in everyday social work is more likely to be characterised as *risk-of-bads, and specifically extreme bads* (Macdonald and Macdonald, 2010, p1174).

Furthermore, social workers' experiences of working with risk may be underpinned by anxiety: the fear of blame. The psychological effects of working with risk are beyond the scope of this chapter; however, it is evident that practitioner anxiety may be heightened by unforgiving societal attitudes to the consequences of error (Furedi, 2002; Munro, 2011).

We have established that risk assessments are of necessity characterised by some degree of uncertainty. However, society often assumes that every possibility should be predicted and that blame can be attributed to every accident (Douglas, 2003; Munro, 2011).

It has been argued that a societal preoccupation with blame – what we might term a *blame culture* – has inevitably encouraged defensive, *safety-first* approaches to risk (Furedi, 2002; Munro, 2011). Research by Stanford (2010) reveals that social workers sometimes struggle with balancing the knowledge that social work clients may be at risk, a potential risk to others, but also a risk to social workers themselves. The idea that social workers may be at risk does not just relate to the potential for physical harm or intimidation – although this is an increasingly acknowledged problem in social work (Ferguson, 2011). Social workers are also at risk from the consequences of errors of judgment (see Chapter 14) and their inability to predict every potential contingency from a course of action. It is arguably the case that social workers are required to follow potentially conflicting imperatives: empowering and person-centred practice may be difficult to reconcile with societal demands that social workers should predict, and intervene to prevent, any potential harm to service users or others (Smethurst *et al.*, 2012).

The following sections of this chapter will explore how practitioners reconcile the conflicting demands of social work, by focusing on the specific practices of social work with adults and children and families respectively.

Social work with adults

An unintended consequence of exploring risk assessment in adults' and children's services as distinct and isolated entities is that the similarities may be lost in the attention to their differences. However, readers of this chapter are probably familiar with the fact that one of the key differences between social work with adults and with children and families is a distinct legal and policy framework. Whereas the legislation related to social work with children is primarily covered in the Children Act 1989 and the Children Act 2004, adult social care legislation has developed in a more piecemeal fashion; successive layers of sometimes contradictory legislation building up a framework that still incorporates the National Assistance Act from 1948. At the time of writing this chapter there is a draft bill to modernise adult care and support in England before Parliament. This aims to replace no fewer than 12 different Acts (Department of Health, 2012, online). Until the new legislation is passed, practitioners continue to have to navigate a complex, and sometimes contradictory, legal and policy framework (see Chapter 12).

For local authorities the requirement for the assessment of adults who may have community care needs is set out in s47 (1) of the NHS and Community Care Act 1990. The Department of Health's (2010) *Prioritising need in the context of putting people first: A whole system approach to eligibility for social care, England* has statutory guidance that describes how adults' services must determine their eligibility threshold from four band levels: 'critical', 'substantial', 'moderate' and 'low'. The guidance highlights the need to assess the 'severity' of the presenting risk or risks – whether immediate in nature, fluctuating or over a longer-term period. This means the ability to assess risk is as important as the ability to assess needs.

In practice this means that 'risk' and 'need' have become largely inseparable, both as a means of allocating resources and in the mental frame of reference of practitioners conducting assessments. This is of course contentious and its implications will be explored in the next section.

The principles of risk assessment with adults

The resource base for adult social care has consistently been outpaced by demand for services (Lymbery, 2010). Consequently, publicly funded support has effectively been rationed, with assessment of risk becoming a gatekeeping activity where 'risk' has supplanted 'need' as the means of determining eligibility for support (Kemshall, 2002; Ray *et al.*, 2009; Webb, 2006). It is argued that this can provide a perverse incentive to define service users as being 'at risk' in order to gain access to resources (Ray *et al.*, 2009). However, there is a further complication: that service users may well be 'in need' but that the risk may be assessed as being insufficient to cross the threshold of eligibility for services. Birmingham City Council, faced with a massive cut in its funding, decided to revise its eligibility criteria so that support would only be given to those with critical needs (the highest banding under the Fair Access to Care Guidance 2011). This was successfully challenged under the Disability Discrimination Act 1995 (now Equality Act 2010, Section 149): it was deemed that the council had not sufficiently taken into account the impact upon disabled people nor tried to ameliorate that impact (R(W) v. Birmingham CC 2011). Despite this ruling the shift in eligibility criteria, to focus services on those with substantial or critical needs, appears to be becoming more common across English local authorities.

CASE STUDY

In the case of Elaine McDonald (R v. Royal Borough of Kensington ex parte McDonald [2011] UKSC) (see Chapter 11), she initially received support from a care worker to use a commode at night, but after reviewing her care the council offered incontinence pads instead. Mrs McDonald won a legal action on the basis that the council was not meeting its assessment of her needs. However, the council subsequently reassessed her and redefined her need as to urinate safely. She subsequently lost her case at the Supreme Court, who considered the incontinence pads as a reasonable means to meet her needs taking into account the council's resources (Thornton, 2011).

Comment

Such creative bureaucratic approaches may meet the financial imperatives of an organisation but miss the point of the intervention. Arguably, one of the risks for practitioners and service users is that the priority of saving money trumps other considerations. This can perhaps be seen within the context of a wider problem, where organisations and practitioners become inward-looking; meeting the needs of the organisation rather than of the service user. One manifestation of this behaviour may occur where practitioners adopt defensive, risk-averse practice. This can stem from paternalism, or from the individual and/or organisation seeking to avoid any action that may expose the agency or the practitioner to blame.

A distinction needs to be made between defensive practice and defendable practice, where risks may still be taken, but with a clear rationale behind them. Kemshall (1998, 2002) states that the core components of a defendable risk assessment decision need to make certain that reasonable steps have been taken to ensure the following:

- Reliable assessment methods have been used.

- Information is collected and thoroughly evaluated.

- Decisions are recorded.

- Staff work within agency policies and procedures.

- Staff communicate with others and seek information they do not have.

Within this concept practitioners also need to consider and evidence the following:

- Who does the risk involve: the individual; the carer; the wider community; the referrer; the assessor?

- Is it a chosen risk or is it imposed by a situation or others?

- What is the nature of the risk: physical, sexual, psychological, emotional, financial, neglect, institutional, discriminatory or a combination?

- What is the likelihood of the risk occurring on a scale between minimal and inevitable? Show your evidence for this decision.

- What options are available in relation to the risk: taking the risk or not taking it? Are the options proportionate to the actual level of risk? What alternative courses of action could be considered?

- What values are attached to each option? If positive – how important? If negative – how serious?

- And, finally, what is the balance for and against the risk being taken?

> (taken and adapted from the seven-stage approach: Gaylard, 2011, p63)

CASE STUDY

Mr Stevens is 80 years old. He lives in his own flat and receives personal care on a daily basis. He has failing eyesight and a number of medical conditions that can contribute to dizziness and loss of balance. He has recently had some falls which have left him shaken and with some minor injuries. Because of this his relatives have been pressing his social worker to increase his amount of personal care. However, the social worker has concluded that additional support will do nothing to alleviate the risk of falling. The relatives have been angered by what they see as the social worker's lack of concern.

Comment

The case study is indicative of situations where the call to 'do something' may come from others who have understandable concerns. However, it is not necessarily the case that proposed solutions always alleviate the problem. In the case study additional support may have provided the relatives with a sense of reassurance, but it is unlikely that Mr Stevens would be any less at risk of falling.

The potential for heavy-handed intervention is arguably increased by the societal construction of older people as 'vulnerable'. Vulnerability is a contentious concept, as a person's vulnerability is often caused by their environment and individuals within it. As with all social work practice, context is everything (Mowlam *et al.*, 2007). Referring to a person as 'vulnerable' risks pathologising them (Gaylard, 2011). Consequently, the term 'vulnerable adult' has been replaced by 'adult at risk' in revised multi-agency safeguarding adults policy and procedures (ADSS, 2010).

Empowerment, mental capacity and decision-making

Perhaps the greatest distinction in assessing risk with adults and children centred on the issue of informed decision-making. While social workers aim to empower all service users to have their views heard, for children and adults who lack capacity others have to act in their best interests. Difficulties arise in terms of the age at which young people can make decisions for themselves. The current situation regarding young people is slightly confusing. Children under 16 can give consent for treatment in their own right, provided that they have achieved significant understanding and intelligence to enable them to understand what is proposed (Gillick v. West Norfolk and Wisbech Area Health Authority 1985). Those who are 16 and 17 can consent to treatment but, until the Mental Health Act 2007, parents could overrule a 16- or 17-year-old person's refusal of admission or treatment for a mental disorder (Dimond, 2008). Even now the High Court can act in their *best interest* to overrule their wishes if they refuse life-sustaining treatment, which is why you have to be over 18 to be able to make an *advance decision to refuse treatment* (Mantell, 2011).

When discussing mental capacity it is essential to bear in mind that this relates to a person's capacity to make a specific decision at a specific time. For adults in England and Wales there is a two-stage test of capacity.

1. *The diagnostic test – does the person have an impairment of the mind or brain, or is there some other sort of disturbance affecting the way their mind works?*

2. *The functional test – does that impairment or disturbance mean that the person is unable to make the decision in question at the time it needs to be made?*

(Mantell, 2011, p51)

The function test is determined by a four-stage test.

1. *Does the person have a general understanding of what decision they need to make and why they need to make it?*

2. *Does the person have a general understanding of the likely consequences of making or not making the decision?*

3. *Is the person able to understand, retain, use and weigh up the information relevant to this decision?*

4. *Can the person communicate their decision?*

(Mantell, 2011, p52).

There are five guiding principles to the Act, which are aimed at empowering people to be heard, but also protecting those who lack capacity. However, what may seem like straightforward principles can become less so when assessing risk in the complexities of people's lives.

- *A person must be assumed to have capacity unless it is established that they lack capacity* (Mental Capacity Act 2005, Section 1(2)). This principle guards against the frequent mistake in the past, where whole groups of people were assumed not to have capacity to make any decisions because of, for example, learning difficulty or dementia. A common error is that practitioners just focus on the first part of that statement, *A person must be assumed to have capacity,* and consequently assume capacity. However, they then do not assess for capacity when there are grounds to do so and consequently leave people at great risk (Mantell *et al.*, 2013).

- *A person is not to be treated as unable to make a decision unless all practicable steps to help him to do so have been taken without success* (MCA 2005, Section 1(3)). It is beholden on social workers to ensure they are sufficiently familiar with various ways of communicating with people, such as using alphabet boards, light writers, etc., and to draw on the expertise of others to assist them in that communication. However, they must also be cautious of relying on others; not only can this lead to unintentional or deliberate miscommunication, but a person may be susceptible to their influence, which can make a person who is normally capable of making a decision experience situational incapacity (SA [2006] EWHC 2942 (Fam)).

- *A person is not to be treated as unable to make a decision merely because he makes an unwise decision* (MCA 2005, section 1(4)). We all make unwise decisions at times and would be outraged if that was viewed as evidence that we lack capacity. However, practitioners may experience situations where there is evidence of consistently unwise decision-making and may question whether this is indicative of lack of capacity. Bennett (2010) argues that considering *best interests*, when assessing, enables the consideration of a much broader context in relation to the individual than the mental capacity test which focuses on a specific issue at a specific time. This can be particularly important where a person is at risk of abuse (Mantell, 2011). However, care needs to be taken not to inadvertently breach the other principles of the Act (Mantell, 2011).

- *An act done, or a decision made, under this Act for or on behalf of a person who lacks capacity must be done, or made in his best interests* (MCA 2005, section1(5)). This means taking into account all relevant circumstances, including the person's past and present wishes, beliefs and values and the views of those who are close to them.

In addition, every effort must be made to encourage and enable the person to take part in making a decision.

- *Before the act is done, or the decision is made, regard must be had to whether the purpose for which it is needed can be as effectively achieved in a way that is less restrictive of the person's rights or freedom of action* (MCA 2005, section 1(6)). When acting to reduce the risk of harm to a person, we must always bear in mind the impact we are having on the person's life. The opportunity costs for the individual of our actions can be considerable – our actions may well make a person physically safe but impact negatively on their quality of life, to the detriment of their psychological well-being.

Personalisation and risk

The personalisation agenda is perhaps the greatest opportunity for empowering people to have control and choices over how they are supported to live their lives (Carr, 2010). The personal budget, a stream of social services funding delivered through self-directed support, is a programme developed by In Control (Duffy, 2011). Under self-directed support the person self-assesses their needs, then a resource allocation system is used to determine their personal budget and the person develops a plan to meet their needs. This personal budget may be provided through direct payment; indirect payment (direct to 'suitable person' or Trust); brokered payment (a broker who manages the payment and arranges the services); individual service fund (money provided to a specific service); or care managed (after Close, 2009). In practice, delivery has been more successful with some groups, such as those with physical disabilities, than, for example, those with dementia (Kinnaird, 2010).

ACTIVITY **13.3**

Why do you think the uptake by people with dementia has been so low?

Comment

Moore and Jones (2012) have argued that practitioners have not been promoting self-directed support in the mistaken assumption that people with dementia do not have the interest or ability to go through the process. Likewise they found that people with dementia and their families also had similar concerns that the process would be too complicated and bureaucratic (Moore and Jones, 2012). Lightfoot in 2010 (cited in Moore and Jones, 2012) found that some practitioners were not aware that if a person lacked capacity to manage their budget a suitable person such as a family member could be appointed. Arguably these examples illustrate risk-averse behaviour by practitioners; risk-averse behaviour that is informed by incorrect information or stereotypical assumptions about people with dementia.

The benefits of personal budgets, particularly in terms of the flexibility that they can offer, can be significant in situations where needs may change rapidly and crises occur. However, they are also beneficial in terms of ensuring that people who are attending to your intimate personal care are people you choose. As a family carer for someone with dementia told Moore and Jones (2012, p73): *I now have control over who comes through my door.* In terms of risk factors and individuals' well-being, surely that should not be too much to ask?

Social work with children

Working with children and families is a complex and challenging task. The role of the social worker is one of negotiator and intermediary, continually balancing the competing needs of protecting children from harm, working in partnership with families and ever-increasing demands on diminishing resources.

However, a comprehensive legislative and policy framework provides clear guidance around the duties and responsibilities of both social workers and local authorities to enable the identification, assessment and protection of children at risk of harm.

All children require some level of intervention in their lives. The majority of children will only require access to universal services such as education, health, libraries, and leisure centres but there are a small number who will require the intervention of statutory services to ensure they are able to achieve their full potential without risk of harm.

The three key areas for assessment for children requiring statutory intervention are:

- Common Assessment Framework (CAF);
- Children in need (also known as Section 17 or CIN);
- Child protection or children at risk of significant harm (also known as Section 47).

Common Assessment Framework

The Common Assessment Framework (CAF) was developed by the Children's Workforce Development Council and Department for Education as part of the *Every child matters: Change for children* programme (2003). The purpose of CAF is to assist in the early identification of a child's additional needs and promote a co-ordinated provision of services to meet those needs. Guidance has been provided with key expectations for workers but each local authority has developed its own interpretation of this guidance. Given that any professional working with a child can be the lead professional for a CAF assessment there is a wide interpretation of this guidance.

A CAF is designed to be used when:

- a practitioner is worried about how well a child or young person is progressing (e.g. concerns about their health, development, welfare, behaviour, progress in learning or any other aspect of their well-being);

- a child or young person, or their parent/carer, raises a concern with a practitioner;

- a child's or young person's needs are unclear, or broader than the practitioner's service can address.

The process is entirely voluntary and informed consent is mandatory, so families do not have to engage and if they do so they can choose what information they want to share.

The CAF process is not a 'referral' process but a 'request for services'.

The CAF is part of a wider programme to provide early intervention and improve on multi-agency working. The CAF will provide a more standardised approach to assessing and responding to a child's and family's needs in a more co-ordinated manner.

The process includes the early identification of a child's need that requires a co-ordinated multi-agency response; an assessment that draws information together from all those involved, including the views of the child and family; a team around the child (TAC) planning process that draws those involved around the family to agree a plan aimed at achieving change and specific outcomes; a review process that measures the change achieved against the outcomes set; an ending of the process when outcomes are achieved or a co-ordinated response is no longer needed.

It is of note that a CAF assessment does not include any component to specifically address risk for workers. When risk of harm to a child is identified, intervention by social care is then required, either through a Section 17 child in need assessment (see Chapter 12) or a section 47 Child Protection assessment (both under the Children Act 1989).

Assessment of children at risk, or likely risk of harm (section 47)

The Children Act 1989 introduced significant harm as the threshold that justifies compulsory intervention in family life in the best interests of children. Significant harm is any physical, sexual, or emotional abuse, neglect, accident or injury that is sufficiently serious to adversely affect progress and enjoyment of life.

Harm is defined as the ill-treatment or impairment of health and development. This definition was clarified in section 120 of the Adoption and Children Act 2002 so that it may include, *impairment suffered from seeing or hearing the ill-treatment of another.* This would therefore include a child who witnessed domestic violence towards their mother, for example.

There are no absolute criteria on which to rely when judging what constitutes significant harm. Sometimes a single violent episode may constitute significant harm but more often it is an accumulation of significant events, both acute and long-standing, which interrupt, damage or change the child's development.

The duty of the local authority is set out in the Children Act (1989), section 47 as follows.

Where a Local Authority –

a) are informed that a child who lives, or is found in their area –

>*i) is the subject of an emergency protection order*
>*ii) is in police protection; or*

b) have reasonable cause to suspect that a child who lives, or is found in their area is suffering, or is likely to suffer significant harm, the Authority shall make, or cause to be made, such enquiries as they consider necessary to enable them to decide whether they should take any action to safeguard or promote the child's welfare.

Section 47 of the Children Act (1989) also places a duty on education departments, housing departments, any health service and police to assist the local authority with their enquiries (see Chapter 8 on collaborative working), legally enabling the sharing of information about a child and their family without parental consent.

Governing principles for all assessments of children

Regardless of the type of assessment being undertaken, there are key skills and standards that should be at the forefront of every social worker's thinking when working with children and families.

- Listening – without trivialising or being dismissive of issues raised.
- Regular and predictable contact with children and their families.
- Being non-judgmental.
- Being honest and open.
- Clear and accurate recording (consider that each assessment is a legal document).
- Working in partnership with children, their families and other professionals to ensure effective relationships.
- Talking and non-verbally communicating with children to ensure that, regardless of age, their views and feelings are represented throughout the assessment.
- Being able to recognise strengths and protective factors within families.

- Ensuring that decision-making and analysis are evidence-based.

- There should be an assessment of risk in each and every case.

Risk assessment

None of the assessment tools or assessment guidance, set out in law or policy, include a specific risk assessment. Assessment of risk, or potential risk, is absolutely essential when considering a child's needs and there are many different risk assessment tools to assist social workers in addressing this. Risk assessment tools do not provide firm predictions but do enable an identification of the most vulnerable children and likely risk indicators (Hart cited in Horwath, 2001).

As stated above, when considering risk to children this must also be balanced with recognition of the strengths and protective factors within a child's life, be it from within their family, immediate or wider, or their wider social environment. For example, using a parental mental health diagnosis as a risk indicator, an assessment might state: *Mother has a diagnosis of schizophrenia*. Statements like this, where a parent is labelled by a diagnosis, can imply risk and a negative presentation: *there is a clear danger of setting up stereotypical expectations which have profoundly negative and discriminatory implications* (Thompson, 1993, p144).

ACTIVITY 13.4

Taking the example above of the mother who is diagnosed with schizophrenia, how would you record this information in an assessment?

Comment

To provide a clear picture of both risks and strengths, it would be good practice to expand on the initial statement, for example: *Mother has a mental health diagnosis of schizophrenia that is stable and well managed and with continued monitoring by professionals is unlikely to impact on mother's ability to recognise and meet the needs of her unborn child*. By presenting the risk indicator as a label and single statement, judgments and decisions could have been made leading to unnecessary interventions for the child.

The same kinds of dangers around assumed risk can be found within assessments regarding substance misuse. A study by Chaffin *et al.* (1996) stated that parental substance misuse is the single most common predictor of child abuses of various kinds and can triple the risk of maltreatment. Conversely, a study by Forrester in 2000 showed that workers were making uninformed judgments about parental drug use. Drug use was automatically seen to be placing a child at risk regardless of pattern, frequency and type of use or support systems available. These contrary statements only serve to increase the uncertainty for professionals when identifying potential risk of harm and increase anxiety around whether risks can be safely managed.

One assessment tool that can assist the worker in identifying actual risk, potential risk and strengths within a family is Brearley's (1982) model of risk assessment. The following case study illustrates the application of Brearley's model.

CASE STUDY

Ms Jones is a prescription methadone user and is currently 18 weeks pregnant. She relapsed and took street heroin in the first six weeks of pregnancy and suddenly withdrew herself from methadone during her second trimester. The drug and alcohol team are very concerned about the potential risks when the child is born. Ms Jones's family live in another part of the country and she has no familial support locally. Ms Jones has talked about feeling depressed and lonely. She has told her midwife that her partner and the father of her child, Mr Wagner, can be very aggressive and that she has heard from other people that he can be violent. Ms Jones has said she thinks this might be worse when Mr Wagner has been drinking.

ACTIVITY 13.5

- *What are the immediately identifiable dangers?*
- *What are the hazards, both situational and predisposing, within this case study?*
- *What could the potential strengths be to alleviate some of the identified hazards?*

Comment

The case study is typical of the referrals encountered by children and families social workers. It is easy to view situations such as these in terms of a list of concerns, each one appearing to amplify the other. Social workers may become overwhelmed, particularly if the anxieties of others act to further amplify the original concerns. In addition, social workers may be working under considerable pressure, both in terms of workload and through working with uncertainty and partial information. Consequently, it may be helpful to untangle the complexities of a case using a diagram to work through the issues (see Table 13.1). This can help clarity of thinking and decision-making, but also help identify any missing elements that are needed to ensure that a robust assessment is made. It is also worth noting that it is essential to interrogate the elements of the assessment to be certain that what is written is supported by the available evidence. Social workers and other practitioners can fall into the trap of making assumptions upon faulty evidence. For example, practitioners can sometimes confuse a parent's love and willingness to care for a child with their *ability* to do so (Barber, 2005; Cousins, 2005).

This model not only identifies risks but specifically enables the social worker to identify strengths and protective factors within a family and also their wider

Table 13.1 Example of using Brearley's (1982) model of risk assessment for this case study

Dangers	Predisposing hazards	Situational hazards	Strengths
Neglect of the baby	Mother's substance misuse	High needs of a new baby, particularly if baby suffering withdrawal	Mother's commitment to withdrawal programme
Emotional harm to the baby	Mother's lack of self-esteem	Risk of relapse when mother under increased pressure with a new child	Planned baby
Physical harm to the baby	Mother's depression		Parents in stable relationship for five years
	Little familial support due to location		Parents' engagement with professionals
	Father's previous history of violence; last conviction ten years ago		Parents' acceptance of concerns
	Father's previous misuse of alcohol		

needs. The model also provides a pictorial representation of the risks and strengths within a family, enabling the social worker to have a simple table of indicators that can be completed with the family. According to Taylor *et al.* (1994, p38): *a view which includes strengths as well as areas for growth helps the client and family to feel positive about the prospects.*

A critique of this model, and all models of risk assessment, is that they are static and provide a snapshot of the immediate circumstances with little scope as an ongoing reference point when working with families. However, as Munro (2008) recognises, if the practitioner completing the tool accepts the fallibility of risk assessment tools and the inexact science of prediction of risk, it enables them to use the tool as a measure of change and a device for the continual review of risk of harm.

The simplicity and breadth of the Brearley (1982) model allows for this to be an aid and not a dictation or definite prediction of risk. It is not a certain representation of what will happen but it is an indicator of risks and strengths that contribute to an ongoing process of effective care planning and consequently better outcomes for children.

CHAPTER SUMMARY

The chapter has explored how risk is a defining feature of contemporary social work practice. The differing legal and policy frameworks for adults' and children's services have been explored within the context of societal constructions of risk and the extent to which these inform practice. It is evident that practitioners cannot divorce their own practice from wider societal and organisational imperatives. However, social workers need to be aware that these imperatives may challenge, or contradict, principles of good social work practice. Both Webb (2006) and Calder (2008) promote the use of any risk assessment tool, but as an aid to professional judgment and not to dictate decision making.

FURTHER READING

Brearley, CP (1982) *Risk and social work.* London: Routledge and Kegan Paul.

A classic text exploring the issues around risk, but do read it in conjunction with some more contemporary texts.

Stanford, SN (2010) 'Speaking back' to fear: Responding to the moral dilemmas of risk in social work practice. *British Journal of Social Work*, 40 (4), 1065–80.

Explores the broader contexts that shape the climate in which social workers assess risk.

Webb, S (2006) *Social work in a risk society.* Basingstoke: Palgrave Macmillan.

A comprehensive discussion around the construction of risk and a 'risk society'.

REFERENCES

Alberg, C, Hatfield, B, and Huxley, P (1996) *Learning materials on mental health. Risk assessment.* Manchester: University of Manchester.

Association of Directors of Social Services (2010) *Safeguarding adults: A national framework of standards for good practice and outcomes in adult protection work.* Available at: www.adass.org.uk/images/stories/Safeguarding%20Adults/SAFEGUARDING%20 ADULTS%20pdf.pdf (accessed 24 February 2013).

Bachelor, L (2012) Car insurance: Black box that's young female drivers' accessory of choice. *The Observer*, 16 December 2012 (online). Available at: www.guardian.co.uk/money/2012/ dec/17/car-insurance-female-drivers (accessed 22 February 2013).

Barber, N (2005) Risking optimism: Practitioner adaptations of strengths-based practice in child protection work. *Child Abuse Protection Newsletter,* 13(2),10–15.

Bennett, J (2010) Assessing mental capacity. *Social care and neurodisability*, 1(3), 44–8.

Brearley, CP (1982) *Risk and social work.* London: Routledge and Kegan Paul.

Calder, M (2008) *Contemporary risk assessment in safeguarding children.* Russell House: Lyme Regis.

Calder, M and Hackett, S (2003) *Assessment in child care – Using and developing frameworks in practice.* Lyme Regis: Russell House.

Carr, S (2010) *Personalisation: A rough guide*, Second revised edition. London: Social Care Institute for Excellence.

Chaffin, M, Kelleher, K and Hollenberg, J (1996) Onset of physical abuse and neglect: Psychiatric, substance abuse and social factors from prospective community data. *Child Abuse and Neglect,* 20 (3).

Cousins, C (2005) But the parent is trying: The dilemmas workers face when children are at risk from parental substance use, *Child Abuse Prevention Newsletter* 13(1), 3–6.

Department for Education and Skills (2006) *Every child matters – Working together to safeguard children.* London: The Stationery Office.

Department of Health (2000) *Framework for the assessment of children in need and their families.* London: The Stationery Office.

Department of Health (2010) *A vision for adult social care: Capable Communities and Active Citizens.* Available at: http: //www.dh.gov.uk/prod_consum_dh/groups/dh_ digitalassets/@dh/@en/@ps/documents/digitalasset/dh_121971.pdf (accessed 7 September 2011).

Department of Health (2012) *Draft bill to modernise adult care and support in England included in Queen's Speech.* Available at: www.dh.gov.uk/health/2012/05/draftadultcarebill/ (accessed 22 February 2013).

Dimond, B C (2008) *Legal aspects of mental capacity,* Oxford: Blackwell.

Douglas, M (2003) *Risk and blame: Essays in cultural theory, Volume 12.* London: Routledge.

Duffy, S (2011) *A fair society and the limits of personalisation.* Sheffield: The Centre for Welfare Reform.

Ferguson, H (2011) *Child protection practice.* London: Palgrave Macmillan.

Forrester, D (2000) Parental substance misuse and child protection in a British sample: A survey of the children on the child protection register in an inner London district office. *Child abuse review,* 9 (4), 235–46.

Furedi, F (2002) *Culture of fear: Risk taking and the morality of low expectations.* London: Continuum.

Gaylard, D (2011) Policy to practice. In Scragg, T and Mantell, A (eds) *Safeguarding adults in social work.* Exeter: Learning Matters.

Horwath, J (2001) *Child's world: Assessing children in need.* London: Jessica Kingsley.

Kemshall, H (1998) *Risk in probation practice.* Aldershot: Ashgate.

Kemshall, H (2002) *Risk, social policy and welfare.* Buckingham: Open University Press.

Kemshall, H (2010) Risk rationalities in contemporary social work policy and practice. *British Journal of Social Work,* 40 (4), 1247–62.

Lymbery, M (2010) A new vision for adult social care? Continuities and change in the care of older people, *Critical Social Policy,* 30(1),5–26.

Macdonald, K and Macdonald, G (2010) Safeguarding: A case for intelligent risk management. *British Journal of Social Work,* 40 (4), 1174–91.

Mantell, A and Clarke, A (2011) Making choices: The Mental Capacity Act 2005. In Scragg, T and Mantell, A (eds) *Safeguarding adults in social work.* Exeter: Learning Matters.

Mantell, A, Weeks, E and Holloway, M (2013) *Mental capacity and traumatic brain injury: A critical comparison of England and New Zealand's legislative responses.* 7th International Conference on Health and Mental Health. Los Angeles, 23–27 June 2013.

Moore, D and Jones, K (2012) *Social work and dementia.* Exeter: Learning Matters.

Mowlam, A, Tennant, R, Dixon, J and McCreadie, C (2007) UK study of abuse and neglect of older people: Qualitative findings. London: Comic Relief and Department of Health. Available at: http://assets.comicrelief.com/cr09/docs/older_people_abuse_report.pdf (accessed 24 February 2013).

Munro, E (2008) *Effective child protection.* 2nd edition. London: Sage.

Munro, E (2011) *The Munro review of child protection: Final report. A child-centred system.* London: The Stationery Office.

O'Hagan, K (1996) *Competence in social work practice.* London: Jessica Kingsley.

Parton, N (2006) *Safeguarding childhood.* London: Palgrave Macmillan.

Ray, M, Bernard, M and Phillips, J (2009) *Critical issues in social work with older people.* Basingstoke: Palgrave Macmillan.

Smethurst, C, Killner, V, Smallbones, D and Wright, C (2012) Skills in working with risk, in B Hall and T Scragg (eds) *Social work with older people: Approaches to person-centred practice.* Maidenhead: Open University Press.

Stanford, SN (2010) 'Speaking back' to fear: Responding to the moral dilemmas of risk in social work practice. *British Journal of Social Work,* 40 (4), 1065–80.

Szmukler, G (2000) Homicide inquiries: What sense do they make? *The Psychiatrist,* 24, 6–10.

Taylor, B and Devine, T (1994) *Assessing needs and planning care in social work.* Aldershot: Ashgate.

Thompson, N (1993) *Anti-discriminatory practice.* Macmillan: Basingstoke.

Thornton, A (2011) Blurred vision: Direct payments, funding cuts and the law. *Social Care and Neurodisability,* 2 (4), 218–25.

Titterton, M (2005) *Risk and risk taking in health and social welfare.* London: Jessica Kingsley.

Webb, S (2006) *Social work in a risk society.* Basingstoke: Palgrave Macmillan.

Chapter 14

Decision-making

Paul Tavender and Grahame Tooth

This chapter will help you to develop the following capabilities from the **Professional Capabilities Framework**:

- **Critical reflection and analysis**

  Apply critical reflection and analysis to inform and provide a rationale for professional decision-making.

- **Contexts and organisations**

  Engage with, inform, and adapt to changing contexts that shape practice. Operate effectively within your own organisational frameworks and contribute to the development of services and organisations. Operate effectively within multi-agency and inter-professional settings.

- **Professionalism**

  Identify and behave as a professional social worker committed to professional development.

- **Values and ethics**

  Apply social work ethical principles and values to guide professional practice.

- **Diversity**

  Recognise diversity and apply anti-discriminatory and anti-oppressive principles in practice.

It will also introduce you to the following standards as set out in the 2008 social work subject benchmark statement:

4.7 Make appropriate use of research in decision-making about practice and in the evaluation of outcomes

5.1.4 Social work theory

7.4 Subject-specific and other skills

Introduction

Many decisions you make during your social work career will arise out of co-operation and consent among parties to a decision. However, you will regularly be faced with competing evidence and perspectives, the strength of feelings of self, service users, carers, practitioners and managers and resource limitations. In the midst of this state of flux you will need to maintain a focus on what is relevant information to the decision in question. You will encounter a number of imponderables, none more so than the adequacy of available evidence to inform best-interest decisions and manage pressure from agencies and others who may oppose what you believe is right and just, and all within a plethora of differing environments: Adults, Children, Statutory, Voluntary, Family centres, Provider services; and client groups: Care leavers, Learning difficulties, Youth offending, Mental health, Substance misuse, Asylum seekers, Older people, Physical impairment.

Thereafter you must negotiate the limitations, whilst managing that inevitable element of self doubt, that fear that you lack the necessary ability or experience to make such an important judgment. Mediating within and living in this decision-making environment is the spirit of social work. Whether decision-making is co-operative or not, it is important that you develop the ability to present, reiterate and justify reasons for chosen courses of action and to develop processes to help keep your bearings. This chapter explores some building blocks for effective decision-making and emphasises the importance of values in shaping effective decisions.

Defining decision-making

The Oxford English Dictionary definition of decision-making includes:

> *The action of deciding (a controversy, a contest, question etc). The making up of one's mind on any point or on a course of action; a resolution or determination. The final and definite result of examining a question; a conclusion or judgement.*

ACTIVITY 14.1

Take a few moments and list five decisions you have made recently in your practice setting.

Use these decisions to write a list or diagram of the stages you typically follow to arrive at a decision.

Comment

Decision-making occurs all the time. It switches between small and large, minor and major, complex and simple, stressful and easy, multi-agency or single practitioner. Sometimes you will initiate a decision. At others, someone else will be asking you to act because you have access to relevant resources, skills and authority derived from legal, value or procedural requirements linked to your role. The decision may be small for you but major for the person and vice versa. If you compare your results to other students in your group you may be quite surprised by the variety of approaches that are possible.

It is also worth undertaking this activity as a group and then reflecting on how you found that process (see Chapter 1). This can be easier due to the synergy created by group work, in that you are able to contribute more than you could individually by bouncing ideas off each other. It can also be easier because the responsibility can be shared. However, you might also find it a frustrating process, you might feel that your views have not been sufficiently heard or that you are not happy with the decision of the group (see Chapter 9).

Elements of a decision-making process

So how do social workers make decisions? Figure 14.1 identifies some elements that social workers need to engage with. This diagram represents a synthesis from the research presented in this chapter and experience of working in both Adults' and Children's Services. Although the elements appear sequentially, in everyday practice, there is an ebbing and flowing between them.

Although you will be addressing these individual elements, there are two questions you need to ask yourself throughout any decision-making activity.

Firstly, which element/s in this process do I want to focus on in order to arrive at a decision? For example:

- I need to seek clarity about the hypothesis. At this point I will be contacting other networks who know the situation or reading relevant literature, for example, in relation to child behaviour and diet.

- Am I happy about the way the adult is being excluded from the safeguarding process? Do I need to focus on making sure the person is included?

Secondly, do I need to take charge of the process or are people managing? This last question touches on developing an ability to make effective use of your own resources of time, energy, emotional well-being and assertiveness (see Chapter 2). It is also about keeping others empowered to do what they do well, whether it is a service user, carer, practitioner, manager or community group.

Is there a decision to be made?

This is such a simple question and yet there is a tendency in practice to think that because a problem is presented to us we must act. Effective assessments (see Chapters 12 and 13) will help with making this judgment but it is good practice to routinely ask:

- Is there a decision to be made here?

- If so, what is it? If not, surely there is nothing to be done.

- Is it me that needs to act?

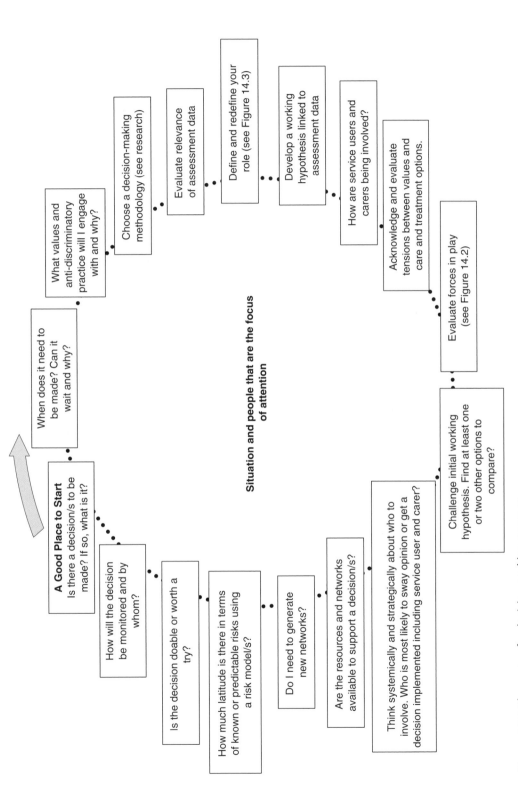

Figure 14.1 Elements of a decision-making process

229

Alternatively ask:

- Is there a problem and if so what is it?

- Does it need solving, why and why now?

Most practitioners will have experience of being privy to unnecessary interventions because these fundamental questions are not addressed. Most statutory practitioners will be required at some stage of their career to oversee an initial response system, where their responsibility will be to respond to initial enquiries be it within Adults' or Children's Services. It is often the case that in such circumstances initial information received, when taken at face value, may appear to require an immediate intervention. It is easy for the anxiety of others to become contagious. An emergency response is immediately prompted without asking *is there a question to be answered?* or *is there a decision to be made?*

It is suggested that these questions can prove invaluable in gaining clarity, creating boundaries, saving time and sometimes allowing and empowering service users and carers time to find their own solutions rather than services jumping in too quickly. In supported care settings it is important to ask:

- What decisions do we tend to make for people?

- Is this necessary?

- How can we promote and maintain levels of independence?

- How much time do I have and what do I do in an emergency?

CASE STUDY

A Community Consultant Psychiatrist contacts Adult Services to report that he has been to visit Claire, 92, and been unable to gain entry because she has lost her keys so can't unlock her door. After climbing through a window, the Consultant reports that Claire, who has had no previous involvement with Adult Services, appears very confused, unkempt and has no food in her fridge and cupboards other than a pint of milk and half a loaf of bread. The Consultant informs that he is in the process of arranging for an emergency locksmith to come and change the locks.

Comment

There are times when you have to act quickly to ensure someone's well-being and so the thinking process will be quick and based on information you have available at the time. However for Claire, the practitioner should reflect upon the information presented to them prior to reacting. This will be framed around questions like: *How has Claire come to be 92 years of age without coming to the attention of Adult Services previously? Who referred Claire to the Consultant and why did they not feel it necessary at that point to refer directly to Adult Services also? Are there any existing support networks already in place, for example family, neighbours, the local church?* Information gathering should always be the first consideration in early intervention and until these facts are established questions may have to be asked as to the appropriateness of changing the locks. With any situation, there are a number of possible scenarios that can explain the reasons for a service user's initial presentation. For example, in this it could be that Claire receives daily visits from a relative or care service which she funds privately and they have a key which is their only point of access and, as part of that support, they visit her with a meal every evening and sit with her to ensure that she eats it. This vital support may be compromised if the locks are changed.

It may be the case however that the presenting issues are indeed an accurate reflection of Claire's circumstance. It may also be that Claire lacks the capacity to know what she is doing and that a best interest intervention is warranted. The Mental Capacity Act 2005 empowers practitioners to decide whether Claire has capacity using a two-stage test and the common-law concept of 'reasonable belief'. Reasonable belief means making a decision the best you can at the time with the knowledge and experience you have to hand. If your decision is later challenged, you will be able to point to objective evidence as to why Claire did or did not lack capacity. If you reasonably believe Claire lacks capacity you can then make a decision for her, in accordance with what is believed to be in her best interests.

Values/anti-discriminatory practice/ empowering service users and carers

The importance of values and anti-discriminatory practice in shaping decision-making cannot be overstated.

CASE STUDY

John is currently in a deep depression (loss of motivation, a sense of no hope, thinking it would better if he was dead, believing he has failed his family). This is sapping his ability to make effective decisions. The team agree that John's depression is causing him to self-neglect and get into financial debt. You know that eventually he will recover his abilities and would be devastated if things are allowed to deteriorate.

ACTIVITY **14.2**

Applying different values as circumstances change

*With reference to the HCPC Codes of Practice for social care (**www.hpc-uk**.org):*

What values would you use to guide decision-making given John's present situation?

What values would you engage with as John becomes more able to make decisions again?

Comment

However little John may be able to do for himself at this time, the focus will be on supporting him to do whatever he can. This starting point means you will be supporting John's strengths, affirming his identity, encouraging him to do the little things and supporting networks and friends from the outset. At this point in John's situation, you would also be likely to bias towards being more directive and not give a lot of choice, as this overwhelms him. The focus would be on protecting him from harm or neglect; for example, making sure the flat gets cleaned, taking his washing to the laundrette, actively contacting financial agencies with John's consent, taking him to out-patients or arranging for mental health services to see him at home. You may get others in his network to do these things and provide support to him.

As John regains motivation and physical energy you would begin to build on promoting independence and decreasing the emphasis on a directive approach.

When does discrimination set in?

There will be a point where being directive becomes welfarist – a point where practitioners and carers assume they are experts on John's situation regardless of John recovering his abilities. Welfarism undermines John's capacity and right to make his own decisions. This point could also be marked by a disablist perspective – a point where the person with mental health problems (John) is labelled as unable to make his own decisions or is unreliable (Thompson, 1998). John becomes an object of professional curiosity and decision-making and his identity and abilities are ignored or undervalued.

I hope that you can see that the values above are being applied relatively across time. However, values such as respect and dignity are absolute and unchanging throughout the period of support.

Challenging stereotypes and decision-making

Often you will experience joint practice that is in tune with current values. However, there will be times when you will need to adopt an active role and challenge contemporary discriminations and promote a more democratic and humane way of living. You will need to decide how power relations will be shaped, challenged and managed.

Dominelli (2002) outlines three types of power used in relation to disadvantaged groups.

- **Power over** Practitioners and society make decisions for groups even if this is not justified. This is characterised by dominance over others and favours the dominant group. For example, services assuming that older people should be in risk-free environments (care home) rather than live at home.

- **Power to** People and groups exercise agency to resist oppressive situations. Older people are able to speak out, perhaps with the help of others, including social workers, to claim the right to take risks.

- **Power of** People and groups draw on collective strengths to achieve a common goal. National organisations for older people and among the famous older generation a movement is developing that challenges current stereotypes of older people and demands different services. You could consider drawing on the strength of such movements by helping service users engage with them.

Finally, it is worth considering how much change the service user or carer wants. In many situations people have little choice but to go through the experience of big changes in life (and this can be particularly the case for children), but it is worth asking people what the person thinks is momentous and what is small. De Mello (1997) cites this story. A man had lived in his house for 50 years and suddenly moved next door. Surprised local reporters asked why. The man replied *I guess it's the gypsy in me.* A small change but a huge adventure.

Evaluating assessment information

The content of assessment tools and proformas is shaped by agency policy and purpose, laws, practitioners, research (service user, carer and practitioner) and values. Implicitly or explicitly all assessment formats guide the practitioner to a conclusion about the relevance of the contents in each tool. For example, assessment focused on a social model (role changes, housing insecurity, wandering at night with no awareness of road safety, debt, harassment, etc.) may omit relevant biological or psychological needs. Similarly, a psychiatric diagnosis for dementia is likely to focus on biological and cognitive processes rather than the service user's worry about his/her partner's failing physical health, financial stress or elder abuse as factors causing confusion or anxiety. Social workers using the Common Assessment Framework (Department of Health 2000) with children and families can find themselves focusing on deficits in the meeting of the *child's developmental needs*, such as emotional and behavioural development, and inadequacies in *parenting capacity*, such as guidance and boundaries. This can lead to the pathologising of parents whilst ignoring *family and environmental factors*, such as poor housing and community resources, which may be very relevant but costly to address.

No one assessment tool is better or worse than another. The choice to be made is which tools are likely to provide the most useful assessment to help with decision-making that reflects the service user's or carer's circumstances. Time and risks permitting, a legitimate decision may be to seek further assessment.

> ### CASE STUDY
>
> **Domestic violence and substance misuse**
>
> *Debbie is 36 years old and presented to services with symptoms of depression. Debbie's husband was upset at her withdrawal from household tasks and child care and wanted help as this was disrupting the division of labour at home and causing arguments. Debbie's withdrawal was interpreted by practitioners as a sign of depression and Debbie was prescribed medication. At subsequent home visits by a social worker to support activities and recovery, Debbie revealed a long and continuing history of domestic violence that had not been asked about at assessment. Stanley et al. (2011) have found that only a limited number of families are offered an initial assessment following domestic violence incidents and time restraints meant that social workers had a lack of engagement with perpetrators of domestic violence.*

> ### CASE STUDY
>
> **A difficult person who can't be helped or someone struggling with meaning and purpose?**
>
> *Sixty-year-old Malcolm has had a stroke that caused significant right-sided paralysis and mental confusion. Prior to his stroke he was an active community member. He is refusing necessary home care and practitioners express frustration and consider withdrawing services which would precipitate a crisis. Luckily, a worker took the time to ask him about what his beliefs told him about dealing with adversity and receiving help. Malcolm replied,* accept your fate, medication should be avoided, stand on your own two feet . . . *Subsequently, someone with a similar faith was found to talk this through and Malcolm accepted help.*

Assessment tools are an essential part of any practitioner's repertoire. However, any tool may leave out important information or the assessor may omit to ask important questions. As a decision-maker you need to satisfy yourself that relevant information has been gathered as part of the decision-making process. Ask yourself and others at your placement:

- What assessment tools have been used?

- Does their content represent a holistic picture of the service user's or carer's situation?

- Have relevant questions been asked and adequately answered?

- Are the assessment tools up to date and effectively used?

Until recently, domestic violence and gender, race and sexuality discrimination were absent from assessment forms. Spirituality and religion are on most forms but practitioners rarely explore or record these critical areas of some people's lives. Good supervision, researching and connecting with anti-discriminatory practice will keep this area alive for you.

Generating a working hypothesis – unless you know why there is a problem you can't know how to address it

Are the symptoms of depression or anxiety arising because of poverty, discrimination, poor housing, spiritual conflict or doubt, isolation, family relationships, grief, biological dysfunction, role change conflict, a network problem, lack of service creativity? Can s/he help acting in this way or is s/he responsible for her behaviour? How big is the risk? Is it a combination of factors and which ones are most important to target to achieve change? These types of debates are commonplace to social work practitioners who contend with multiple dilemmas as they seek solutions to diverse lifestyles and circumstances.

Mental health teams regularly debate whether aggressive behaviour could be viewed as an aspect of mental illness, a feature of personality or culture, a reflection of childhood family abuse, an indication of social isolation linked to paranoia, poverty leading to financial stress, persecution by local youths or the poor response of agencies (mental health teams, housing or social security) to requests for help or support in times of need.

Service user and carer research (Faulkner, 2000) emphasises the importance of asking the person what helps or what might make a difference, even where you might be invoking statutory or duty of care actions.

For each 'why is this happening' hypothesis above there will be 'how to resolve it' interventions. Below are five actions to help with hypothesising.

- Gather relevant research, theory and values that help to hypothesise about the 'why' of a problem.

- Get to know what the service user, carers, networks, communities and practitioners think about why there is a problem and what to do about it.

- Settle on a working hypothesis for why the problem exists, even if this is tentative. It may be the best you can get at the time.

- Develop a 'how to resolve it' working hypothesis.

- Check that there is a link between the 'why' and the 'how to resolve it' hypotheses.

Without some clarity in this process you will not be able to evaluate outcomes, engage others meaningfully or justify your interventions.

> **CASE STUDY**
>
> *You are the social worker assessing a situation in which Terry, a single dad has come to an office appointment concerned about having to physically restrain his son, Ashley (11) who has Asperger's syndrome. When you meet he says he is fatigued by being kept awake part of most nights and trying to stop Ashley leaving the house, as he is considered to be unsafe and would get lost. He restrains him and this is causing bruising on his arms and cuts where he knocks against furniture in the struggles. He can't think of another way of dealing with the situation and now seems desperate for some kind of help.*
>
> *Your initial 'why' hypothesis might be that Terry is a well-intentioned father who is finding it increasingly difficult to keep his son safe. He can cope with being awake at night but not with his persistent attempts to run away from home. The 'how to resolve it' hypothesis might lead to the use of sedation (medical solution), telecare support, family aid workers (social solutions).*
>
> *Terry is reluctant but agrees to your visiting Ashley at home. When you arrive the house looks clean and well cared for. However, when you meet Ashley he looks malnourished and when you approach him to introduce yourself he looks frightened and wets himself. Terry won't allow Ashley to answer your questions and eventually insists you leave, saying there is no problem and he doesn't know why he asked you for help in the first place.*
>
> *Your 'why' hypothesis will now have shifted with the evidence to the likelihood that Terry is abusing Ashley and that his intentions are not in Ashley's best interests. The original 'how to resolve it' hypothesis will have shifted away from supporting Terry's benign concerns to one of protecting Ashley. The 'how to resolve it' question will not now be about additional care and will shift to considering what needs to be done to protect Ashley from abuse.*

Risk and decision-making

Risk is currently the subject of much debate and has become an increasingly central feature of many areas of social policy (Kemshaw 2009). Baker and Kelly (2011) describe risk assessment as a multifaceted activity that can be undertaken for a variety of purposes. For each person you help, it is necessary to have a grasp of which risk models are being used.

Bruce Thornton (2013) has developed a two stage risk screening and assessment tool for children and surmises on his website that the critical components of assessing risk include:

- Understanding the capacity of the parents/carers;
- Understanding the needs of the child;
- Assessing the level of harm;

- Classifying the harm;

- Predicting the likelihood of future harm;

- Summarising risk;

- Considering whether the harm is significant;

- Making decisions;

- Follow up actions.

Along with other risk-taking models, Thornton's approach acts as an antidote to potential and sometimes unintended policy and practice pressures towards risk elimination rather than minimisation.

CASE STUDY

Charlotte lives with husband, Mike, a recovering alcoholic and their four children, Justin, aged 14, Amy, aged 10, and twins Nigel and Beatrice in a two bedded flat in a tower block on a poor estate. Justin has mild learning disabilities and is currently being taught in a pupil referral unit, as his attendance has been poor and he has been very disruptive in class. Amy is reported to be a bright pupil, who is doing well at school but is often said to be tired and is painfully thin. The twins have recently had their two year health check after which no concerns were raised. Charlotte endured many years of domestic violence from Mike when he was drinking heavily although there have been no such incidents since he abstained from alcohol two years ago following the birth of the twins. However, after a heated argument about Justin's increasingly difficult behaviour Mike went to the local pub. He turned up later that evening, drunk, and not only proceeded to beat up Charlotte but threw Justin across the room when he tried to intervene to protect his mother. Amy had the presence of mind to call the police who arrived and arrested Mike immediately and placed him in custody. Charlotte does not want to press charges, blaming herself for the argument and has stated to the police that she wants Mike to return the family home as does Justin who says he is missing his dad.

Comment

A positive risk-taking model could seek to build on the strengths of this family's way of being and promote social networks by suggesting more needs to be found out about their circumstances than just the problems above. Working closely with the family to facilitate open dialogue and discussed decision-making, might enable all parties to contribute their views including the children, who should not be viewed just as victims but be actively engaged in dealing with the problems and involved in seeking solutions (Hague, Mullender, Kelly, Imam, Males 2002).

Acknowledging known predictors of domestic violence, for example standard of living, stress, poverty and inadequate housing should be central to shaping the decision-making process. Poverty can be a major stress factor that can lead to people who would normally have adequately coped not being able to do so and pushing them into neglectful parenting Beckett (2007). Children in economically deprived households have a higher risk of mental health problems such as depression, low self-confidence and peer conflict and these can be as a direct result of poor housing and violence in the home (Hutson 1991). Furthermore, the parental management of Justin's learning difficulties may be an ongoing source of anxiety and stress (Burke 2008) and have contributed towards Mike's reaction to him.

Reviewing Justin's present support services, advocating to the Local Housing authority, engaging Mike in an alcohol rehabilitation programme, sourcing counselling, introducing the family to a local family centre or Sure Start initiative and organising for the children to participate in after school activities clubs are operational interventions geared towards managing risk through the shared ethos of keeping the family together through promotion of well-being.

Positive risk-taking is a good starting point for any decision-making, but one that needs to be balanced out with a realistic evaluation of risks to family breakdown and long-term health issues for Charlotte and her children. As the children have been subject to violence the progression from the initial assessment would be for a section 47 of the Children Act 1989 investigation to be completed. The paramount consideration is the welfare of the children and whether there is an imminent risk of significant harm occurring. *Working Together to Safeguard Children* (2010) indicated the importance of multi-disciplinary working and it would be essential to liaise with the police and the schools and any wider family involved with the children to inform the decision-making process. A positive risk-taking focus can overemphasise an individual's needs above other important dilemmas and risks that may have an adverse effect on the family as a whole. Different risk models need to be used alongside each other.

Other forces shaping decision-making

The knowledge and value bases acquired by practitioners to assess and intervene are important to effective decision-making. There is a constantly developing state of knowledge about social, spiritual, biological and psychological factors affecting people's lives. Such understandings have developed more humane responses to behaviours that were previously not understood; for example, autism, challenging behaviours, brain injury and dementia.

However, Figure 14.2 shows other potent forces at work in shaping decision-making. As a general rule of thumb these forces will be time-, location- and agency-specific and demand of the social worker that s/he maintains an up-to-date awareness.

Political forces include media or government attitudes to risk; individual rights and duties versus community responsibility and capacity (how far should family

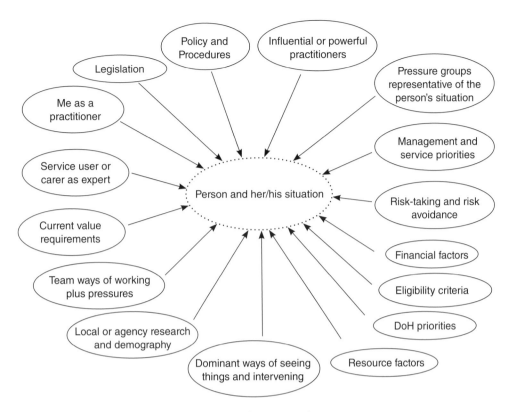

Figure 14.2 Analysing the forces at play in decision-making

and community carry the burden of caring or will the state provide?); the promotion of domestic violence and adult abuse as no longer acceptable. Citizen-led forces include service users and carers as experts in their own lives, campaigning to stop domestic violence, and campaigns for the rights of homosexuals. Economic forces include the money and resources available to develop and provide services. Value forces include challenges to racism, sexism, classism in accessing education and numerous other current discriminations. Dominant ways of seeing could include the use of 'power over' (Dominelli, 2002) medical perspectives in assessment and intervention.

ACTIVITY **14.3**

Choose a service user or carer situation you are involved with. Use Figure 14.2 to consider the following questions.

- *Which forces would you want to raise or reduce the profiles of?*
- *Which forces are beyond your control?*
- *Which resources or people might you engage to manage these forces?*

Comment

Figure 14.2 demonstrates the number of variables that might be in play for any decision. This variety can be a source of great possibility in so far as any elements put together have great power to act positively. They are also important as you can draw on authority from a range of sources to justify a decision. For example, combining policy, values on service user involvement, pressure group influence, laws on discrimination and statutory funding to ensure a person can access care services and make her/his own risk decisions.

Here are some ideas about how other forces influence decision-making. The outcome of local service user and carer consultations may change how care is given for minority ethnic groups. National reactions to the latest local or national tragic event (suicide, murder) may lead to risk avoidance that challenges the service value of promoting independence. Neglect in a care home may lead to social work reviews directed towards monitoring restricted areas of concern rather than quality of life care planning.

In this environment you may develop an idea of what a preferred decision might look like but be unable to implement it. It is important to remember that a decision is not a decision unless it can be implemented.

Policies change but decision-making thrives

The current policy trend for adults is towards personalisation (DoH, 2007a, b) based on self-assessment by a person whereby needs are represented by outcomes. Money is then allocated to her/him to reach those outcomes. This represents a shift in decision-making away from practitioners to service users and to managers implementing financial formulae to apportion money. However, social workers will continue to support people through the self-directed process, to make complex decisions in relation to the most vulnerable and to support those unable to make their own decisions. Decision-making will continue to thrive.

Policy promotion and society today tend to use the language of superlatives that set up expectations of the 'most' radical and creative thinking, the 'best' innovative change, 'full' assessments and 'inclusive' partnerships that will 'transform' well-being and lead to 'fulfilled' lives. The public are told practitioners will deliver. As a practitioner it is difficult not to be affected by this pressure. While many recent policy changes are to be applauded, there is a need to acknowledge with a degree of humility that many service users want to maintain an ordinary quality of life and that services and practitioners do not always have the knowledge or resources to bring about tumultuous changes (Munro, 2003; Brandon, 2000). Try to keep a mental note of how you are responding and staying creative in the culture of perfection.

Partnership and networking

Partnerships, networks and multi-agency working are crucial to effective decision-making. Chapter 8 covers this in detail and it is useful to refer back to the comments sections there to see how you might respond to the questions below.

ACTIVITY **14.4**

Take time now to reflect on the quality of decision-making partnerships in your work setting.

- *Are they supportive and consistent and do they help you to analyse and understand?*
- *Do they assist with resources and flexible responses to diverse situations?*
- *Are you doing all you can to support and develop partnerships? There is a tendency for practitioners to focus only on what others can do and to neglect this question.*

Paying attention to yourself

The daily expectations and pressures on social workers to make best decisions will inevitably raise tensions and conflicts, especially where services are unable to provide for a service user's needs or outcome-based services. You may feel disillusioned or ill-equipped in your quest to find a way forward; situations are complex and volatile and decisions are finely judged. This is a reality of being a social worker, be it in adults' or children's services and one you will inevitable experience at some time or another. You may also have unreasonably high expectations of yourself. Figure 14.3 outlines some personal anchors that can be useful when making decisions.

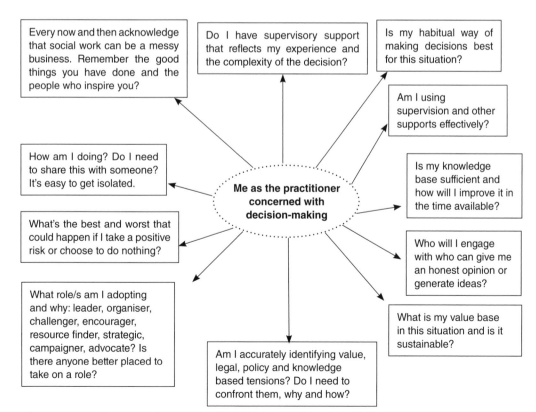

Figure 14.3 Paying attention to myself

ACTIVITY **14.5**

Spend some time reflecting on these questions.

- *Find a metaphor, other than 'anchor', that works for you.*

- *How do you approach decision-making? For example, do you jump in with both feet and get people organised? Do you just want to get things sorted to relieve your own or others' worries? Do you tend to sit back and let things happen? Do you find making decisions difficult? Do you have a patient and measured approach?*

Comment

There is nothing inherently right or wrong in different ways of decision-making. Each approach has to be judged on its value as part of the decision-making process. However, you do need to be able to recognise your preferred styles so you can adjust.

And lastly, be clear what you want from others. They will find it a lot easier to give something if they know what you want, whether it is a request for emotional support, expert advice, clarification or action (see Chapters 1 and 4).

RESEARCH SUMMARY

Munro (2003) reviews two types of decision-making. The first is pattern recognition, which is often used by experienced and knowledgeable workers engaging intuition (practice experience), sifting information selectively, metaphor and storytelling. Pattern recognition biases decision-making towards 'satisficing'. This means the tendency to settle on the first good-enough solution that presents itself even if it is not the best available.

Pattern recognition can work well for less significant or less complex decisions. For example, relieving poverty through a benefits application, treating biological depression pharmacologically or arranging home care. Practitioners can rapidly develop a story around a person's situation based on practice experience of similar situations and some process of checking with the person or others. Experienced practitioners run the risk of excluding important information when using pattern recognition. Inexperienced practitioners run a similar risk, but due to lack of knowledge of what information is important for any presenting problem.

In contrast to pattern recognition, formal decision-making follows a prescribed set of questions, a process that aims to think broadly and to generate several options for intervention. The processes and information are represented through a decision-making tree tool. Advantages might include having a wide range of information available about the person and her/his circumstances, generation of a wide range of options for intervention, transparency and a best-outcomes decision. The main disadvantages are that it can be time-consuming, unnecessary information is collected, service users' and carers' privacy is unnecessarily intruded on and resources may not be available.

Gambrill (2006) discusses research on how decisions are made, outlines useful bullet-pointed lists and charts and describes barriers to effective decision-making. Gambrill's research overview on decision-making highlights that:

- *similar decision-making processes are common to all areas of human activity;*

- *you can improve the quality of your decision-making capacity;*

- *reflection and thinking time are crucial to effective consideration of factors relevant to the decision at hand;*

- *barriers that prevent effective decision-making need to be identified, interpreted and removed wherever possible;*

- *it is important to have contact with others who will encourage lateral and focused thinking and if necessary challenge you;*

- *mistakes will happen but you can learn from them.*

Edmund (2012) has developed an 11-stage process based on an analysis of decision-making across a wide range of occupational groups. His Short Problem Solving Model Formula (SM-4) format contains the four elements:

- *problem definition;*

- *alternatives sought by searching for information and generating solutions;*

- *evaluating or selecting the best option based on evidence;*

- *challenging or checking whether this is the best option.*

Edmund also urges you to work creatively, to engage with your own resourcefulness.

The thousands of effective and creative decisions practitioners make daily rarely come to public light. Occasionally things can and do go wrong. The essence of effective practice, whether things go right or wrong, is captured by Munro (2003) when she says that decisions should not be judged by their outcome: fallibility is an inevitable aspect of the work. They should be judged on the way they were reached. *Popper (cited in Gambrill 2006, p198) emphasises a practitioner's need to* recognise our duty to minimize avoidable mistakes.

ACTIVITY **14.6**

- *Briefly review one decision you made recently. Which of the methods above did you use and why?*

- *What messages do Munro's and Popper's comments above carry for you?*

- *What actions will you take now to develop your decision-making abilities?*

Comment

The decisions you take throughout your career will vary in complexity and nature and will be influenced by which path you choose to pursue your social work career. Many of the decisions you take may directly affect the lives of those you support, be it children or adults. With that responsibility however comes the reality that not every decision taken will be the correct one. In frontline social work you will not have the benefit of hindsight. It is therefore imperative when mistakes do occur that you find time to reflect upon what you can learn from them (see chapter 1). Whilst in placement consider the benefits of seeking advice from more senior colleagues and ask them to share their experiences as, no doubt, they will have made mistakes too. You may also wish to consider blocking out some time to consider the processes you utilise when making decisions through your supervisory structure.

CHAPTER SUMMARY

This chapter has explored ways of structuring thinking and actions for effective decision-making. It has reviewed the influence of values, anti-discriminatory practices and the wider forces that shape decision-making. It makes the case that social work holds an almost unique role among other helping groups in needing to take a holistic view of situations when making decisions and in being concerned with how social forces and the distribution of power affect outcomes. As such you will need to develop and maintain a familiarity with the wide range of variables addressed in this chapter as they apply to your service setting. The points below give some ideas for staying alive to decision-making as a skill in its own right.

- *Develop your ability to describe the process you travelled to arrive at a decision and include your ability to challenge your own hypotheses.*
- *Actively cultivate your internal and external supports and reflective capabilities using the ideas in this chapter. Ask yourself, what can I do to develop a healthy resilience to the pressures of decision-making that doesn't leave me overwhelmed or detached?*
- *Clarify the values and value tensions inherent in any decision-making activity and be prepared to swim against the tide of opinion to support what you believe to be right.*

FURTHER READING

DoH (2007) *Independence, choice and risk: A guide to best practice in supported decision-making.* London: The Stationery Office.

Includes a supported decision tool focused on risk.

Kemshall, H. and Wilkinson, B. (eds) (2011) Good practice in assessing risk current knowledge, issues and approaches. Jessica Kingsley Publishers London and Philidelphia.

A comprehensive overview on risk assessment for both adult and children's services.

Knott, C. and Scragg, T. (2007) *Reflective practice in social work.* Exeter: Learning Matters.

A good introduction to the reflective process essential for effective decision-making.

Milner, J. and O'Byrne, P. (1998) *Assessment in social work.* Basingstoke: Macmillan.

Contains a section on prospect theory (barriers to effective decision-making and risk).

O'Sullivan, T. (1999) *Decision-making in social work.* Basingstoke: Macmillan.

Very helpful and succinct information and discussions that develop the knowledge and practice issues contained in this chapter.

Segal, J. et al. (2007) *Depression in older adults and the elderly.* www.helpguide.org/mental/depression/elderly.htm

Provides a summary of signs and causes of depression and suggests kinds of decisions.

Taylor, B. and Devine, T. (1995) *Assessing needs and planning care in social work.* Aldershot: Ashgate.

Includes a section on decision-making and some useful diagrams and charts.

REFERENCES

Baker, K. and Kelly, G. (2011) 'Risk assessment and young people', in Kemshall, H. and Wilkinson, B. (eds) *Good practice in assessing risk: Current knowledge, issues and approaches.* London: Jessica Kingsley.

Beckett, C. (2007) *Child protection: An introduction*, 2nd Edition. London: Sage.

Brandon, D. (2000) *The tao of survival – Spirituality in social care and counselling.* Birmingham: Venture Press.

De Mello, A. (1997) *The heart of the enlightened.* London: Harper Collins.

Department of Education (2010) 'Working together to safeguard children', London: Department of Health https://www.education.gov.uk/publications/standard/publicationdetail/page1/DCSF-00305-2010 (accessed 10 October 2013).

Department of Health (2000) *Framework for the assessment of children in need and their families.* London: The Stationery Office.

Dominelli, L. (2002) *Anti-oppressive social work theory and practice.* Basingstoke: Palgrave Macmillan.

Edmund, N.W. (2012) *Short problem solving model formula – SM-4.* www.problemsolving.net (accessed 8 July 2013).

Gambrill, E. (2006) *Social work practice – A critical thinker's guide.* Oxford University Press.

Hague, G., Mullander, A., Kelly, L., Imam, U. and Males, E. (2002) 'How do children understand and cope with domestic violence?', *Practice*, 14(1): 17–26.

Hutson, A. (1991) *Children in poverty.* Cambridge: Cambridge University Press.

Kemshall, H. (2009) 'Risk, social policy and young people', in J. Wood and J. Hine (eds) *Work with young people.* London: Sage.

Munro, E. (2003) *Effective child protection.* London: Sage.

Stanley, N., Miller, P., Foster, H. and Thomson, G. (2011) 'A stop start response: Social services' interventions with children and families notified following domestic violence incidents', *The British Journal of Social Work,* 41(2): 296–313.

Thompson, N. (1998) *Promoting equality.* Basingstoke: Palgrave Macmillan.

Conclusion

This book has explored the skills necessary for competent social work and developing best practice. The content has highlighted concepts and values that inform the application of skills and illuminated complex practice dilemmas. The book has aimed to help you think for yourselves about ideas and values that you can use to influence and shape your practice. Central themes have aimed to promote the rights and welfare of children, young people, carers and those who use services, as well as the benefits of partnership working between professionals.

In the first edition of this book I noted that high sickness rates (*The Times*, 2008) and the acute shortage of experienced social workers (*The Times*, 2008, p4) pointed to a wider organisational dilemma. Cree and Myers observed that: *Good social work must have an organisational context that allows it to thrive* (Cree and Myers, 2008, p158). Since then the financial climate has deteriorated, as the public sector continues to be subject to cuts in the fallout from the credit crisis. In a period when more people are turning to services, the welfare safety net is becoming increasingly threadbare.

In light of this the book recognises that social workers do not act alone and are shaped as much by their employing organisations as by their training and values. At the time of writing, universities are planning for the implementation of the new degree, shaped around the Professional Capabilities Framework (PCF) rather than the National Occupational Standards (NOS). This will hopefully encourage more critical and reflective practice; yet we must also take care that the simultaneous introduction of fast-track routes into social work does not renew a mechanistic culture of tick-box practices.

This second edition has explored ways to achieve reliable and effective social work interventions within organisations affected by the pressures and challenges of restructuring and perennial budgetary restraints. It is in such environments that good practice becomes even more essential, to safeguard the needs and rights of children, carers, service users and ultimately your own integrity.

In the first part of the book (Chapters 1, 2, 3 and 4) we focused on your own development, to build a firm foundation from which to look at working with others. Chapter 1 provided a practical introduction to applying dominant theories in developing reflective practice. In Chapter 2 we explored how your values, attitudes and behaviour impact upon the way you present yourself. This chapter highlighted the need for self-awareness and assertiveness; factors that will enrich not only your professional development but also your personal growth. Self-awareness requires reflection to produce positive, constructive change. Chapter 3 explored the potential positive and negative impacts of the way we present ourselves in writing, arguing for an anti-oppressive approach. Chapter 4 explored the skills for surviving the challenges inherent in twenty-first-century social work. It recognised that you require support in developing the complex skills discussed within this text and sought to provide suggestions on how you can utilise support from your peers, supervisors and employing organisations. It will help you to stay a safe practitioner on your journey to becoming an accomplished one.

The second part of the book (Chapters 4, 5, 6 and 7) considered not only how we build relationships with others but also the type of relationships we seek to develop. In Chapter 5 the nature of our interventions and attempts at advocacy and promoting participation were challenged, emphasising the need for genuine person-centred planning to promote empowerment. Engaging and communicating with people is at the heart of social work but is also given direction by our commitment to empowering practice. The importance of empowerment continued as a primary theme throughout the book. Chapter 6 reasserted the need for creating meaningful relationships with children, young people, carers and service users. Chapter 7 focused on how communication can contribute to or undermine those relationships, drawing on examples from more complex practice situations.

The third part of the book (Chapters 8, 9 and 10) concentrated on specific areas of how we work with others. Decisions are increasingly made by multi-disciplinary teams and Chapter 8 considered how to collaborate more effectively with other professionals, highlighting the need for clarity and understanding of the roles of others. It demonstrated how collaboration can enable professionals to become more than the sum of their parts. Chapter 9 looked at the broader range of groups in which we operate and the tensions, power dynamics and dilemmas that can occur. Competing perspectives and agendas require good negotiation skills and these were the focus of Chapter 10. This requires sensitivity to power imbalances and an understanding of others' perspectives to achieve 'win–win' situations rather than impasse or potentially oppressive practice.

In the final part of the book we explored the complexity of the world in which these skills are practised. Chapter 11 emphasised that it is not sufficient for social workers to have a clear and up-to-date understanding of the legislation, but must also develop skills in applying it to deliver anti-oppressive practice. Chapters 12 and 13 argued that effective assessment: are the basis for achieving successful interventions but, as Chapter 12 makes clear, it is essential to identify what are the criteria for your assessment: are you concerned with gatekeeping or needs or rights or risks? Chapter 13 scrutinised what we mean by risk and navigated ways of managing risk within the context of a risk-averse society and often a culture of blame. The final chapter (Chapter 14) explored further the factors that impact upon our decision-making process and offered strategies to help guide you through this potential minefield. It emphasised the importance of being sensitive to but critical of external influences and our own thought processes and values. In this way, it can be seen that the end of this book leads us back to the beginning and the crucial role of reflective practice in the development and application of social work skills.

We hope this book has stimulated you to practise the skills discussed and explore with your supervisors and colleagues the dilemmas raised. The book has explored social work skills for working with children, young people and adults and highlighted some of the differences and similarities in working in these different areas of practice. As we stated at the start of this book, whatever area of practice you are in, it is often about working with families and their wider ecosystems (Bronfenbrenner, 1979), but at different points in their life course.

Whether you are qualified or qualifying, we encourage you to cultivate and retain a commitment to the knowledge and principles contained in this book; and to be prepared to constantly hone, update and critically review your practice and that of, your organisation and others with whom you work. Reflection and feedback are essential aspects of such practice.

REFERENCES

Bronfenbrenner, U (1979) *The ecology of human development.* Cambridge, Mass.: Harvard University Press.

Cree, V and Myers, S (2008) *Social work: Making a difference.* Bristol: Policy Press.

The Times (2008) Social work sick leave. Wednesday, 11 June.

Appendix 1

Professional Capabilities Framework

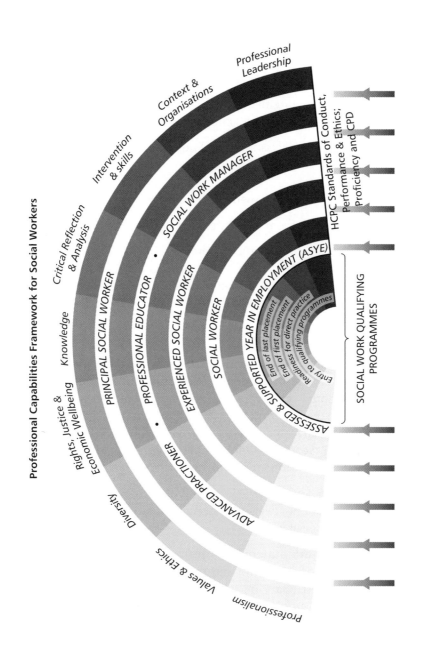

Professional Capabilities Framework for Social Workers

Professional Leadership

Context & Organisations

Intervention & skills

Critical Reflection & Analysis

Knowledge

Rights, Justice & Economic Wellbeing

Diversity

Values & Ethics

Professionalism

SOCIAL WORK MANAGER

PRINCIPAL SOCIAL WORKER

PROFESSIONAL EDUCATOR

EXPERIENCED SOCIAL WORKER

SOCIAL WORKER

ASSESSED & SUPPORTED YEAR IN EMPLOYMENT (ASYE)

ADVANCED PRACTITIONER

End of last placement

End of first placement

Readiness for direct practice

Entry to qualifying programmes

HCPC Standards of Conduct, Performance & Ethics; Proficiency and CPD

SOCIAL WORK QUALIFYING PROGRAMMES

Appendix 2
Subject benchmark for social work

3 Nature and extent of social work

3.1 This subject benchmark statement covers social work as an applied academic subject at honours level. It sets out expectations concerning:

- the subject knowledge, understanding and skills of an honours graduate in
- social work
- the teaching, learning and assessment methods employed in their education
- the standards expected of them at the point of graduation.

3.2 Legislation establishing regulatory bodies in social work and introducing statutory registration of social workers was passed across the UK from 2000 onwards. These acts also recognise the terms 'social work' and/or 'social worker' as protected titles. Anyone using the title 'social worker' is required to be registered with the relevant care council.

3.3 Professional social work qualifications in the UK are linked to a specific level of academic achievement and may be attained through undergraduate or postgraduate study. Convergence of academic and professional awards established an undergraduate honours degree as the minimum required qualification for social workers. The curriculum design and assessment of academic work and practice within the respective social work degrees is determined by the specific requirements in England, Scotland, Wales and Northern Ireland. The NOS and the subject benchmark statement for social work inform these requirements.

The *Codes of Practice for Social Care Workers and Employers* should also shape the curriculum. This statement covers only honours degrees that constitute a professional qualification in social work.

3.4 This subject benchmark statement informs descriptions of professional competence for registration by identifying the required academic level and the range of subject matter necessary for an undergraduate degree. The process of establishing undergraduate degree programmes in social work should only be undertaken in partnership with other stakeholders including regulatory bodies, employers, professional bodies, providers of practice-learning, service users and carers, and those who work within social work and social care.

3.5 Honours degree programmes in social work may be studied in full-time, part-time, open and distance-learning, work-based, and post-experience modes. Irrespective of learning mode, all honours degree programmes covered by this statement must include structured opportunities for supervised or directed practice in relevant and appropriate practice-learning settings.

3.6 In addressing the content and standards of honours degrees, this statement takes account of European and international contexts of social work, including the Bologna Process and the desirability of the mutual recognition of social work qualifications within the European sector of the International Federation of Social Workers.

3.7 Contemporary social work increasingly takes place in an inter-agency context, and social workers work collaboratively with others towards interdisciplinary and cross-professional objectives. Honours degree programmes as qualifying awards are required to help equip students with accurate knowledge about the respective responsibilities of social welfare agencies, including those in the public, voluntary/independent and private sectors, and acquire skills in effective collaborative practice.

3.8 To facilitate broad access to honours degree programmes in social work, holders of sub-degree and vocational qualifications (normally in social care) may be offered entry with advanced standing by means of approved procedures for the recognition of prior (experiential) learning. Honours degree programmes must, however, ensure that all such arrangements enable students to achieve fully the standards required by the relevant care council. Advanced standing is not available in respect of the practice learning requirements in the degree.

3.9 The term 'service user' is used in this statement to cover the wide and diverse set of individuals, groups and organisations who are involved in, or who benefit from, the contribution of social work to the well-being of society. This group will include some that are involuntary or unwilling recipients of social work services. The term 'carer' is used in this statement to cover people who provide unpaid care to a member of their family or to another person, and who work in partnership with social workers to deliver a service. It should be recognised that students and staff may also be, or have been service users and/or carers. In providing services, social workers should engage with service users and carers in ways that are characterised by openness, reciprocity, mutual accountability and explicit recognition of the powers of the social worker and the legal context of intervention. Service users and carers are required by the four care councils to be integrally involved in all aspects of the design, delivery and assessment of qualifying honours degree programmes.

4 Defining principles

4.1 As an applied academic subject, social work is characterised by a distinctive focus on practice in complex social situations to promote and protect individual and collective well-being. This underscores the importance of partnerships between HEIs and service providers to ensure the full involvement of practitioners, managers, tutors, service users and carers with students in both academic and practice learning and assessment.

4.2 At honours level, the study of social work involves the integrated study of subject-specific knowledge, skills and values and the critical application of research knowledge from the social and human sciences, and from social work (and closely related domains) to inform understanding and to underpin action, reflection and evaluation. Honours degree programmes should be designed to help foster this integration of contextual, analytic, critical, explanatory and practical understanding.

4.3 Contemporary definitions of social work as a degree subject reflect its origins in a range of different academic and practice traditions. The precise nature and scope of the subject is itself a matter for legitimate study and critical debate. Three main issues are relevant to this.

- Social work is located within different social welfare contexts. Within the UK there are different traditions of social welfare (influenced by legislation, historical development and social attitudes) and these have shaped both social work education and practice in community-based settings including residential, day care and substitute care. In an international context, distinctive national approaches to social welfare policy, provision and practice have greatly influenced the focus and content of social work degree programmes.

- There are competing views in society at large on the nature of social work and on its place and purpose. Social work practice and education inevitably reflect these differing perspectives on the role of social work in relation to social justice, social care and social order.

- Social work, both as occupational practice and as an academic subject, evolves, adapts and changes in response to the social, political and economic challenges and demands of contemporary social welfare policy, practice and legislation.

4.4 Honours graduates in social work should therefore be equipped both to understand, and to work within, this context of contested debate about nature, scope and purpose, and be enabled to analyse, adapt to, manage and eventually to lead the processes of change.

4.5 The applied nature of social work as an academic subject means that practice is an essential and core element of learning. The following points clarify the use of the term 'practice' in the statement.

- The term 'practice' in this statement is used to encompass learning that not only takes place in professional practice placements, but also in a variety of other experiential learning situations. All learning opportunities that bear academic credit must be subject to methods of assessment appropriate to their academic level and be assessed by competent assessors. Where they form part of the curriculum leading to integrated academic and professional awards, practice learning opportunities will also be subject to regulations that further define learning requirements, standards and modes of assessment.

- In honours degree programmes covered by this statement, practice as an activity refers to experiential, action-based learning. In this sense, practice provides opportunities for students to improve and demonstrate their understanding and competence through the application and testing of knowledge and skills.

- Practice activity is also a source of transferable learning in its own right. Such learning can transfer both from a practice setting to the 'classroom' and vice versa. Thus practice can be as much a source of intellectual and cognitive learning as other modes of study. For this reason, learning through practice attracts full academic credit.

- Learning in practice can include activities such as observation, shadowing, analysis and research, as well as intervention within social work and related organisations. Practice-learning on honours degrees involves active engagement with service users and others in practice settings outside the university, and may involve for example virtual/simulated practice, observational and research activities.

4.6 Social work is a moral activity that requires practitioners to recognise the dignity of the individual, but also to make and implement difficult decisions (including restriction of liberty) in human situations that involve the potential for benefit or harm. Honours degree programmes in social work therefore involve the study, application of, and critical reflection upon, ethical principles and dilemmas. As reflected by the four care councils' codes of practice, this involves showing respect for persons, honouring the diverse and distinctive organisations and communities that make up contemporary society, promoting social justice and combating processes that lead to discrimination, marginalisation and social exclusion. This means that honours undergraduates must learn to:

- recognise and work with the powerful links between intrapersonal and interpersonal factors and the wider social, legal, economic, political and cultural context of people's lives

- understand the impact of injustice, social inequalities and oppressive social relations

- challenge constructively individual, institutional and structural discrimination

- practise in ways that maximise safety and effectiveness in situations of uncertainty and incomplete information

- help people to gain, regain or maintain control of their own affairs, insofar as this is compatible with their own or others' safety, well-being and rights

- work in partnership with service users and carers and other professionals to foster dignity, choice and independence, and effect change.

4.7 The expectation that social workers will be able to act effectively in such complex circumstances requires that honours degree programmes in social work should be designed to help students learn to become accountable, reflective, critical and evaluative. This involves learning to:

- think critically about the complex social, legal, economic, political and cultural contexts in which social work practice is located

- work in a transparent and responsible way, balancing autonomy with complex, multiple and sometimes contradictory accountabilities (for example, to different service users, employing agencies, professional bodies and the wider society)

- exercise authority within complex frameworks of accountability and ethical and legal boundaries

- acquire and apply the habits of critical reflection, self-evaluation and consultation, and make appropriate use of research in decision-making about practice and in the evaluation of outcomes.

5 Subject knowledge, understanding and skills
Subject knowledge and understanding

5.1 During their degree studies in social work, honours graduates should acquire, critically evaluate, apply and integrate knowledge and understanding in the following five core areas of study.

5.1.1 **Social work services, service users and carers**, which include:

- the social processes (associated with, for example, poverty, migration, unemployment, poor health, disablement, lack of education and other sources of disadvantage) that lead to marginalisation, isolation and exclusion, and their impact on the demand for social work services

- explanations of the links between definitional processes contributing to social differences (for example, social class, gender, ethnic differences, age, sexuality and religious belief) to the problems of inequality and differential need faced by service users

- the nature of social work services in a diverse society (with particular reference to concepts such as prejudice, interpersonal, institutional and structural discrimination, empowerment and anti-discriminatory practices)

- the nature and validity of different definitions of, and explanations for, the characteristics and circumstances of service users and the services required by them, drawing on knowledge from research, practice experience, and from service users and carers

- the focus on outcomes, such as promoting the well-being of young people and their families, and promoting dignity, choice and independence for adults receiving services

- the relationship between agency policies, legal requirements and professional boundaries in shaping the nature of services provided in interdisciplinary contexts and the issues associated with working across professional boundaries and within different disciplinary groups.

5.1.2 **The service delivery context**, which includes:

- the location of contemporary social work within historical, comparative and global perspectives, including European and international contexts

- the changing demography and cultures of communities in which social workers will be practising

- the complex relationships between public, social and political philosophies, policies and priorities and the organisation and practice of social work, including the contested nature of these

- the issues and trends in modern public and social policy and their relationship to contemporary practice and service delivery in social work

- the significance of legislative and legal frameworks and service delivery standards (including the nature of legal authority, the application of legislation in practice, statutory accountability and tensions between statute, policy and practice)

- the current range and appropriateness of statutory, voluntary and private agencies providing community-based, day-care, residential and other services and the organisational systems inherent within these

- the significance of interrelationships with other related services, including housing, health, income maintenance and criminal justice (where not an integral social service)

- the contribution of different approaches to management, leadership and quality in public and independent human services

- the development of personalised services, individual budgets and direct payments

- the implications of modern information and communications technology (ICT) for both the provision and receipt of services.

5.1.3 **Values and ethics**, which include:

- the nature, historical evolution and application of social work values

- the moral concepts of rights, responsibility, freedom, authority and power inherent in the practice of social workers as moral and statutory agents

- the complex relationships between justice, care and control in social welfare and the practical and ethical implications of these, including roles as statutory agents and in upholding the law in respect of discrimination

- aspects of philosophical ethics relevant to the understanding and resolution of value dilemmas and conflicts in both interpersonal and professional contexts

- the conceptual links between codes defining ethical practice, the regulation of professional conduct and the management of potential conflicts generated by the codes held by different professional groups.

5.1.4 **Social work theory**, which includes:

- research-based concepts and critical explanations from social work theory and other disciplines that contribute to the knowledge base of social work, including their distinctive epistemological status and application to practice

- the relevance of sociological perspectives to understanding societal and structural influences on human behaviour at individual, group and community levels

- the relevance of psychological, physical and physiological perspectives to understanding personal and social development and functioning

- social science theories explaining group and organisational behaviour, adaptation and change

- models and methods of assessment, including factors underpinning the selection and testing of relevant information, the nature of professional judgement and the processes of risk assessment and decision-making

- approaches and methods of intervention in a range of settings, including factors guiding the choice and evaluation of these

- user-led perspectives

- knowledge and critical appraisal of relevant social research and evaluation methodologies, and the evidence base for social work.

5.1.5 **The nature of social work practice**, which includes:

- the characteristics of practice in a range of community-based and organisational settings within statutory, voluntary and private sectors, and the factors influencing changes and developments in practice within these contexts

- the nature and characteristics of skills associated with effective practice, both direct and indirect, with a range of service-users and in a variety of settings

- the processes that facilitate and support service user choice and independence

- the factors and processes that facilitate effective interdisciplinary, interprofessional and interagency collaboration and partnership

- the place of theoretical perspectives and evidence from international research in assessment and decision-making processes in social work practice

- the integration of theoretical perspectives and evidence from international research into the design and implementation of effective social work intervention, with a wide range of service users, carers and others

- the processes of reflection and evaluation, including familiarity with the range of approaches for evaluating service and welfare outcomes, and their significance for the development of practice and the practitioner.

Subject-specific skills and other skills

5.2 As an applied subject at honours degree level, social work necessarily involves the development of skills that may be of value in many situations (for example, analytical thinking, building relationships, working as a member of an organisation, intervention, evaluation and reflection). Some of these skills are specific to social work but many are also widely transferable. What helps to define the specific nature of these skills in a social work context are:

- the context in which they are applied and assessed (eg, communication skills in practice with people with sensory impairments or assessment skills in an interprofessional setting)

- the relative weighting given to such skills within social work practice (eg, the central importance of problem-solving skills within complex human situations)

- the specific purpose of skill development (eg, the acquisition of research skills in order to build a repertoire of research-based practice)

- a requirement to integrate a range of skills (ie, not simply to demonstrate these in an isolated and incremental manner).

5.3 All social work honours graduates should show the ability to reflect on and learn from the exercise of their skills. They should understand the significance of the concepts of continuing professional development and lifelong learning, and accept responsibility for their own continuing development.

5.4 Social work honours graduates should acquire and integrate skills in the following five core areas.

Problem-solving skills

5.5 These are sub-divided into four areas.

5.5.1 **Managing problem-solving activities**: honours graduates in social work should be able to plan problem-solving activities, ie to:

- think logically, systematically, critically and reflectively

- apply ethical principles and practices critically in planning problem-solving activities

- plan a sequence of actions to achieve specified objectives, making use of research, theory and other forms of evidence

- manage processes of change, drawing on research, theory and other forms of evidence.

5.5.2 **Gathering information**: honours graduates in social work should be able to:

- gather information from a wide range of sources and by a variety of methods, for a range of purposes. These methods should include electronic searches, reviews of relevant literature, policy and procedures, face-to-face interviews, written and telephone contact with individuals and groups

- take into account differences of viewpoint in gathering information and critically assess the reliability and relevance of the information gathered

- assimilate and disseminate relevant information in reports and case records.

5.5.3 **Analysis and synthesis:** honours graduates in social work should be able to analyse and synthesise knowledge gathered for problem-solving purposes, ie to:

- assess human situations, taking into account a variety of factors (including the views of participants, theoretical concepts, research evidence, legislation and organisational policies and procedures)

- analyse information gathered, weighing competing evidence and modifying their viewpoint in light of new information, then relate this information to a particular task, situation or problem

- consider specific factors relevant to social work practice (such as risk, rights, cultural differences and linguistic sensitivities, responsibilities to protect vulnerable individuals and legal obligations)

- assess the merits of contrasting theories, explanations, research, policies and procedures

- synthesise knowledge and sustain reasoned argument

- employ a critical understanding of human agency at the macro (societal), mezzo (organisational and community) and micro (inter and intrapersonal) levels

- critically analyse and take account of the impact of inequality and discrimination in work with people in particular contexts and problem situations.

5.5.4 **Intervention and evaluation:** honours graduates in social work should be able to

use their knowledge of a range of interventions and evaluation processes selectively to:

- build and sustain purposeful relationships with people and organisations in community-based, and interprofessional contexts

- make decisions, set goals and construct specific plans to achieve these, taking into account relevant factors including ethical guidelines

- negotiate goals and plans with others, analysing and addressing in a creative manner human, organisational and structural impediments to change

- implement plans through a variety of systematic processes that include working in partnership

- undertake practice in a manner that promotes the well-being and protects the safety of all parties

- engage effectively in conflict resolution

- support service users to take decisions and access services, with the social worker as navigator, advocate and supporter

- manage the complex dynamics of dependency and, in some settings, provide direct care and personal support in everyday living situations

- meet deadlines and comply with external definitions of a task

- plan, implement and critically review processes and outcomes

- bring work to an effective conclusion, taking into account the implications for all involved

- monitor situations, review processes and evaluate outcomes

- use and evaluate methods of intervention critically and reflectively.

Communication skills

5.6 Honours graduates in social work should be able to communicate clearly, accurately and precisely (in an appropriate medium) with individuals and groups in a range of formal and informal situations, ie to:

- make effective contact with individuals and organisations for a range of objectives, by verbal, paper-based and electronic means

- clarify and negotiate the purpose of such contacts and the boundaries of their involvement

- listen actively to others, engage appropriately with the life experiences of service users, understand accurately their viewpoint and overcome personal prejudices to respond appropriately to a range of complex personal and interpersonal situations

- use both verbal and non-verbal cues to guide interpretation

- identify and use opportunities for purposeful and supportive communication with service users within their everyday living situations

- follow and develop an argument and evaluate the viewpoints of, and evidence presented by, others

- write accurately and clearly in styles adapted to the audience, purpose and context of the communication

- use advocacy skills to promote others' rights, interests and needs

- present conclusions verbally and on paper, in a structured form, appropriate to the audience for which these have been prepared

- make effective preparation for, and lead meetings in a productive way

- communicate effectively across potential barriers resulting from differences (for example, in culture, language and age).

Skills in working with others

5.7 Honours graduates in social work should be able to work effectively with others, ie to:

- involve users of social work services in ways that increase their resources, capacity and power to influence factors affecting their lives

- consult actively with others, including service users and carers, who hold relevant information or expertise

- act cooperatively with others, liaising and negotiating across differences such as organisational and professional boundaries and differences of identity or language

- develop effective helping relationships and partnerships with other individuals, groups and organisations that facilitate change

- act with others to increase social justice by identifying and responding to prejudice, institutional discrimination and structural inequality

- act within a framework of multiple accountability (for example, to agencies, the public, service users, carers and others)

- challenge others when necessary, in ways that are most likely to produce positive outcomes.

Skills in personal and professional development

5.8 Honours graduates in social work should be able to:

- advance their own learning and understanding with a degree of independence

- reflect on and modify their behaviour in the light of experience

- identify and keep under review their own personal and professional boundaries

- manage uncertainty, change and stress in work situations

- handle inter and intrapersonal conflict constructively

- understand and manage changing situations and respond in a flexible manner

- challenge unacceptable practices in a responsible manner

- take responsibility for their own further and continuing acquisition and use of knowledge and skills

- use research critically and effectively to sustain and develop their practice.

6 Teaching, learning and assessment

6.1 At honours degree level, social work programmes explicitly recognise and maximise the use of students' prior learning and experience. Acquisition and development of the required knowledge and skills, capable of transfer to new situations and of further enhancement, mark important staging posts in the process of lifelong learning. Social work models of learning are characteristically developmental and incremental (ie, students are expected to assume increasing responsibility for identifying their own learning needs and making use of available resources for learning). The context of learning should take account of the impact of the Bologna Process and transnational learning. The overall aims and expected final outcomes of the honours degree, together with the specific requirements of particular topics, modules or practice experiences, should inform the choice of both learning and teaching strategies and aligned formative and summative assessment methods.

6.2 The learning processes in social work at honours degree level can be expressed in terms of four inter-related themes.

- **Awareness raising, skills and knowledge acquisition** – a process in which the student becomes more aware of aspects of knowledge and expertise, learns how to systematically engage with and acquire new areas of knowledge, recognises their potential and becomes motivated to engage in new ways of thinking and acting.

- **Conceptual understanding** – a process in which a student acquires, examines critically and deepens understanding (measured and tested against existing knowledge and adjustments made in attitudes and goals).

- **Practice skills and experience** – processes in which a student learns practice skills in the contexts identified in paragraph 4.4 and applies theoretical models and research evidence together with new understanding to relevant activities, and receives feedback from various sources on performance, enhancing openness to critical self-evaluation.

- **Reflection on performance** – a process in which a student reflects critically and evaluatively on past experience, recent performance, and feedback, and applies this information to the process of integrating awareness (including awareness of the impact of self on others) and new understanding, leading to improved performance.

6.3 Honours degree programmes in social work acknowledge that students learn at different rates and in diverse ways, and learn best when there is consistent and timely guidance and a variety of learning opportunities. Programmes should provide clear and accessible information about learning approaches, methods and outcomes that enable students to engage with diverse learning and teaching methods in learning settings across academic and practice environments.

6.4 Approaches to support blended learning should include the use of ICT to access data, literature and resources, as well as engagement with technologies to support communication and reflection and sharing of learning across academic and practice learning settings.

6.5 Learning methods may include:

- learner-focused approaches that encourage active participation and staged, progressive learning throughout the degree

- the establishment of initial learning needs and the formulation of learning plans

- the development of learning networks, enabling students to learn from each other

- the involvement of practitioners and service user and carer educators.

6.6 Students should engage in a broad range of activities, including with other professionals and with service users and carers, to facilitate critical reflection. These include reading, self-directed study, research, a variety of forms of writing, lectures, discussion, seminars/tutorials, individual and group work, role plays, presentations, projects, simulations and practice experience.

6.7 Assessment strategies should show alignment between, and relevance to, social work practice, theory and assessment tasks. They should also be matched with learning outcomes and learning and teaching methods. The purpose of assessment is to:

- provide a means whereby students receive feedback regularly on their achievement and development needs

- provide tasks that promote learning, and develop and test cognitive skills, drawing on a range of sources including the contexts of practice

- promote self-evaluation, and appraisal of their progress and learning strategies

- enable judgements to be made in relation to progress and to ensure fitness for practice, and the award, in line with professional standards.

6.8 Assessment strategies should be chosen to enhance students' abilities to conceptualise, compare and analyse issues, in order to be able to apply this in making professional judgements.

6.9 Assessment methods normally include case-based assessments, presentations and analyses, practice-focused assignments, essays, project reports, role plays/simulations, e-assessment and examinations. The requirements of honours degree programmes in social work frequently include an extended piece of written work, which may be practice-based, and is typically undertaken in the final year. This may involve independent study for either a dissertation or a project, based upon systematic enquiry and investigation. However, the requirements of research governance may restrict opportunities available to students for research involving human subjects. Where practice competences have to be assessed, as identified through national occupational standards or equivalent, opportunities should be provided for demonstration of these, together with systematic means of development, support and assessment. Assessment methods may include those listed above, in addition to observed practice, reflective logs and interview records.

6.10 Honours degree programmes in social work assess practice not as a series of discrete practical tasks, but as an integration of skills and knowledge with relevant conceptual understanding. This assessment should, therefore, contain elements that test students' critical and analytical reflective analysis. As the honours degree is an integrated academic and professional award, the failure of any core element, including assessed practice, will mean failure of the programme.

7 Benchmark standards

7.1 Given the essentially applied nature of social work and the co-terminosity of the degree and the professional award, students must demonstrate that they have met the standards specified in relation to **both** academic and practice capabilities. These standards relate to subject-specific knowledge, understanding and skills (including key skills inherent in the concept of 'graduateness'). Qualifying students will be expected to meet each of these standards in accordance with the specific standards set by the relevant country (see section 2).

Typical graduate

7.2 Levels of attainment will vary along a continuum from the threshold to excellence. This level represents that of typical students graduating with an honours degree in social work.

Knowledge and understanding

7.3 On graduating with an honours degree in social work, students should be able to demonstrate:

- a sound understanding of the five core areas of knowledge and understanding relevant to social work, as detailed in paragraph 5.1, including their application to practice and service delivery

- an ability to use this knowledge and understanding in an integrated way, in specific practice contexts

- an ability to use this knowledge and understanding to engage in effective relationships with service users and carers

- appraisal of previous learning and experience and ability to incorporate this into their future learning and practice

- acknowledgement and understanding of the potential and limitations of social work as a practice-based discipline to effect individual and social change

- an ability to use research and enquiry techniques with reflective awareness, to collect, analyse and interpret relevant information

- a developed capacity for the critical evaluation of knowledge and evidence from a range of sources.

Subject-specific and other skills

7.4 On graduating with an honours degree in social work, students should be able to demonstrate a developed capacity to:

- apply creatively a repertoire of core skills as detailed in section 5

- communicate effectively with service users and carers, and with other professionals

- integrate clear understanding of ethical issues and codes of values, and practice with their interventions in specific situations

- consistently exercise an appropriate level of autonomy and initiative in individual decision-making within the context of supervisory, collaborative, ethical and organisational requirements

- demonstrate habits of critical reflection on their performance and take responsibility for modifying action in light of this.

Index